Undermining resistance

Manchester University Press

**PROGRESS IN
POLITICAL ECONOMY**

Series editors: Andreas Bieler (School of Politics and International Relations, University of Nottingham), Gareth Bryant (Department of Political Economy at the University of Sydney), Mònica Clua-Losada (Department of Political Science, University of Texas Rio Grande Valley), Adam David Morton (Department of Political Economy, University of Sydney), and Angela Wigger (Department of Political Science, Radboud University, The Netherlands).

Since its launch in 2014, the blog Progress in Political Economy (PPE) – available at www.ppesydney.net/ – has become a central forum for the dissemination and debate of political economy research published in book and journal article forms with crossover appeal to academic, activist and public policy related audiences.

Now the Progress in Political Economy book series with Manchester University Press provides a new space for innovative and radical thinking in political economy, covering interdisciplinary scholarship from the perspectives of critical political economy, historical materialism, feminism, political ecology, critical geography, heterodox economics, decolonialism and racial capitalism.

The PPE book series combines the reputations and reach of the PPE blog and MUP as a publisher to launch critical political economy research and debates. We welcome manuscripts that realise the very best new research from established scholars and early-career scholars alike.

To buy or to find out more about the books currently available in this series, please go to https://manchesteruniversitypress.co.uk/series/progress-in-political-economy/

Undermining resistance

The governance of participation by multinational mining corporations

Lian Sinclair

MANCHESTER UNIVERSITY PRESS

Published by Manchester University Press
Oxford Road, Manchester M13 9PL

www.manchesteruniversitypress.co.uk

British Library Cataloguing-in-Publication Data
A catalogue record for this book is available from the British
Library

ISBN 978 1 5261 7333 1 hardback
ISBN 978 1 5261 9791 7 paperback

First published 2024
Paperback published 2026

EU authorised representative for GPSR:
Easy Access System Europe – Mustamäe tee 50,
10621 Tallinn, Estonia
gpsr.requests@easproject.com

Typeset by Newgen Publishing UK

Contents

Figures

Tables

Preface and acknowledgements

I have always been fascinated by mining. Growing up in Western Australia, on the beautiful lands of the Noongar people, in an economy dominated by mining, there are few degrees of separation between any social, political or economic activity and the mining industry – our sports teams, arts sector and universities are all sponsored by mining. I completed high school followed by an undergraduate degree at the University of Western Australia during the last global commodity super-cycle – or 'mining boom' – circa 2005–2014. Witnessing the promise, growth and wealth that mining brought alongside the arrogance, corruption, pollution and inequality of the 'two-speed economy' sparked a lifelong interest in political economy, uneven development and social change surrounding extractive industries.

This book is the culmination of eight years' hard work and deep engagement with questions about how Australian-based multinational mining corporations operate in our closest neighbour – Indonesia. It is much more than an exposé of corporate 'behaviour'. I have centred people affected by mining – usually relegated as external stakeholders – in processes of resistance, participation and governance.

My greatest debt is to my research participants, most of whom must remain anonymous. In Kulon Progo, thanks for trusting me with your fierce defiance. Special thanks to Mas Widodo. I hope to do you all justice. In North Halmahera, for incredible hospitality while sharing the joys and frustrations of living, especially Ibu Afrida and family. In West Kutai, to everyone who shared their pain and resilience, including the tireless Pak Pius Nyompe. This book is dedicated to you, and to the many more searching for justice whose names we will never know.

The beautiful cover image – a custom illustration I commissioned from Andi Bhatara, a friend, artist and activist based in Bandung, Indonesia – centres a giant '*gunungan hasil bumi*', the fruit of the earth that is customarily paraded during harvest festivals in Yogyakarta, representing the pride, resilience and defiance of agrarian communities. The produce inside the open pit mine represents the fecundity of resistance despite land grabbing, while the mine pit seems to be undermining the peasants' resistance, productive and reproductive activities. The figures across the top represent the confusing and often shadowy realm of consultations, negotiations and corporate sites of participation, while the geology art in the bottom third represents both the mineral and spiritual wealth contained within the earth.

In writing this book I have attempted to consider the broadest possible audience, and hope that it is accessible for scholars, students, professionals, activists and policymakers alike. I have tried to balance rich historical and ethnographical detail with theoretical interpretation and explaining implications. While there is an overall arc of development from start to finish, each chapter should make sense on its own, so feel free to pick and choose relevant chapters if need be.

In the process of writing this book, I must thank several people. First, the continued dedication of Garry Rodan, despite wishing to enjoy his retirement in peace. My deepest gratitude goes to my dedicated mentors Shahar Hameiri and Jane Hutchison; your belief in my ability and project often exceeded my own. The Asia Research Centre (now relaunched as the Indo-Pacific Research Centre) at Murdoch University was my intellectual home for over eight years. I would like to thank Rebecca Meckelburg, Jacqui Baker, Kanishka Jayasuriya, Trissia Wijaya, Agung Wardana, Melissa Johnston, Charan Bal, Martin Brueckner, Charles Roche, Rochelle Spencer, Ian Wilson, Jeffrey Wilson, Carrol Warren, Ghamal Satya Mohammad and Sia Kozlowski.

I was lucky enough to receive detailed feedback from three external readers, Jojo Nem-Singh, Matthew Allen and Pascale Hatcher, whose encouragement spurred the process of writing this book at an early stage. I also must acknowledge the comradely community of the Australian International Political Economy Network, which was fertile testing ground for many of the ideas in this book.

Thanks also to Adam Morton and the other editors of the Progress in Political Economy series, for providing excellent guidance and feedback on the book proposal. Thanks go to Robert Byron, Humairaa Dudhwala and the team at Manchester University Press, along with the anonymous reviewers whose provocative feedback pushed me towards a more definitive theoretical contribution.

A slightly revised version of the book will be simultaneously released in Indonesia by INSISTPress as *Di bawah tanah: Melawan Pertambangan Multinasional di Indonesia*, translated by Nidya Paramita, who was also my translator, interpreter and companion during fieldwork. Thanks also go to Mas Achmad Choirudin, executive editor at INSISTPress. To friends in WALHI, AMAN and JATAM, especially Merah Johansyah, Hidup perjuangan!

My eight months of fieldwork in Indonesia and three-month internship were funded by an Endeavour Postgraduate Award for Long Term Fieldwork from the Department of Education and the Australian Government's Research Training Program Stipend and Murdoch University's top-up scholarship.

My fieldwork was hosted in Indonesia by the Centre for Peace and Security Studies at Universitas Gadjah Mada. Special thanks to my hosts Professor Sigit Riyanto and Professor Najib Azca. Also at UGM, the staff and students at the Institute of International Studies, especially Ibu Ayu Diasti Rahmawati, for a friendly academic environment.

The Agrarian Resource Centre in Bandung became my second intellectual – and sometimes literal – home during a three-month internship in 2017. Pak Dianto Bachriadi, Ibu Hilma Safitri, Pak Asep, Syafiq, Zulfi and Thiara, thanks for an inspiring example of organic academia.

In 2023, I found a new home in the School of Geosciences at the University of Sydney, working with Neil Coe on critical mineral global production networks. I thank him and all my new colleagues for their support and understanding in the final stages of preparing this manuscript. I am indeed happy to be dedicating renewed effort to understanding uneven development surrounding the boom in critical minerals amidst the global energy transition – an area that I highlight as one of two crucial avenues for future research in the conclusion of this book – surrounded by world-class scholars.

Finally, thanks to my parents, sister, grandparents, and family for supporting me on this mysterious journey. As the first person in my family to attend university, I hope to make you proud.

This book was mostly written on the lands of the Noongar Whadjuk people and I pay respect to their elders past and present for their custodianship of their *boodja* (country) since time immemorial. I extend this respect to First Nations peoples across the continent of Australia, the archipelago of Indonesia and around the world where traditional lands are affected by mining.

Special thanks to Kanishka Jayasuriya and Garry Rodan for extensive troubleshooting of Chapter 1 while revising this book.

I would like to thank Rebecca Meckelburg, Agung Wardana and Neil Coe for generous comments on earlier versions of Chapter 3.

I would like to thank Pak Pius Nyompe and Jeff Atkinson for their helpful comments on draft versions of Chapter 4. Representatives from PT KEM were also provided with a draft, but declined to comment further.

Abbreviations

ADB	Asia Development Bank
AMAN	*Aliansi Masyarakat Adat Nusantara*, Alliance of Indigenous Communities of the Archipelago
ASM	artisanal and small-scale miners
BAL	Basic Agrarian Law
BPD	*Badan Permusyawaratan Desa*, village consultative body. Also referred to as the village representative council
CAA	Community Aid Abroad, now Oxfam Australia
CAO	Compliance Advisor Ombudsman (IFC)
CSR	corporate social responsibility
DFID	Department for International Development (UK)
EITI	Extractive Industries Transparency Initiative
ESG	Environmental Social Governance (standards)
FKMA	*Forum Komunikasi Masyarakat Agraria* – Agrarian Communities Communication Forum
FPIC	free prior informed consent; also corrupted as free prior informed consultation
GAM	*Gerakan Aceh Merdeka* – Free Aceh Movement
GMI	Global Mining Initiative
ICMM	International Council on Mining and Metals
IFC	International Finance Corporation
JATAM	*Jaringan Advokasi Tambang* – the Mining Advocacy Network
JMI	PT Jogja Magasa Iron – operating company owned by Indomines Limited and JMM
JMM	PT Jogja Magasa Mining – owned by members of the royal families of Yogyakarta
KEM	PT Kelian Equatorial Mining – majority owned by Rio Tinto
KPM	*Komite Penasehat Masyarakat* – Community Advice Committee

LKMTL   *Lembaga Kesejateraan Masyarakat Tambang dan
                 Lingkungan* – Council for Environment and Mining
                 Communities Prosperity
MCA   Minerals Council of Australia
MCSC   Mine Closure Steering Committee – KEM
MMSD   Mining, Minerals and Sustainable Development initiative
                 of the Global Mining Initiative
MNC   multinational corporation
NHM   PT Nusa Halmahera Minerals – majority owned by
                 Newcrest Mining Limited
NGO   non-governmental organisation – not including business
                 associations
OEM   original equipment manufacturer
PPLP   *Paguyuban Petani Lahan Pantai* – Association of
                 Shoreline Farmers, Kulon Progo
TNI   Tentara Nasional Indonesia – The Indonesian Army
UNDP-LEAD   United National Development Programme-Legal
                 Empowerment and Assistance for the Disadvantaged
UUK   *Undang-undang keistimewaan Yogyakarta* – the Special
                 Yogyakarta Law
UUPA   *Undang-undang pokok agrarian* – the Basic Agrarian Law
                 (BAL) of 1960
VOC   The Dutch East India Company
WALHI   *Wahana Lungkungan Hidup Indonesia* – Friends of the
                 Earth Indonesia
WBG   World Bank Group
WWF   World-Wide Fund for Nature

Introduction: mining and participation in global capitalism

Large-scale corporate mining has an extraordinary ability to generate controversy. The exploration for, extraction, processing, refining, transport and distribution of coal, minerals and metals is inextricably associated with environmental pollution, land grabbing, human rights abuse, poor governance, inequality and violent conflict. No book on mining would be complete without mention of the 'resource curse' – the correlation of natural resource abundance and poor development outcomes.[1] Yet the global mining industry continues to enjoy enormous support. Its promise of economic development and modernisation appeals across national borders and social classes (Hatcher and Grégoire 2022). Indeed, most modern conveniences and technologies that we enjoy would be in short supply without mining. This cycle of modernisation-development-conflict is only intensifying in the 2020s as we embark on a new global boom in 'critical minerals' for 'green-technologies' like renewable energy and electric vehicles (Kramarz et al. 2021; IEA 2022).

The positive and negative sides of mining stem from its ability to generate rapid economic, social and political change. Land grabbing and changes in land use – from sites of subsistence, small-scale mining, agricultural production, ecology or residence to sites of large-scale resource extraction – disrupt and demand new *social relations of production and reproduction*. Such disruption threatens the basis of people's livelihoods (Ballard and Banks 2003). Large mines come to dominate local economies and can cause localised or national inflationary pressures and exacerbate inequalities (Devi and Prayogo 2013; Perreault 2018). Such changes inevitably produce winners and losers according to the distribution of impacts and opportunities. Even within villages or geographic communities, various 'sets of subgroups and individuals' (Horowitz 2011, 1385) develop differing opinions about the benefits and costs of mining. The resultant contestation needs to be managed by corporations or states lest it manifest in forms of conflict that threaten the profitability of capital.

Multinational mining corporations are continuously reforming their social and environmental practices in response to conflicts with people affected by mining. Since the 1990s, multinational miners, along with their political allies and financiers, have developed a global network of self-regulatory standards and organisations to reconstitute their legitimacy as responsible corporate actors. Together with international financial institutions, they have subverted, avoided, reconfigured, undermined or depoliticised resistance, opposition and conflict through new participatory mechanisms (Hatcher 2014). Corporate social responsibility, community development, 'gender mainstreaming' and environmental monitoring are neither simple outcomes of corporate ethics nor mere greenwashing strategies. Rather, participation is a mechanism to undermine opposition and create social relations amenable to extractive accumulation. Yet, in 2019, 20 years since the mainstreaming of corporate social responsibility (CSR), participation and community development in the mining sector, controversy, violence and environmental destruction persist.

This book is concerned with the rise, forms and effects of corporate participation as mechanisms for *undermining resistance to extractive accumulation*. I present two related arguments:

1. Multinational mining corporations develop participatory mechanisms to secure their legitimacy and undermine opposition by people affected by mining and non-governmental organisations (NGOs).[2]

At international scales this takes the form of a global network of self-governance standards and associations. At local scales, these mechanisms include participatory CSR, community development, environmental monitoring and consultative committees. These mechanisms all have implications for the distribution of political, social and economic goods. They have ideological *and* material effects.

2. People affected by mining will secure more benefit from participatory mechanisms or most effectively resist them through their control of land, histories of organisation, alliance structures and ideological conceptions of the world. Together, these four factors underpin the capacity and desire of groups of people affected by mining to participate in or resist mining developments.

Extractive accumulation is the collection of strategies and relationships at local, national and global scales that enables corporations to first secure natural resources and then profit from their extraction. The initial acquisition of resource deposits (resource grabbing) necessitates a dispossession from someone else, generating conflict and consequent rapid changes to existing political, social and economic relations – social relations of production and reproduction. These changes and conflicts are increasingly managed through new modes of participation. The effectiveness of participation rests on the ideological receptivity of potential participants.

Crises in global mining and the rise of participation

Mining corporations began to employ participatory approaches to CSR,[3] community development, consultation and environmental management in the late 1990s following increased media and NGO attention to sustainability, human rights, environmental devastation, and even civil war (Kirsch 2014; Cochrane 2017).[4] Beyond reputational damage, several cases resulted in multinational miners being sued in their home jurisdictions and NGO campaigns to create regulations that would hold multinational miners' foreign operations to the same standards that apply in their home states (Atkinson 1998; Kirsch 2014, 84–126). Conflict with communities is immensely costly for corporations if they develop into blockades, injunctions or otherwise delay or cancel projects (Gobby et al. 2022; Franks et al. 2014).

Reputational damage, regulatory risk and conflict with local communities represent the loss (or failure to establish) a *social license to operate* – the 'ongoing acceptance by society of a company carrying out its activities' (Brueckner and Eabrasu 2018, 218).[5] Activists and other critics consciously attack the 'social licence' or public legitimacy of mining projects they oppose, just as they might challenge environmental permits through courts (Brueckner and Sinclair 2019).

Sustained reputational, regulatory and community opposition to multiple projects and corporations within the industry culminates in *crises of legitimacy*.[6] In Gramscian terms, a crisis of legitimacy occurs when a dominant class loses the consensus for its leadership and risks being subjected to (additional) regulation (Filippini 2017, 99; Chapter 3). In this case, multinational mining corporations as a collective were threatened with increased state regulation and community intervention in their operations. Crises of legitimacy and their material cost were not limited to multinational miners but extended to their financiers and political supporters, notably the World Bank Group (Fox and Brown 2000; Danielson 2002; World Bank 2003; Hatcher 2014).

Multinational miners and their financiers sought to address their collective crisis of legitimacy by forming a global network of associations, organisations and standards for the self-regulation of the environmental and social dimensions of mining (Chapter 4; Kirsch 2014; Hatcher 2020). Ideological fragments and practices from critics and allies – including sustainability,

good governance, participatory development and community empowerment – were incorporated into new standards. Together these form the ideological basis and institutional structures for new *modes of participation*
(Rodan 2018). More specifically, they promote non-democratic ideologies
of representation to restore legitimacy without conceding decision-making
power (see Chapter 2). At the project level, corporations employed new
participatory mechanisms based in internationally constituted modes
of participation and in response to local risks to directly engage people
affected by mining.

These strategies have not eliminated problems of environmental devastation, human rights abuse, violence or corruption. Of recent infamy
is BHP's fight against liability and compensation claims following the
collapse of the Samarco mine's tailings dam, 50% owned by BHP, that
destroyed the Brazilian village of Bento Rodrigues (Ong 2016; Ferguson
2016). Recent Indonesian examples include ongoing conflict, protests,
and police killing workers around nickel mines and smelters in Sulawesi
(Morse 2021). In Australia, both the corporate sector and government
promote Australian mining corporations as world leaders in best practice associated with all aspects of extractives and extractive development
(DISR 2023). However, Australian multinationals are still undermining the rights of Indigenous peoples to free, prior and informed consent (FPIC), like Rio Tinto did when they exploded the Juukan Gorge
ancient cultural heritage site (Nagar 2021). Of course, participation has
not been able to entirely replace violence as a mechanism of undermining
resistance.

Together, global self-governance networks and local participatory mechanisms have been effective strategies to entrench the power of multinational miners in the face of challenges. With corporations becoming more
involved in community development programs, environmental monitoring
and stakeholder consultation, incentives are created for people affected by
mining to engage with corporate actors. The forms that conflict takes are
continuously changing as participatory mechanisms evolve in response to
ongoing contestation with critics and people affected by mining (Kurniawan
et al. 2022). Indeed, the main effect of CSR programs is to change the
dynamics of conflict, rather than eliminate it (Li 2015). Participatory mechanisms shape and contain conflict, but often in quite unpredictable ways,
in some cases opening up new opportunities for conflict (Arellano-Yanguas
2011; Leifsen et al. 2017; Jaskoski 2022). New opportunities for conflict
range from outright resistance to the pursuit of alternative mechanisms of
participation (Kröger 2020).

Explaining divergent outcomes

The key contribution of this book is to develop empirical and theoretical understandings of how and why groups embrace, co-opt, disrupt, resist or build alternatives to participatory mechanisms and how their reactions drive the emergence of new governance arrangements. This is achieved by situating mining conflict within broader processes of economic, political and social transformations across local, national and global scales and across state, corporate and autonomous sites of participation.

While there is a large volume of literature describing the emergence of participation, governance initiatives and the reactions of people affected by mining to participatory mechanisms (Jaskoski 2022; Kurniawan et al. 2022), there is very little that explains why and how people affected by mining choose to participate or not in corporate mechanisms. Groups of people affected by mining make strategic decisions to embrace, co-opt, resist, create alternatives, or subvert attempts to elicit their participation (Nem Singh and Camba 2016; Conde and Le Billon 2017). Participatory mechanisms can be manipulated by groups and individuals to accommodate desires they were not designed for (Horowitz 2015). Yet what determines the capacity and desire of groups of people affected by mining to participate or not and how?

The lacuna in answering this question can be explained by the tendency in existing literature to adopt a methodological or epistemological focus on particular sites or scales (national institutions, international organisations, individual corporations etc.) of conflict and participation to the exclusion of others. While institutional approaches produce detailed descriptions of the regulation and governance of social dimensions of mining, they treat institutions as a *deus ex machina* (Hameiri 2019). They tend to ignore the multiscalar social-economic contestations that drive the creation and transformation of institutions themselves. Institutionalist approaches can be divided into *neo-institutionalism* and *historical institutionalism*.

Neo-institutionalism is the more influential approach that underpins international organisations' current approach to participation, conflict and extractive industries (World Bank 2014; Fanthorpe and Gabelle 2013; Ali et al. 2017). Neo-institutionalists recognise that institutions play important roles in shaping human behaviour and that states require the capacity to create and support markets and confront threats to their effective operation (North 1990; 2005; Stiglitz 2003). In response to threats to private-sector-led development, neo-institutionalists advocate problem-solving reforms that increase privatisation, transparency, ownership, accountability, participation and stability to promote private-sector-led economic growth. Foundational for this approach to mining was the World Bank's *Extractive Industries Review* (World Bank 2003), which famously recommended the standard of free prior informed *consent*, while the World Bank Group in fact adopted the lesser free prior informed *consultation*. Neo-institutionalism also underpins the United Nations' understanding of conflict (Grzybowski 2012) and initiatives such as the Extractive Industries Transparency Initiative and the Kimberley Process (Haufler 2017).

Historical institutionalists recognise that there can be a fundamental conflict between the goal of states to generate revenue through extractive developments or to facilitate private sector growth and protect the rights of citizens, promote democracy, or address inequality (Thorp et al. 2012; D. H. Bebbington 2011). Kristiansen and Sulistiawati (2016, 215) argue that land conflicts in Eastern Indonesia are triggered by weak and competing insti-tutionalisations of land rights in Eastern Indonesia. Similarly, Robinson's (2016, 141–42) analysis of conflict in Sorowako, South Sulawesi, concludes that 'much of the conflict over land has its roots in the lack of clarity, or lack of enforcement, of the legal instruments that permit mining, includ-ing regulation of the entry of foreign miners'. In this view, land conflict and human rights violations could be avoided through improved legislation, better enforcement and more participation. This methodological and onto-logical privileging of institutional politics overlooks the fundamental diver-ging political and economic interests of the actors involved.

On the other hand, post-structuralist and constructivist accounts move beyond blaming conflict on institutional failure and provide descriptions of contests and 'micro-power relations' between actors.[7] Post-structuralist scholars begin with how mining companies, NGOs and state actors create, control, maintain and marginalise knowledges, rationalities and strategies to constitute supportive discourses, 'truths' and populations (Wesley and MacCallum 2014). For Welker (2014, 188):

> The proliferating standards, indicators, and metrics adopted by [mining com-panies] tend to bureaucratize, depoliticize, and render technical the social, envi-ronmental, and economic impacts of business. Many are developed through consensus-based 'multistakeholder' processes; civil society participants lend these processes and their products legitimacy and hegemonic force, even when they may not endorse the results.

In this view, participation is a technology for defining legitimate knowl-edge and forming compliant subjects. Through participation, persuasion, seduction and manipulation, corporations and states create new 'extrac-tive subjectivities' (Frederiksen and Himley 2020). Ultimately, while post-structuralist approaches offer rich descriptions of conflicts surrounding extractive industries and are sensitive to the way legitimate knowledge is produced, their explanatory power is limited by the focus on knowledges and discursive power at the expense of structural power within changing capitalist relations of production.

There are few accounts of participation and conflict in extractive industries that analyse how local, national and global contestation over the social and environmental dimensions of mining overlap and constitute each other. The most notable contributions that do this are Kirsch's *Mining Capitalism* (2014) and Kröger's *Iron Will* (2020). To understand both how, when and why multinational miners deploy participatory mechanisms *and* how groups of people affected by mining participate or not and the ways these two decisions are related, we must move past methodological focus on specific scales, sites and institutions to view extractive accumulation as an integrated set of strategies, institutions and relationships.

Critical political economy

Mining corporations often become embroiled in conflicts that predate their presence but may have found little visible expression. This is because social, economic and political divisions pre-exist extractive developments, including class, ethnic, gender and political tensions (Borras and Franco 2013; A. Bebbington 2011; Arellano-Yanguas 2011). Histories of dispossession, colonialism and marginalisation may become entangled, especially where mining affects Indigenous people (Coumans 2008; Angelbeck 2008; Guichaoua 2012). The analytical task is to unmask the dynamics of conflict, the role extractive developments play and how expressions of conflict are managed or perpetuated through corporatised participatory mechanisms.

For critical political economists, conflicts over mining take place within broader historically produced structures and social relations. Explanations for conflict are found in the political, social and economic relations surrounding mining within capitalism (Colley 2001; Hatcher 2014).[8] Critical political economy therefore rejects the idea that development is a value-neutral good or institutions can always be reformed to produce 'win-win' solutions. However, critical political economy remains divided between macro and micro variants. This division has implications for which social forces and conflicts at which political scales are thought to drive political and economic change.

The macro, or structural variant,[9] best represented by Veltmeyer and Petras's (2014) research into 'the new extractivism', is concerned with how ongoing crises in global capitalism and neoliberal modes of accumulation drive states' developmentalist strategies. According to Mentan (2018, 12), 'extractivism is a form of internal colonialism managed by elites of the former colonies operating under the structural power of supranational institutions like the World Trade Organization, World Bank and International Monetary Fund'. Other scholars of extractivism emphasise technological change in driving 'political, territorial and environmental struggles' Dougherty (2016, 6).

In structural political economy, development, resource extraction and processes of governance, participation and corporate responsibility are driven by 'dynamics of power relations between states, on the one hand and international financial institutions and private capital, on the other' (Nem Singh and Bourgouin 2013, 5; see also Hatcher and Grégoire 2022; Hatcher 2020). Hatcher argues that the World Bank's enshrining of participation within national mining codes results from mining investors' need for 'participatory schemes as a management tool to circumscribe the risks faced' (2015, 340).

Structural critical political economy thus provides an analysis of the national and international drivers of governance, institutions and contestation, and is a powerful explanation of why (but not necessarily when and how) participation emerges as a conflict-management strategy. The over-emphasis on the power of international and national actors like international financial institutions, multinational corporations and national governments underestimates the agency and power of people affected by mining activists and NGOs.[10] Furthermore, these approaches offer no explanation for the variation of participatory mechanisms that emerge within the same or similar jurisdictions. They also offer no explanation for why people affected by mining take wildly divergent responses to participatory mechanisms, which are key concerns of this book.

In contrast, the micro variant of critical political economy is a collection of critical approaches to studying conflict from below. These approaches intersect with political ecology (Horowitz 2011; Peluso 2016; Allen 2018) and critical agrarian studies (Lucas and Warren 2013; Bachriadi and Suryana 2016; Lahiri-Dutt 2018), and more recently have given rise to the 'everyday political economy' approach (Hobson and Seabrooke 2001; Elias and Rethel 2016).[11]

These approaches give methodological and analytical weight to the agency, strategy and relations of non-elite or 'local' actors and argue that by 'stressing the ordinary weapons of relatively powerless groups, we are able to understand how ordinary people devise their livelihood and resistance strategies as they become integrated in global circuits of production and consumption' (Nem Singh and Camba 2016, 51). Here, local social relations[12] are taken to shape how economic and political change manifests (Elias et al. 2016). Nem Singh and Camba (2016) use this approach to show how some communities are more militant while others are more legalistic.

These approaches are sensitive to the influence that gendered and racialised social relations can have on conflict and participation (Mahy 2011b; Lahiri-Dutt 2012). They do this by privileging a broader array of actors – peasants, workers, village officials, subnational NGOs, religious organisations, individual corporations, community relations managers and so on – and adopt greater sensitivity to how company–community conflicts play out around the mine site. Through the focus on local social relations, micro approaches provide strong explanations for how and when participatory mechanisms are implemented and the specific forms they take.

The danger and limitations here are reversed. Micro approaches to political economy can give too much weight to the agency of actors at local scales and underestimate the barriers and opportunities presented by established governance regimes and powerful economic actors. Because of the multiscalar nature of mining conflicts, it is critically important not only to recognise that conflicts between multinational mining corporations and people affected by mining are embedded in local, national and global capitalist social relations but also to analyse the ways in which sets of relations at each scale shape each other.

While the following chapter develops my theoretical framework of extractive accumulation in detail, for now it is enough to emphasise the danger of reifying particular social actors, scales, sites or manifestations of conflict. Combining macro and micro critical political economy approaches conceptualises scales, sites, structures and agencies as internally related parts of a social whole. It is in this combination that we can find explanations for when, how and why corporate participatory mechanisms emerge *and* how people affected by mining choose to participate or not.

Modes of participation and scales of contestation

To explain the forces behind participation, its governance, the forms that it takes, and how groups of people affected by mining respond to participatory mechanisms, I adopt the 'modes of participation' framework. Modes of participation are 'the institutional structures and ideologies that shape the inclusion and exclusion of individuals and groups in the political process' (Jayasuriya and Rodan 2007, 774). The advantage of this approach is the focus on historically constituted social forces and the root causes of conflict in processes of capitalist development, not merely its visible and institutional manifestations.

While the framework was developed to analyse how state institutions use participation as a technique for securing legitimacy (Rodan 2018), I adapt it to examine corporate sites of participation. This reflects the increasing need for mining corporations to contain contradictions and conflicts resulting from extractive developments – particularly from acts of primitive accumulation or land grabbing. Beyond simply reacting to conflict, mining corporations use participatory mechanisms, CSR and particularly participatory community development work to construct social relations of production favourable to large-scale mining.[13]

The second adaptation I make, given that participatory mechanisms operate largely at local scales while standards for their implementation and ideological legitimacy are enshrined at international scales, is to combine the modes of participation framework with a 'politics of scale'. In political geography, the concept of scale refers to the spatial level (from local, metropolitan and provincial to national, regional and global) of social, political and economic activities (Smith 2008). The production of scale, along with the issues governed at any particular scale, is never given *a priori* but is the result of capitalist development, environmental factors and political contestation (Smith 2003, 181–90; Swyngedouw and Heynen 2010; Allen 2018). Following this, in this study I use 'local scale' or simply 'local' to refer to the areas surrounding a mine site that are directly impacted by or impact extractive developments. The *local scale*, then, is an outcome of capitalist development but always also involves political contestation over who should be considered local for the purposes of community development, compensation or preferential employment among other benefits.

Because different opportunities, allies and resources are available at any given scale, actors strategically contest issues at scales, or across multiple scales, that are the most beneficial to their interests (Hameiri and Jones 2015, 56; Allen 2018). For example, social movements often attempt to 'jump scales' to the national or international where they can access allies, resources and media and invite public scrutiny (Escobar 2001; Kirsch 2014). Alliances which operate across political scales are a crucial factor in how effectively people affected by mining can campaign if they decide to reject participation – or how much knowledge and support they can receive to participate.[14]

I use the term 'people affected by mining' or 'groups of people affected by mining' and generally avoid 'local community' to signal that in any given locality, different individuals and groups of people will be affected and react differently.[15] To be sure, the very act of proposing a mining project can play a role in creating or splitting new scales and sites of political, economic and social relations as various actors and groups organise to contest or benefit from resource extraction.

In this approach, participatory mechanisms are not merely an ethical imperative or greenwashing exercise (e.g. Mzembe and Downs 2014; see O'Faircheallaigh 2008). Rather, they are a political tool for multinational corporations to manage conflict and risk generated by rapid changes in social relations of production and reproduction caused by large-scale mining. Conflicts are not limited to local scales or sites of production but spill over national and global scales through alliances of critics, supporters and governance networks. It is this complex, multiscalar conflict over the institutional and ideological bounds of participation that determines the diverse outcomes of participatory mechanisms.

In turn, affected peoples' capacity to participate or not depends on their access to economic and political resources, their strategic assessment of negative and positive impacts of mining, and their ideological receptivity to forms of participation on offer. Communities, or groups within communities, will gain more concessions and compensation when they organise to increase their power outside of and regardless of CSR programs, community development agreements and other forms of participation. Their power and agency to do so is rooted in their historically produced social relations. More specifically, groups' capacity to embrace, co-opt, resist or subvert participatory mechanisms is based on their control of land, history of organisation, alliances and ideologies. These four factors were identified through empirical fieldwork and are not meant to be an exhaustive list. Of these factors, ideology plays a special role. Ideologies are influenced by and influence how people conceive of their relationship to land, their organisation of production and social reproduction and their choice of allies. I argue that these factors explain why and how groups of people affected by mining often respond differently in what appear to be similar situations.

Methodology and methods

Social conflict theory,[16] on which the modes of participation framework is based, employs an historical sociological analysis to understanding transformations producing 'the global set of class relations attending capitalism, and the manner in which these relate to locally variegated patterns of investment, production and consumption, as well as geopolitical contestation' (Hameiri and Jones 2020, 17). It is sensitive to how 'even the most localised contest is ultimately nested within a wider set of power relations that now span the globe' (Hameiri and Jones 2020, 16). I therefore adopt a methodology that places individual and group decision making within a broader structural political economy analysis. To explain local variability within political and economic structures, Horowitz (2008; 2011) combines wide-angle political economy analysis with focused micro-political 'actor-oriented' approaches. Such a methodology strikes a balance between the equally inadequate economic determinism and political spontaneism that conceptualise actors as either without agency or unbounded by structural factors, and takes as its unit of analysis 'actors-in-context' (Murdoch and Marsden 1995).[17] Bieler and Morton (2018, 49) also warn about treating agency and structure as separate ontological categories that interact and influence each other externally. Analysis, therefore, 'commences with a focus on the structuring conditions of capitalist social relations of production, which by default implies that structure matters' (Bieler and Morton 2018, 44).[18]

Case study methods provide the opportunity to examine how political economic structures change through multiscalar conflicts and changing social relations. Qualitative case studies are an ideal research strategy to explain 'how' and 'why' questions (Yin 2003, 6). They allow detailed examination of phenomena without losing sight of trends and pressures across societies. Multiple-case studies help to produce theoretical replication across cases with different political outcomes (see Yin 2003, 47).

The research methodology draws from a single country case – Indonesia – with three local cases chosen to demonstrate the diversity of corporate–community participation. In selecting three cases, a balance was struck between replication of theoretical explanations of divergent outcomes while still having the time and resources for sufficiently detailed investigation.[19] Each of the three cases, introduced below, represents one of Yin's three categories: Kelian is a *critical case*, Gosowong a *typical case* and Kulon Progo an *extreme case*.[20]

Each case study primarily focuses on how and why participatory mechanisms are used by multinational corporations and how and why people affected by mining react to them. Yet each case study also has exploratory elements examining factors determining the capacity and desire of groups of people affected by mining to participate or not.[21] This reflects the inductive/deductive split in my research questions. It is deductive because I apply the modes of participation framework to provide explanations for how multiscalar contestations shape participatory mechanisms. It is inductive because it was through fieldwork and analysis that the factors determining the capacity and desire of affected groups to participate – control of land, histories of organisation, alliance structures and ideologies – were identified. The questions in Table 0.1 guided the four-year investigation across the three cases in Indonesia, each involving Australia-based mining corporations.

Research methods involved literature review, document analysis, participant observation and, most importantly, in-depth semi-structured interviews in Indonesian or English. Semi-structured interviews create space for participants to make observations not predicted or anticipated by the researcher (Fife 2005), while participant observation helps 'ensure the [interview] questions [reflect] the respondents' concerns and

Table 0.1 Research questions

---

1. How do multinational mining companies attempt to control risks posed by conflict with people affected by mining?

2. What factors explain when, why, how and the degree to which multinational mining corporations use participatory mechanisms to manage conflict with people affected by mining?

3. How do participatory mechanisms shape, contain or change the forms that social conflict takes?

4. How and why are participatory mechanisms contested, co-opted, embraced or ignored by grassroots and non-governmental organisations?

5. What factors, including access to resources, land use, alliance structures and strategies or ideologies affect the responses to participatory mechanisms of people affected by mining?

---

assumptions, not those of the researcher' (Mills 2014, 38). Participant observation allows researchers to observe and confirm data that participants have divulged.

Fieldwork was conducted across three case study locations plus Jakarta between 2015 and 2018. I conducted formal interviews with 80 individuals – some were interviewed multiple times, to check back and update data over time. Formal interviews were supported by many more conversations, participant observation and fieldnotes. Most participants were people affected by mining, with a range of pro, contra or neutral voices included from each area. Representative sampling was used to ensure that different opinions and voices were included, including representation of people of different ages, genders and ethnicities, where relevent and possible. Snowball sampling aided in reaching data saturation among each group. Triangulation of data was also provided by interviews with company employees, managers and government officials.

Sometimes, difficulty in obtaining data can be illuminating. In the case of Kulon Progo, the Australian parent company declined offers to be interviewed, while community relations staff in the Indonesian subsidiary initially agreed but later cancelled arranged interviews. In Gosowong and Kulon Progo, women and men were both well represented in formal interviews with people affected by mining, whereas in Kelian eight out of ten interviews were with men. This reflects the painful history of gendered violence associated with the Kelian gold mine and the ethical imperative to not force participants to revisit past trauma. Table 0.2 provides a summary of formal interviews.

Data analysis involved constant 'zigzagging' between literature, data collection, analysis, theoretical development and drafting. Early drafts of

Table 0.2 Formal interviews

Case, location and corporation	Type of interviewee	Number of formal interviews
Kelian gold mine	People affected by mining	10
West Kutai, East Kalimantan	Local organisers	2
PT Kelian Equatorial Mining	Regency and village government officials	5
Rio Tinto	District and provincial NGO workers and activists	2
	Company employees	3
Gosowong gold mine	People affected by mining	4
North Halmahera, North Maluku	Local organisers	1
PT Nusa Halmahera Minerals	Provincial, regency and village government official	9
Newcrest Mining Limited	Provincial NGO workers and activists	2
	Company employees	1
Kulon Progo sand iron mine	People affected by mining	25
Kulon Progo, Yogyakarta	Local organisers	5
PT Jojga Magasa Iron	District and village government officials	5
Indo Mines Ltd	Provincial NGO workers and activists	5
	Company employees	0

chapters based on case studies were translated into Indonesian and copies provided to key informants during follow-up fieldwork in 2018, providing further opportunities for informants to approve quotes, correct information or provide further details. The final section of Chapter 3 outlines the analytical procedure applied to each case study.

Case study selection

Indonesia presents a meta case containing three location-based cases. Each case then includes several embedded cases (Yin 2003, 52) – different groups of affected people who are offered different forms of participation or react differently to the same participatory mechanisms. Indonesia presents an ideal country to study contestation over the social and environmental impacts of mining for several reasons. From 2010 to July 2023, mining made up 25.7% of Indonesian exports and 7.1% of GDP (Bank Indonesia 2023b; 2023a), while between 2016 and 2020 mining contributed 5.6% of state revenue (EITI Indonesia 2022). This means the extractive sector is significant but not entirely dominant. This allows examination of the extractive sector as part of broader phenomena in political economy and suggests Indonesia presents a typical case, like countries with significant extractive sectors such as the Philippines, Brazil or Australia.[22]

Indonesia is a significant country for metal and mineral extraction, ranked ninth in the world for value of metallic minerals and coal extracted in 2020, down from fourth in 2019 (ICMM 2022). Extractive industries have been involved in many forms of conflict, from armed separatist wars to political protest and high-profile legal cases. Indeed, in Indonesia, high-profile cases contributed to global crises of legitimacy for multinational miners as well as generating national and local crises (Guáqueta 2013). Freeport's Grasburg mine in West Papua is notorious for its links with the Indonesian Military (TNI), clashes with organised labour and toxic waste (Bachriadi 1998; Leith 2003). Exxon's gas-field development played a role in independence conflicts in Aceh (Robinson 1998; Harker 2003; Aspinall 2007). The terrifying Lapindo mud volcano, triggered by drilling in a gas well, focused world attention on extractives and corruption in post-New Order Indonesia (Tapsell 2012; Tingay 2015).

Finally, archipelagic Indonesia presents a diverse range of political and social contexts within which extractives operate, allowing a bounded comparative study. There is a range of techniques used by corporate and state actors to manage conflict and a diversity of reactions from people affected by mining. This allowed the selection of case studies where different strategies are employed within the same nation. Indeed, the three cases in this book are from disparate areas of Indonesia: Kalimantan, Java and Maluku (Fig. 0.1). The following subsections introduce each of the three cases.

The rise of resource nationalism in Indonesia since 2014 has spurred the return of debates about the developmentalist state (Wilson 2015; Warburton 2016; Gellert 2019; Tilley 2021). Indonesia therefore presents a peculiar dynamic, as power is rebalanced between domestic conglomerates, the national government and multinational corporations. Indeed, the selection of Indonesia during the resurgence of 'resource nationalism' shows that corporations remain the dominant governors of social dimensions of mining *despite* this assertion of state power.

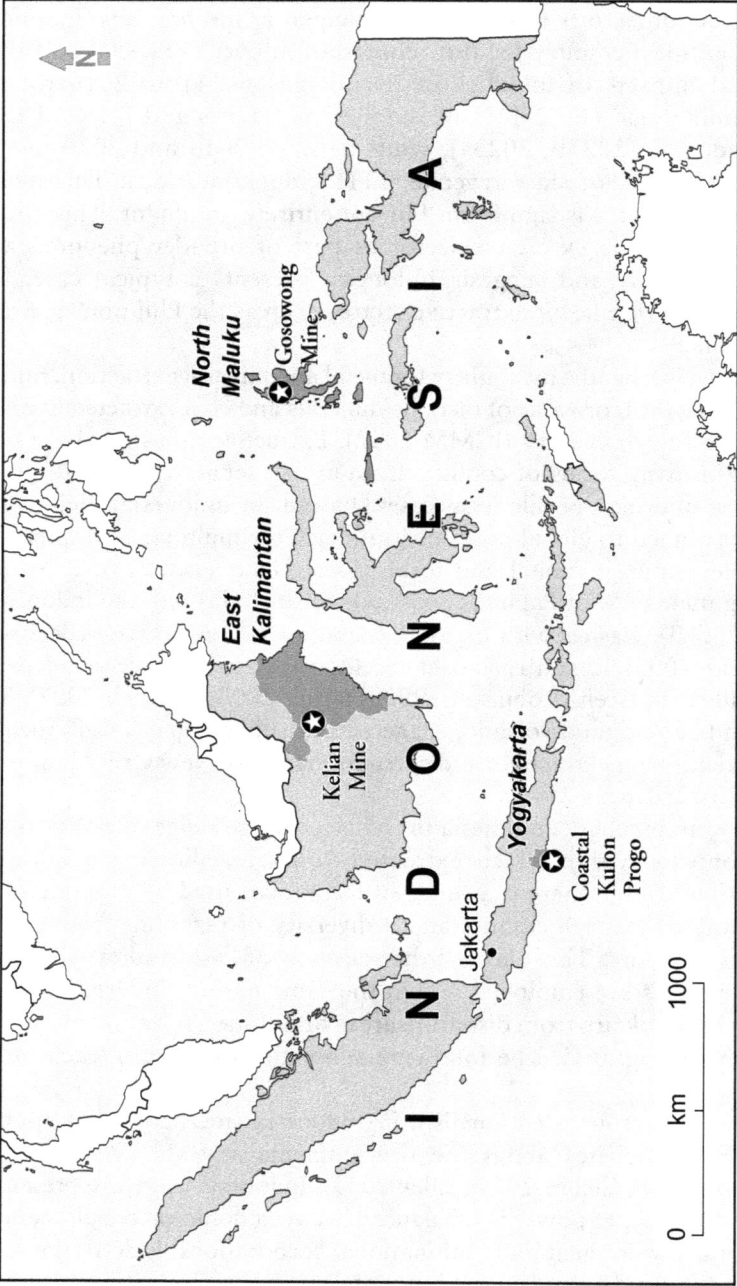

Figure 0.1 Case study locations.

Kelian Equatorial Mining – Rio Tinto's legacy

Rio Tinto's former gold mine on the Kelian River in East Kalimantan operated from 1991 until 2005. It provides a rare insight into the conflict management strategies applied before and after modes of participation emerged globally. The case is important because of Rio Tinto's leadership role in developing self-governance standards and associations. Human rights abuses and extreme inequality characterised the relationship between local communities and Rio Tinto's subsidiary, Kelian Equatorial Mining (KEM) until local activists were able to form national and international alliances and force KEM to negotiate. Then, following the fall of the authoritarian New Order regime, space opened for organisations to campaign at local and national scales. Pressure on Rio Tinto, across multiple political scales, resulted in an expansion of participatory community programs, including the negotiation of compensation for evicted families and victims of human rights abuse. It is a critical case because of the timing at the creation of a new democratic political regime domestically and new global governance regime– providing insight into the conflicts that spurred the creation of new regimes.

Nusa Halmahera Minerals – Newcrest's Gosowong gold mine

Nusa Halmahera Minerals' (NHM) Gosowong mine, majority owned by Newcrest Mining Limited until 2020, presents a typical representative case of a multinational mining corporation following international standards to respond to conflict with people affected by mining. The Gosowong mine in North Maluku has been producing gold and silver since 1999. In contrast to KEM, NHM employed community development programs from the beginning. However, this did not stop the mine becoming embroiled in violent conflict between politicians over Indonesia's decentralisation process. However, after the conflict ended, NHM was able to shape social relations amenable to extraction through community development, and negotiations with local leaders. One percent of annual revenue from the mine is spent on community development projects 'based on proposals developed by village teams elected by the communities' (Fletcher 2012). This kind of participatory community development program is typical – and can be taken to be representative of contemporary participatory mechanisms implemented by multinational miners.

Jogja Magasa Iron – IndoMine's Kulon Progo sand iron proposal

Finally, the case of Jogja Magasa Iron presents an extreme or rare case (Yin 2003, 40) where a group of peasants[23] overcame the odds to successfully resist the mining company. This project was a joint venture between Australian mining company Indo Mines Ltd, the royal family of Yogyakarta and domestic conglomerate Rajawali Corp. The association of shoreline farmers (*Paguyuban Petani Lahan Pantai* – PPLP) refused and actively obstructed attempts to elicit their participation and even disrupted community development projects and consultation sessions. The rare success of a group of peasants refusing to participate and overcoming an elite coalition tests the theoretical framework in a case that deviates from the typical or representative case. Being a rare outcome, it also provides crucial insights into the factors that contribute to the capacity and desire of groups to resist mining.

Organisation of this book

This book is organised into six chapters, plus this Introduction and the Conclusion. Chapter 1 develops a critical political economy of 'extractive accumulation', uniting and extending existing critical political economy approaches to extractive dispossession and extractivism. This is then combined with the modes of participation framework (Rodan 2018) to understand how political–economic contestation results in a variety of participatory mechanisms. Social reproduction theory (Federici 2004; Bhattacharya 2017b) explains how conflict generated by mining – and especially land grabbing – is not limited to formal political institutions or sites of production but encompasses social relationships that sustain and reproduce livelihoods. Gramscian 'common sense' (Gramsci 1971; 1996) is used to explain the ideological receptivity of people affected by mining to participation. Together this creates a critical political economy of extractive accumulation and resistance. The original contribution of this combination of approaches is to understand how histories and ideologies of people affected by mining shape diverse outcomes of participatory strategies in the mining sector.

   Chapter 2 applies a politics of scale to the historical development of global self-governance networks for the social and environmental dimensions of mining, and accounts for how localised conflicts combined and jumped scales to produce global crises of legitimacy for the mining industry in the 1990s. The response of multinational miners was to produce networks of global governance mechanisms for the social and environmental dimensions of mining. Language and practices of sustainability, participation and responsibility have been adopted by multinational mining corporations and combined with consultative ideologies of representation. Mechanisms based in international standards are implemented at local scales, extending and entrenching the power of multinational corporations.

Rather than this being seen as a decrease of state sovereignty through globalisation, most governments have been happy to allow corporations to self-regulate or regulate through partnership. This is certainly the case in Indonesia, the subject of Chapter 3, where an analysis of extractivism as a national development strategy reveals that because of alliances between domestic oligarchs, foreign capital, senior bureaucrats and politicians, corporations are left to self-regulate. People affected by mining and their allies continue to fiercely resist the social and environmental impacts of mining. The balance of power between and within these alliances is constantly shifting, along with the dominant regimes and ideologies of development. Changing opportunities for alliance building, defending land and building autonomous organisations means there is a vast array of reactions by people affected by mining towards participation and mining.

Chapters 4, 5 and 6 analyse fieldwork data from case studies in Kelian, Gosowong and Kulon Progo, respectively. Each chapter explains how participatory mechanisms came about, who participated, on what terms and who was excluded. Each case demonstrates the power of the modes of participation framework to explain diverse outcomes. In Kelian, participatory mechanisms were employed in reaction to threats to mining. As local groups increased in power, they demanded forms of participation suiting their interests. However, the outcomes of participatory mechanisms reflected the balance of power between the actors involved. In Gosowong, modes of participation offered by NHM were compatible with pre-existing common sense understandings of political participation and were easily integrated into pre-existing structures. Various groups were able to organise to extract benefits from NHM based on ideologies of indigeneity, cross-class alliances and physical blockades, although the mine's operations were never seriously threatened. In Kulon Progo, the mining company and government allies failed to present forms of participation that agreed with local actors' common sense understandings of the world. Because of their independently organised modes of production and strong communitarian relations of social reproduction, peasants were powerful enough to resist the mine's development. In fact, the experience of marginalisation, resistance and alliance formation has strengthened the peasants' organisations and given rise to more equal gender relations across five villages.

Finally, the Conclusion extends the analysis and argument developed throughout the book while identifying limitations. New modes of participation, enshrined through networks of global governance, provide the institutional and ideological structures with which multinational mining companies respond to contemporary and future conflicts with local communities. These structures are not static but continue to evolve in relation to ongoing multiscalar conflicts, new technologies and production processes. Technological development is behind a new boom in 'critical minerals' needed for green technologies, especially lithium-ion batteries and renewable energy. There are already several new governance standards for batteries and critical minerals that follow the same pattern of conflict-crisis-governance-participation described in this book. While the expansion and globalisation of capital and mining corporations from China, India and Russia are established phenomena, it is yet to be seen whether corporations from these countries will integrate and modify existing modes of participation, whether they will face a similar crisis of legitimacy to established multinational corporations, or whether they will produce alternative and competing global standards to manage the environmental and social dimensions of mining. The modes of participation framework contains the potential for further analysing, predicting and understanding these and other emerging developments in the global extractive industries.

Notes

1 The 'resource curse hypothesis' emerged in the 1990s to explain decades of ambiguous economic and social development and high rates of conflict in resource-rich countries (Auty 1993; Ross 2018). The hypothesis is that large natural resource endowments and high contributions of natural resources to total exports are correlated with durable authoritarian regimes, corruption, slower economic development, civil war and violent conflict (Sachs and Warner 1999).

2 Throughout this book, I use the term NGO to refer to private (non-state), not-for-profit formal organisations, organised around a social purpose such as environmentalism and human rights.

3 In this book, I mostly use the term 'corporate social responsibility' (CSR), especially when talking about the history and emergence of the practice, even though the term has largely been replaced in industry reports by 'environment social governance' (ESG).

4 'Participation' in mining borrows heavily from earlier lessons in 'participatory development' by international organisations like the World Bank (White 1996; Cooke and Kothari 2001, 5; Leal 2007; Guggenheim 2006). Likewise, the critical literature on participation in mining builds on critiques of participatory development which argue, for example, participatory techniques are employed 'as a technical method of project work rather than as a political methodology of empowerment' (Hickey and Mohan 2005, 242).

5 'Social license to operate' is a metaphor developed by business in the late 1990s in response to the increasing salience of 'sustainability' (Brueckner and Eabrasu 2018). Obtaining a 'social license' represents a shift on the part of corporations to actively manage and promote their social credentials (Prno and Slocombe 2012).

6 Also synonymous with crisis of authority, confidence or hegemony; see (Gramsci 1971, Q13§23; 210–11).

7 Fabiana Li's analysis, for example: 'Instead of taking transparency and participation as the end point of the analysis (the desired outcome that will prevent or reduce the incidence of conflicts), I consider how mechanisms of audit, environmental management, and accountability take shape and become enmeshed in the controversies. What I am proposing is an analysis that gets beyond common sense understandings of the "conflicts" as a failure of state and corporate accountability' (2015, 12).

8 Conflict is inherent in contestations over the impacts of development and between competing pathways of development. Interventions into conflict are not created *ex nihilo* but are driven by social groups with interests in particular kinds of solutions.

9 Also drawing on critical political geography.

10 The privileged analytical position given to national and international scales often overshadows how developments in social relations of production shape both structure and agency (Bieler and Morton 2018).

11 They build on classic work on subaltern actors' agency such as Scott's (1985) *Weapons of the Weak*, Peluso's (1992) 'Repertoires of resistance', and Kerkvliet's (1990) *Everyday Politics*.

12 Local social relations may be capitalist or non-capitalist and encompass class, gender, ethnic relations and so on.

13 Here, 'social relations of production' is meant in the broad sense, as 'everyday patterns of behaviour involved in the production and consumption of physical goods as well as the discursive institutional and cultural tactics established to ensure the hegemony of existing social relations' (Bieler and Morton 2018, 37), and includes social relations of reproduction.

14 Indeed, in all three cases in this book, people opposed to mining sought to create alliances with groups who could help attract national and international resources and legitimacy.

15 A micro political economy approach to community formation emphasises localised relationships that enable production and distribution of resources as a *process* of community creation (Roseberry 1989; Li 1996).

16 This approach, based in Marxist and Gramscian sociology, has also been referred to as 'structural political economy' (Hutchison et al. 2014) or 'the Murdoch school of critical political economy' (Hameiri and Jones 2020).

17 This methodological approach places this research in critical realist epistemology that 'takes the middle road through positivism and constructivism in asserting the existence of fixed structures within which society functions, while

acknowledging that we have the capacity to exert influence through the constructions that result from social interaction' (Birks 2014, 20).

18 The same danger of reification applies to political scales, which are not separate
realms but co-produced and internally related through the historical globalisation of capitalist relations.

19 Furthermore, several insightful single or dual case studies of social conflict and
mining in Indonesia have been written (Bachriadi 1998; Welker 2014; Peluso
2016; Robinson 2016). I build on their insights while producing a greater level
of replication.

20 Robert Yin (2003, 40) outlines the utility of the critical case for 'testing a well-
formulated theory'; the extreme or unique case where an occurrence 'may be
so rare that any single case is worth documenting and analysing' (2003, 41);
and the representative or typical case where 'lessons learned from these cases
are assumed to be informative about the experiences of the average person or
institution' (2003, 41). Selecting critical, typical and extreme cases helps to
demonstrate theoretical replicability over different case types as opposed to, for
example, testing three typical cases.

21 Yin (2003, 6) explains that *exploratory* case studies (or any other exploratory
research method) are those that ask 'what', 'who' and 'where' questions – 'In
contrast, "how" and "why" questions are more *explanatory* and likely to lead
to the use of case studies, histories and experiments as the preferred research
strategies'. Thus, case studies, along with a small handful of other qualitative
research strategies, are uniquely placed to test theories that explain why and
how particular outcomes arise.

22 The Philippines, Brazil and Australia were ranked 43rd, 30th and 15th by
the ICMM (2022) in 2020 in terms of mining's contribution to exports, GDP
and government revenue. Indonesia was ranked 36th. Countries with a higher
proportion of mining contributions where mining is the dominant industry
include Mongolia, PNG and the DRC, which are ranked 2nd, 10th and 12th,
respectively.

23 I use 'peasant' to refer to agrarian smallholders. Following Lucas and Warren
(2013, 27), I translate the Indonesian *'petani'* as 'peasant', 'implying traditional village ties and semisubsistance household based economic orientation'
as opposed to 'more commercially oriented "farmer"'.

1

Extractive accumulation and modes of participation

Extractive accumulation, encompassing both the initial acquisition of natural resources and their ongoing profitable extraction, requires particular global, national and local conditions to be established and maintained. It is part of global capitalism, but may at times contradict or conflict with alternative accumulation strategies. The theoretical approach developed in this book is intended to unite and extend several existing frameworks and concepts to explain the ongoing evolution of global governance mechanisms as a reaction to multiscalar conflict and crises of legitimacy. As crises emerge from intersecting conflicts, new governance arrangements and modes of participation are created which (attempt to) undermine resistance to mining, until new conflicts emerge.

Extractive accumulation builds on existing concepts of 'primitive accumulation', 'accumulation by dispossession', and 'extractive dispossession', but also includes the ongoing maintenance of social relations of production and reproduction. It moves beyond the methodological nationalism often present in 'extractivism', which is usually used to mean national strategies for state developmentalism via extractive industries.[1]

To set the theoretical foundation for extractive accumulation and participation, this chapter first provides an account of institutions, development and contestation from a social conflict theory perspective. Social conflict theory's advantage is that it seeks to understand the social roots of conflict, not merely its visible manifestations. The second section covers contestations and manifest forms of conflict that are distinctive, but not unique, to extractive accumulation. In affected communities surrounding mine sites, both dispossession and ongoing profiteering generate rapid changes in previously existing political, social and economic relations. Land grabbing, primitive accumulation, changing modes of production, and the disruption to social reproduction are features of extractive capitalism that explain the roots and manifestations of company–community conflict. Such rapid changes require the creation and management of amenable social relations of production and reproduction. The third section therefore turns to feminist social reproduction theory to explain how mining companies become active in forming the social reproduction of communities surrounding mine sites. Social and political management techniques are increasingly participatory, although violence has not been abandoned as a technique of control.

The fourth section introduces the politics of scale because extractive conflicts are not limited to scales and processes of production but take on multiscalar dimensions as groups seek to resolve conflicts across various fora. The fifth section expands on the modes of participation framework to explain why forms of participation emerge at given moments and places. Participation is regarded as a political technique to contain and transform manifestations of conflict that threaten profitability, creating new sites for contestation to (re)define boundaries for legitimate social and political conflict. In other words, participation undermines resistance to create social relations of reproduction compatible with extractive accumulation. In the sixth section, to understand the reactions of people affected by mining to attempts to elicit their participation, I turn to Gramscian concepts of ideology and common sense. The ways in which people affected by mining understand the world, and their ideological receptivity to modes of participation, shape the ways in which they are likely to participate or not. Common sense understandings are both influenced by and influence the ways in which people affected by mining control land, organise production and politics, and form alliances.

Social conflict theory

Social conflict theory understands society as groups of actors who pursue their interests in struggles over how power and wealth are produced and distributed. Following Hutchison et al. (2014, 79), 'development is never merely a public good, but is rather a perpetual process of resource redistribution that is fought over by class-based groups'. Social and political change is understood as driven by conflict between competing social groups.[2] Visible forms of conflict are treated as manifestations of contestation and contradictions generated through processes of capitalist development. The advantage of this approach is the focus on social forces and the root causes of conflict, not merely its visible and institutional manifestations.

This has ontological implications for how the state, institutions and corporations are conceptualised. States and institutions are not taken as pre-existing facts, unified subjects, or tangible objects standing apart from each other (Jessop 2007, 123). Rather they are mutually constituted with society and permeated by conflicts between groups of actors with different interests. More precisely, institutions are understood as both the outcomes of and terrain for political and social conflict (Rodan et al. 2006). In this view, institutions shape political contestation and the form that conflict takes but do not elevate politics above society (Hutchison et al. 2014, 80). Institutional configurations are not static but change as new social forces or conflicts emerge (Nguyen 2014).

Institutional mechanisms and practices that attempt to contain conflict may be designed by powerful actors, yet often, as in the case of 'sustainable development' and corporate social responsibility, they are co-opted and adapted from critics. This means that critics and critical discourses are often included within new practices to pacify or co-opt opposition. In this way, various mechanisms of rule are tested and the ones that work survive in a continuing 'evolutionary process of variation, selection [and] retention' (Jessop 2006b). Of course, institutional containment is always successful; oppositional groups can use institutional inclusion to open up conflict over broader issues of inequality or resource distribution (Rodan 2018, 218).

The social conflict approach is useful in analysing the political power of multinational mining corporations because it rejects the reification of governance institutions, markets and even corporations. Instead, institutions, markets and corporations are sites where different actors come together in cooperation and conflict. Social conflict theory recognises participatory mechanisms as an institutionalisation of relations between mining corporations, states and people affected by mining. Therefore, analysis remains focused on how actors in corporations, NGOs, people affected by mining and their allies contest the social, environmental and economic impacts of mining.

The approach opens analytical space to examine conflict that occurs around and outside formal institutions as well as the agency of subaltern actors.[3] Conflict may occur at sites of production, social reproduction, governance or regulation. This is important for mining conflicts as many critics of large-scale mining refuse to 'work within parameters of reform set by industry participants and state actors' (Nem Singh and Camba 2016, 50). Furthermore, acts of resistance may go unnoticed or be illegible to corporate or state actors, may be organised or spontaneous, can be collective or individual, and occur across multiple political scales. The actions, ideologies and understandings of people affected by mining are critical to how conflicts evolve either within or outside institutional bounds.

This book applies insights from social conflict theory to corporate spaces, processes and institutions. There is a growing interest in studying corporations as political actors or governance institutions[4] (Wilks 2013; Mikler 2018; May 2020; Sinclair 2020). Corporate interests and strategies – like other institutions – change through contestation.[5] Marina Welker, an anthropologist of corporations, examines how corporations are reconstructed through contestation with people affected by mining: 'Without denying profit as a motivation, … people enact corporations in multiple ways … these enactments involve struggles over the boundaries, interests and responsibilities of the corporation' (2014, 1). On the other hand, there is the recognition that 'corporate actors' often have interests outside those of the corporation – for example employees may also belong to affected communities or activist groups (Filer and Le Meur 2017, 23–25).

The crucial point for an analysis of participatory mechanisms, which function at intersections between the state, corporations and society, is how they institutionalise and contain undesirable forms of conflict, undermine resistance, or open spaces for new contestations to emerge in response to the conflicts generated in extractive accumulation.

Primitive accumulation and extractive dispossession

At the local scale (scale of production), the distinctive feature of extractive accumulation is competition and conflict over land use, and especially 'land grabbing' (Perreault 2018). Mining corporations must expropriate land, through legal, illegal, economic or violent means, and repurpose it from previous uses – most often agrarian, traditional Indigenous uses, small-scale extraction or protected ecosystems (Leifsen et al. 2017). Large mines come to dominate local economies and subsume livelihoods, 'redirecting and circumscribing them according to extractivist logics and practices' (Perreault 2018, 346). Even positive changes disrupt social, political and economic relations as 'new sources of income can give rise to major problems because they are often distributed unevenly', which in turn can 'generate social tension through its impact on existing structures of authority' (O'Faircheallaigh 2015, 44). It is this disruption to local economies, politics and culture that produces most conflict between corporate miners and people affected by mining.

Land grabbing is a type of 'primitive accumulation'[6] whereby resources previously unincorporated – or only partially incorporated – into capitalist economic systems are appropriated by corporations, states or development agencies (Hall 2013; Bachriadi and Suryana 2016). The term describes not merely the dispossession of one group of actors to the benefit of others, but a repurposing – a commodification and marketisation – of land itself and the development of capitalist relations (Marx 1990, 873–76; Federici 2004, 12; Veltmeyer and Petras 2014). Roche et al. (2019) coined the term 'extractive dispossession' in recognition of the way that accumulation by dispossession plays out in relation to extractive projects.[7] For previous land users – peasants, Indigenous people or small-scale miners – land might have served multiple uses and values. It might have provided a place of residence, source of income, provided for subsistence needs, served as spiritual or religious sites and/or served ecological functions.[8] Repurposing land means changing social relations surrounding that land. That is, changes in the function of land entail not only a change in relations of production but also relations of social reproduction. It is both the initial dispossession and the medium- to long-term reconfiguring of social, political and economic relations for profitability that constitute extractive accumulation.

Social reproduction theory

To analyse these changes and resultant conflict, I turn to social reproduction theory, which considers how relations of production are co-produced with relations of social reproduction in capitalist economies (Bhattacharya 2017a; Moore 2023b).[9] As changes in one set of relations will produce contradictions and conflict with the other and precipitate change, this approach provides further insight into the terrains of conflict that emerge around extractive development. In social reproduction theory, 'production' involves the production of commodities while social reproduction 'embodies several overlapping but contradictory meanings, including human biological reproduction, the socialization of children, the reproduction of labour power, and the reproduction of the mode of production or of the society as a whole' (Bezanson and Luxton 2006, 27). Reproduction therefore includes health care, education, food, care work, shelter, pensions, leisure facilities and so forth (Abercrombie et al. 1994, 357; Bhattacharya 2017a, 7). It also involves the development and transmission of knowledge, social values and cultural practices, and the construction of individual and collective identities[10] (Bezanson and Luxton 2006, 3).

Silvia Federici's (2004, 63) contribution to the debate on primitive accumulation is that it involves not merely 'the divorcing of the workers from the means of production', expropriation of land from the peasantry 'and the formation of the "free", independent [male] worker'. It separates commodity production from social reproduction, which also becomes terrain for control and resistance.[11]

Indeed, Atkinson (1998, 35) notes how, following the development of large-scale mines, inequality grows between those employed at the mine and those in informal or subsistence occupations, especially between men and women, as 'the [increasing] cost of basic necessities [leads] to more traditional subsistence and cooperative economic activities being regarded as inferior to having a job at the mine'. Inequality and disruption to social relations of production and reproduction can create new conflicts, including between employees and those in informal sectors; between locals (sometimes Indigenous people) and newcomers; between men and women; and between the dispossessed and the corporation.

Contradictions and conflict are also produced because

> social reproduction holds a dual character of reproducing humans *and* society outside of the needs of capital, but also of reproducing labour power for capitalist production, which leads to a constant struggle to further extend capitalist relations into the sphere of how labour power is reproduced and who must bear the costs.
>
> (Meckelburg 2019, 32, emphasis in original)

This follows Rebecca Hall (2016, 102) 'theorising the shifting, mutable relationship between social reproduction, non-capitalist subsistence production and capitalist production', which can all become sites for exploitation *and* resistance, domination *and* agency. Relations of reproduction are not merely instrumental to a particular mode of production but shaped by agency, crises and marketisation (Moore 2023a).

People dispossessed of their land – their means of subsistence, production and reproduction – must find new ways of securing their income and subsistence needs. This situation may result in some people variously finding employment at the mine, opening land elsewhere, 'illegal' mining, engaging in precarious employment or demonstrating against and making demands of the corporation. Tania Li (2011, 286) asks, in relation to plantations in Indonesia, what happens when local people's land is needed but their labour is not? This question is even more pertinent in relation to land grabs for mining where labour requirements are smaller and more specialised than in plantation agriculture. The answer is *often* poverty, inequality and conflict between the dispossessed, migrant labourers and corporate actors and, Li argues, government intervention is needed to manage these negative effects.

State – or corporate – institutions take on the role of 'chief supervisor of the reproduction and disciplining of the workforce' (Federici 2004, 84). State and corporate actors intervene through public assistance and social control programs to avoid forms of social reproduction that could produce recalcitrant populations (Sears 2016). Mining corporations need to produce, in their local areas, social relations conducive to extractive activities. To avoid threats to their operations – blockades, demonstrations, 'illegal mining', theft, sabotage and so on – they must manage some of the inequalities and disruption involved in changing relations of production and reproduction. They do this through a wide range of strategies, including discipline and violence, establishing patronage networks, inviting the participation of potential opponents, sustainable community development work, promoting cash cropping and market economies, education, and ideological intervention. In this way, participatory mechanisms are not only about containing risky forms of conflict but establishing new relations of production and reproduction among people affected by mining so that such disruptive manifestations of conflict are not generated in the first place.

The capacity and desire of people affected by mining to participate or not is largely influenced by their histories of organisation – by their relations of production and social reproduction – which are not always separate but always related. Where the organisation of production and reproduction is more communal, less integrated into state or corporate hierarchies, and less determined by market relations, people affected by mining will be less willing or able to integrate into corporate forms of production or participation. Where social organisation is more hierarchical or fractured by class, gender, ethnicity or age, participation and resistance will reflect this. Control of resources, especially the means of production (land), is perhaps the most direct factor in determining the *ability* of people affected by mining to resist land grabs. Control of land is practical and can be divided into physical control or the ability of groups to exclude other actors; claims which may be based in agrarian law or tradition (*adat*); and legal title or certification. The point is that histories of social organisation of production and reproduction are co-determined with the way that relations with land are organised. There is, of course, an ideological dimension to production and reproduction, which is explored further below.

The politics of scale

Conflicts around extractive industries rarely remain confined to sites of production and social reproduction. Indeed, they often take on national and international dimensions as one or more actors attempt to resolve conflict in their favour through international campaigning or institutional fixes. It is at national and international scales where questions of governance, regulation, rights and alliances become significant. An explicit analysis of the political scales across which conflict occurs allows an understanding of how seemingly separate conflicts are enmeshed in historical contestations over governance, rights and development. It also avoids the reification of institutions that operate at particular scales.

In political and economic geography, the concept of scale refers to the spatial level (from local, metropolitan and provincial to national, regional and global) of particular social, political and economic activities (Smith 2008). The production of scale, along with the issues governed at any particular scale, is never given a priori but is the result of capitalist development, environmental factors, and political contestation (Swyngedouw

and Heynen 2010; Smith 2003). For Smith (2008, 181–90), scale is reproduced through dynamics of capitalist development: local scales have tra-
ditionally been sites of production and socialisation; provincial scales are
reproduced through the mechanics of distribution; and national scales are
reproduced through the support, defence and coordination of capital.[12]
Political scales then, are related parts of a single social-economic whole,
not separate ontological categories. Following this, here I use 'local' to
refer to the areas surrounding a mine site that are directly impacted by or
impact extraction. The local scale, then, is an outcome of capitalist development, but almost always also involves political contestation over who
should be considered local for the purposes of community development or
preferential employment.

Just as scale is not given *a priori*, it is not simply determined by structural
and environmental factors but is also the outcome of political and social
contestation and strategic decisions (Smith 2003; 2008, 229; Hameiri and
Jones 2015, 56; Allen 2018, 16). The politics of scale involves conflicts over
the appropriate scale, or construction of new scales, at which contestation
and governance occur (Jessop 2006a; Hameiri et al. 2017, 69). Because different opportunities, allies and resources are available at any given scale,
actors may attempt to contest issues at scales, or across multiple scales,
that are most beneficial to their interests (Hameiri and Jones 2015, 56). For
example, social movements often attempt to 'jump scales' to the national or
international where they can access allies, resources and media, and invite
public scrutiny (Escobar 2001; Kirsch 2014). National and international
campaigns may jump scales to target investors, particularly governments,
churches and public-facing banks, which may be more sensitive to public
opinion than the operating company (Kirsch 2014, 82). Alliances which
operate across political scales are a critical factor in how effectively people
affected by mining can campaign if they decide to reject participation – or
how much knowledge and support they can receive to participate.[13]

Likewise, multinational miners use scalar strategies to relocate sites of
governance from domestic to global scales – where corporations and their
associations can control the agenda more effectively than governments
(Hatcher 2014; Elbra 2017).[14] They simultaneously attempt to re-localise
conflicts with people affected by mining. Participatory mechanisms can contain threats to multinational miners' international reputations by separating people affected by mining from their national and international allies.
While participatory mechanisms operate on local political scales, global
self-governance establishes their institutional guidelines and ideological
legitimacy. The institutional frameworks and ideological support for participation constitute modes of participation which shape who can participate
on what issues when (Jayasuriya and Rodan 2007; Rodan 2018).

Modes of participation

Participatory mechanisms are a major tool used by mining corporations to contain and depoliticise undesirable forms of conflict. To understand contestations over who can participate on which issues, when, this section details the modes of participation framework – a specific application of social conflict theory. Developed by Jayasuriya and Rodan (2007) and extended by Rodan (2018), this framework analyses how state actors use participation as a technique for securing legitimacy and containing challenges from various groups. It provides a conceptual understanding of why particular forms of participation emerge at given moments and sites. The modes of participation framework is concerned with 'the institutional structures and ideologies that shape the inclusion and exclusion of individuals and groups in the political process' (Jayasuriya and Rodan 2007, 774). Modes of participation range from individual to collective and state-sponsored to autonomous (Rodan 2018, 34). Yet, across various regimes, there has been a growing emergence of state-sponsored extra-parliamentary modes of participation which bypass democratic modes of contesting politics such as political parties and workers' unions. The growth of new modes of participation and ideologies of representation is explained by the need to contain conflicts that emerge from inequities and contradictions of capitalist development and crises (Rodan 2012; Bal 2015).

The *legitimacy* of modes of participation is established when potential participants accept their ideological foundations. The legitimation of ideologies of representation has 'profound implications for whether or not persistent unequal social, political, and economic relationships are subject to scrutiny and potential political mobilization' (Rodan 2018, 23). In other words, legitimated ideologies come 'to define what is realistic and to drive certain goals and aspirations into the realm of the impossible, the realm of idle dreams, of wishful thinking' (Scott 1985, 326). Ideologies are not merely imposed by dominant groups but gain the consent of participants through concessions and co-optations as 'previously germinated ideologies come into contact and confrontation with one another, until only one of them – or, at least, a single combination of them – tends to prevail, to dominate' (Gramsci 1996, 2:Q4§38; 180).[15] Indeed, the modes of participation established by multinational mining corporations appropriate ideological fragments from critics, including ideas of sustainable development and human rights. Yet these are subsumed under an overarching *ideology of representation* and corporate-led development.

In the latest iteration of the framework, Rodan (2018, 29) identifies four ideologies of representation – democratic, populist, consultative and particularist.[16] In democratic ideologies of representation, representatives should be elected or appointed. Populist ideologies 'emphasize direct links between "the people" and the leadership of political movements' (Rodan 2018, 29–31). Consultative ideologies rely on the selection of technical experts in specific policy domains, while particularist ideologies 'emphasize the rights to representation of discrete communities and identities based on ethnicity, race, gender and culture' (Rodan 2018, 32). These are not mutually exclusive, but exist in tension, and particular participatory mechanisms may draw on multiple ideological sources. Ideologies of representation are also linked to broader historically situated ideological struggles.

Participatory mechanisms in the extractive industries are based in and reinforce consultative ideologies, although they may also draw on particularist ideologies and other ideological support. It is now widely accepted that people affected by mining have a right to be consulted. This so-called 'right to consultation' is a compromise offered by industry groups in response to growing pressure for the much stronger right to free prior and informed consent (FPIC) (see Chapter 2). Yet this right to be consulted exists in tension with and even at the expense of democratic forms of participation:

> Consultative ideologies of representation emphasise the problem-solving utility of incorporating stakeholders, interests, and/or experts into public policy processes to ensure the most effective functioning of economic, social, or political governance. These ideologies privilege such problem solving over political competition, thereby limiting the political space for contending normative positions over the fundamental objectives of public policy through spaces of technocratic governance.
>
> (Rodan 2018, 30)

In addition, pro-corporate ideologies support the creation of *corporate* sites of participation. Participatory mechanisms, then, incorporate social groups – usually through representatives – into corporate problem-solving processes without conceding democratic rights. Indeed, with the promise of representation in consultation, participatory mechanisms redirect demands for the right to veto to problem-solving obstacles to extractive accumulation.

This book extends the modes of participation framework to examine corporate-sponsored modes of participation and how they are constructed against state-sponsored and autonomous modes of participation. This reflects the increasing trend and need for mining corporations to contain contradictions and conflicts resulting from extractive developments.

Table 1.1 shows the matrix of sites of participation adapted from Rodan (2018, 34). The middle column, 'corporate-sponsored' sites of participation, is my addition. The level of inclusion may be individual or collective, with collective levels of inclusion incorporating various styles and forms of representation and group participation. This is a typology, not an exhaustive categorisation of sites or examples. The categories are not mutually exclusive and are not intended to represent a sharp delineation between sites; indeed, they are often constituted against each other (Bal 2015, 224). For example, political participation that begins in autonomous sites as individual expression may shift to corporate or state-sponsored sites of collective participation (Langlois 2022, 4). Sites of participation may be co-sponsored by a combination of corporations, states, NGOs or international organisations. Actors may simultaneously participate in corporate fora while maintaining autonomous expression, as is the case when a group enters negotiations with a corporation while maintaining independent protest activity. Likewise, affected people may choose between available corporate and state sites of participation – for example in negotiating directly with corporate actors versus suing them in court. Thus, the potential for particular sites of participation to manage conflict and distribute benefits is partially determined by the opportunities available at other sites. Each site of participation may involve any type of participant. Corporations can participate in state-sponsored sites, state actors may organise protests, and corporations may participate in sites sponsored by other corporations.

The advantage of this approach is that it explains the forms, sites and ideologies of participation in the mining sector as the result of broader conflicts

Table 1.1 Sites of participation

	Sites of participation		
Level of inclusion	State- and trans-state-sponsored	Corporate-sponsored	Autonomous from state and corporations
Individual	Administrative incorporation	Corporate-administrative incorporation	Individualised political expression
Examples:	Public grievance processes.	Corporate grievance mechanisms; Expert cultural advice.	Petitions; Blogs; Sabotage.
Collective	Societal incorporation	Corporate-social incorporation	Civil society expression
Examples:	Consultative councils; Participatory budgeting.	Participatory community development; Consultative committees; Environmental monitoring programs; Negotiations for compensation.	Protests; NGO advocacy; Blockades.

over extractive accumulation described above. Indeed, participatory mechanisms are always situated within broader social relations and processes of national, regional and international capitalist development (Nguyen 2014). Participation is neither the result of a universal 'corporate responsibility' nor simply a public relations exercise – it is the product of multiscalar contestation with people affected by mining and other critics. Furthermore, it is concerned with the development of ideological support and institutional structures that legitimise some forms of representation and participation over others.

The participatory mechanisms of multinational miners are usually collective, although individual grievance mechanisms are also common. Participatory environmental monitoring, sustainable community development programs, consultative committees and negotiations over compensation are all ways in which groups of people affected by mining participate either directly or via representatives. Through societal incorporation, defined groups of people (which may include particular ethnicities, villages or people affected by mining in particular ways) and NGOs participate in the delivery of predefined objectives (delivering community development, environmental monitoring) 'rather than [engaging] in an open-ended debate' (Rodan 2018, 38–39). Participatory mechanisms may also intervene in the political and economic relations of the target groups by privileging particular actors as representatives, redistributing resources, providing education, and ideological interventions.

Through particularistic and consultative ideologies of societal incorporation, conflicts with people affected by mining are (partially) contained within the expanded bounds of corporations. Yet, the concessions made through consultation are influenced by alternative sites of political participation available – autonomous or state – and their ideological legitimacy must be defended against or make concessions to competing ideologies. When groups are dissatisfied with the consultative boundaries of participation, they may find more autonomous forms of political participation – such as protests – or turn to state institutions – such as the court system. Participants or represented groups may also attempt to challenge the terms of participation to expand the issues or actors included (Rodan 2018, 34; Bal 2015).[17]

Ideologies of representation also involve struggles over who has the power to represent whom. Societal incorporation relies on corporations' ability to render communities legible, to determine both the groups that should be represented and who has authority to represent them and then police these boundaries. Often esoteric and complex social relationships are flattened and simplified through bureaucratisation (Borras and Franco 2013). This simplification can trigger new inter-communal conflicts. For example, while discussing representation of communities in the oil-rich Niger Delta,

Guichaoua laments, 'who is entitled to represent the now-reified "communities". In practice, such asymmetrical procedures favour the emergence of brokers co-opted by oil companies or state agents (2012, 148). Likewise, in Bougainville and the Solomon Islands, Allen (2018, 119) shows how struggles over who has the right to represent groups of landowners developed following

> 'trustees' and 'landowners' failing to share proceeds of rental payments and surface access fees, intensified land disputes and struggles over the control of landowner associations, stark asymmetries of knowledge and information, and the marginalisation of women from decision making and benefit-sharing.

So, while corporations will attempt to select representatives of groups most favourable to their interests, this too is subject to contestation by members of represented and excluded groups.

Problems of representation are particularly salient given generational and gender divides within represented groups – especially when, as is often the case, representatives are older men. Allen's (2018, 65) research shows how interests of supposedly homogeneous groups were divided along gender and generational lines:

> Generally speaking, I found that women throughout Bougainville were more likely to speak about [negative impacts on land, subsistence agriculture and village livelihoods – how they would feed their children] in relation to the Panguna question, while men tended to focus on compensation and benefit-sharing.

Therefore, compensation, negotiation and participation can reinforce pre-existing political, social and economic hierarchies by selecting already powerful figures – older men, village officials, etc. – as representatives. Yet it can also open new lines of contestation, for example as women demand to be included as representatives or participants.

Modes of participation also define the scale, or create new scales, at which participation can occur, again limiting who can participate and the availability of resources. For example, through localised grievance mechanisms and consultative committees, mining corporations create scales of political participation that might be more accessible to people affected by mining and bypass NGOs and state institutions such as courts. Of course, corporate grievance mechanisms are used to limit the exposure of corporations to litigation or negative publicity.[18] Participatory practices developed at the 'local' scale have been enshrined in global governance networks that entrench consultative and corporate ideologies and institutional forms as modes of participation.

In the following chapter I detail how organisations such as the International Council of Mining and Metals do less to regulate corporate power and more to legitimise pro-corporate ideologies. Curiously, this creates a split between sites of participation, which are largely local, and the governance and ideological defence of corporate participation, which takes place at international scales. Through this dual scalar strategy, participation and consultation have become the new orthodoxy, if not hegemony, to the exclusion of democratic and rights-based forms of political participation. Immediately, participatory mechanisms aim to manage local conflicts to smooth extractive accumulation while modes of participation attempt to facilitate a wider national and international legitimacy for the mining sector.

The modes of participation framework, as presented here, provides explanations for why forms of participation emerge at given moments and sites; it explains why, how and when mining corporations implement participatory mechanisms. It also explains how ideologies of representation and participatory mechanisms are constructed against and evolve through broader ideological contests. Yet it does not explain where the ideology of people affected by mining comes from. While this could be left as a given, to understand the diversity in reactions to participatory strategies, we must understand the diversity in ideology of people affected by mining. To add this level of analysis, I turn to Gramscian conceptualisations of ideology and common sense.

Common sense and ideological receptivity

So far, I have mentioned ideological dimensions of social conflict, extractive accumulation, and modes of participation. This section explicitly elaborates how ideology and common sense are understood in this book. I draw on Gramscian conceptualisations of ideology as historically produced conceptions of the world which ' "organise" human masses, and create the terrain on which men move, acquire consciousness of their position, struggle, etc.' (Gramsci 1971, 377; Q7§21). Especially for subaltern actors, ideologies 'are an expression of the contradictions of capitalist social relations (exploitations and oppressions) of production and reproduction' (Meckelburg 2019, 40), expressed through activity, resistance and domination. Importantly, ideologies have a material structure (Bieler and Morton 2018, 70).

While 'ideology' connotes a singular coherent world view, in Gramsci's schema, 'common sense' is ideology in its least developed, most incoherent and contradictory form. Rupert (2006, 93–94) defines common sense as 'an amalgam of historically effective ideologies, scientific doctrines and social mythologies … a syncretic historical residue, fragmentary, and contradictory, open to multiple interpretations and potentially supportive of very different kinds of social visions and political projects'. Meanwhile, E. P. Thompson (1978, 156) referred to 'an amalgam of the cultural debris of many different ways of thinking' from which people select 'those parts most calculated to defend their present interests' (1978, 154). Common sense contains 'the "raw material" of a new conception of the world, since it also contains the seeds of the new "systems of ideas"' (Filippini 2017, 20).

Contradictory and fecund, common sense becomes terrain for social conflict as competing actors emphasise ideas and practices that favour their interests. Which element becomes dominant and which others are discarded is the result of competition and cooperation between actors. For Gramsci (1971, Q11§12; 323–343), intellectuals, organisers, political parties and leaders play the role of critiquing 'common sense' – they 'develop the "gastric juices" to digest competing conceptions of social order' (Bieler and Morton 2018, 71). Organisations and actors struggle to emphasise elements within common sense and develop ideologies that best serve their interests as they understand them. It is also through common sense (and critique of common sense) that people understand their interests.

Ultimately, it is the elements which become dominant within common sense understandings that preclude or predispose people to iterations of participatory mechanisms. The forms that participatory mechanisms take are also determined by the contradictions and synergies between the common sense of people affected by mining and corporate ideologies.

The dynamics of ideological conflict within common sense are a matter for detailed empirical investigation. The theoretical point is that people affected by mining are 'historically situated social agents whose actions are enabled and constrained by their social self-understandings' (Rupert 2006, 93). This is most clearly demonstrated in Chapter 6, where fragments of historical ideologies of Javanese feudalism, left-nationalism, syncretic and religious belief of the Kolon Progo peasants mix with newer anarchist and feminist influences to create new common sense understandings of land, resistance and politics.

Common sense understandings enable or privilege some courses of action over others, influencing social organisation, relationships with land, and dispositions towards alliance partners and state and corporate actors. Yet this is a two-way process; the development of common sense is profoundly influenced by histories of social organisation of production and reproduction.[19] Therefore, in this book, feudalism, anarchism, nationalism, feminism and *adat* (indigeneity) are considered as ideologies in so far as they contain or contribute to more or less coherent conceptions of the world.

The modes of participation framework provides a typology of *ideologies of representation* that legitimise forms and sites of participation

(Rodan 2018, 29). Ideologies of representation may intersect and draw support from, yet should not be confused with, a wide range of broader ideologies, such as neoliberalism, corporatism or nationalism. I identified that, in the mining industry, consultative ideologies of corporate–social incorporation are the most prevalent – although administrative incorporation and particularist ideologies are also relevant. While this situation supports and is produced by corporate power, these ideologies are influenced by the broader political environment and must respond to challenges.[20]

To analyse how people affected by mining accept or resist participatory mechanisms, I consider how their ideologies are receptive to, or contradict, ideologies of representation in general, and consultative ideologies of corporate-social incorporation in particular. Where these ideologies are incompatible with extractive capitalism or participation, it is likely that the group will be opposed to participation. Where there is common ground, even if tactical or opportunistic, groups may accept participation, yet may attempt to change the terms of participation. While I identify four factors – control of land, histories and forms of organisation, alliance structures, and ideology – that determine if and how people affected by mining participate, the role of ideology is key. It is through ideology that people affected by mining understand their tactics and agency, relationships to land, how they construct organisations and select allies.

Conclusion

Mining companies have developed participatory mechanisms for three interrelated reasons: in response to crises of legitimacy, both global and local; to attempt to control risky forms of conflict that emerge from extractive developments; and to create social relations of production and reproduction conducive to extractive developments. Participatory mechanisms are developed by multinational mining corporations in response to threats to profitability as methods of accommodating dissent in order to continue accumulating wealth. They therefore have the potential to prolong underlying causes of conflict and entrench inequality.

The political economy of extractive accumulation established here conceptualises visible forms of conflict as manifestations of the conflicting interests within extractive developments and between extractive and competing modes of production. This includes land grabbing, ideological contradictions, conflict over environmental pollution, inequality between mine employees and others, inequality between men and women, and changing relations of social reproduction. The implementation of participatory mechanisms and the forms that they take are explained by the modes of participation framework as techniques for managing these conflicts, contradictions and inequalities. Yet modes of participation are subject to contestation over both their material effects and ideological legitimacy. The ways that the common sense understandings of people affected by mining intersect or contradict ideologies of representation will determine their reactions to them and perhaps the form of participation. This therefore goes halfway to explaining the vast range of outcomes of participation and extractive conflicts.

The next chapter adds nuance to extractive accumulation with a concrete analysis of scale, global governance and multiscalar contestation. An analysis of political scale allows us to move beyond the single scalar focus present in much of the literature. A modes of participation framework sensitive to scalar politics understands that multinational miners implement participatory mechanisms in response to localised conflict, ideological foundations *and* standards set at the global scale, which, in turn, are also the result of contestation between the mining industry and its critics.

To explain why people affected by mining accept or resist invitations to participate, or force corporations to accept their participation, I analyse them as historically situated subjects with relationships to land and resources, forms of organisation based in histories of production and social reproduction, allies, and corresponding common sense understandings of the world. The ways that their common sense understandings contradict or are compatible with corporate ideologies of participation will largely determine their desire to participate and how they participate.

The original contribution of this combination of approaches is to understand how histories and ideologies of people affected by mining explain diverse outcomes of participatory strategies in the mining sector within broader developments in extractive accumulation and global capitalism. The next chapter demonstrates, clarifies and expands this framework by considering in detail the specific forms that participatory mechanisms take in the mining sector and how these are governed at a global scale.

Notes

1 For example, according to Mentan ' "Extractivism" is the policy by which governments finance their economic and political programs by exporting their countries' mineral resources … The term has been especially used by social theorists in Latin America … to describe and criticize the economic policies of the presumably progressive governments of Bolivia, Ecuador, Brazil' (2018, 76).

2 Contestation often occurs between class-based groups or class fractions, while gender, indigeneity, ethnicity and religion are also important social categories that can demark conflicting interests.

3 Approaches including 'everyday political economy' (Elias and Rethel 2016), 'everyday forms of resistance' (Scott 1985; 2012), poor peoples' politics (Hutchison and Wilson 2020), and social reproduction theory (Bhattacharya 2017a) are entirely consistent with how social conflict theory is used in this book, while focusing greater analytical attention on subaltern actors.

4 Corporations can be considered political actors in so far as they act politically and socially to secure their economic interests. They can be considered as governance institutions when they actively create governance standards, networks or regulations, either collectively or in partnership with state actors (Wilks 2013; Sinclair 2020).

5 Scholars from various traditions have problematised the idea of corporate personhood – the legal fiction that corporations are people – pointing out the conflicting interests within corporations between owners, executive management, shareholders, financial mangers (who control stock on behalf of investment funds), workers and other stakeholders (Wilks 2013, 13–15). The balance of these interests changes with national legal frameworks, corporate structures and shifting patterns of ownership and managerialism. Nevertheless, it is often a convenient simplification to treat corporations as unitary actors (May 2020, 6) – and a heuristic simplification that I will use throughout this book without forgetting that it remains an abstraction.

6 Or 'accumulation by dispossession', a term coined by David Harvey (2003), following Rosa Luxembourg's (1951, 348–67) theorising that primitive accumulation was not only the original appropriation of the commons by capital but is an ongoing process driven by crises of over-accumulation and under-consumption.

7 According to them, land grabbing by extractive corporations is typically accompanied by rising gendered inequality; fraudulent consent; displacement; destruction of sacred sites; epistemicide; displacement of traditional economic activities; environmental and social impacts; and militarisation.

8 In Indonesia, a common slogan for peasant unions is 'Land is a social relation, it cannot be bought and sold!' (*Tanah adalah hubungan sosial, tidak bisa dijual-beli!*).

9 As an extension of Marxist theories of production (e.g. Engels 1986), social reproduction theory shares a common heritage with social conflict theory. Both resist deterministic and reductionist interpretations of Marxism. As conceptualised in this book, they are complementary theories for considering how social conflicts exceed sites of production.

10 Ruth Hall et al. (2015, 469) add to this the importance of affective ties and social allegiances. This then links to my treatment of ideology and common sense.

11 Although this argument is given in its most developed form by Silvia Federici, this observation can be traced back to Rosa Luxembourg and through the work of Marxist feminists including Lise Vogel (Čakardić 2017).

12 Ecological factors can also influence the production of scales of conflict and governance.

13 Indeed, in all three cases in this book, people opposed to mining sought to create alliances with groups who could help attract national and international resources and legitimacy.

14 Chapter 2 details how organisations such as the International Council of Mining and Metals, standards such as the Equator Principles and institutions such as the UN Global Compact do less to constrain corporate power and more to establish the legitimacy and ideology of corporate self-regulation.

15 In this note, 'Relations between structure and superstructure', Gramsci is theorising moments in the historical formation of hegemony. However, I avoid using the term 'hegemony' because I am not considering the hegemony of a dominant class over society in general. I am simply considering a single moment – the domination of multinational corporations over the management of social impacts of mining.

16 These are 'conceptual categories', not the 'complete range of ideological perspectives' (Rodan 2018, 28).

17 This was the case in Kelian (Chapter 5).

18 See Chapter 6 for an example involving UNDP-LEAD.

19 Chapter 7 provides the best demonstration of this process.

20 For example, particularist ideologies are most often adopted where an Indigenous group has been able to establish its legitimacy and right to participate. See Ibu Afrida's story in Chapter 6.

2

Global governance, crises and resistance in extractive accumulation

The social and environmental impacts of extraction are increasingly regulated at a global scale by multinational corporations and international organisations. Global private governance networks have emerged in response to successive overlapping global, national and company-specific crises of legitimacy – crises created by multiscalar conflicts over extraction. These governance mechanisms establish the overarching institutional and ideological structures of participation for people affected by mining and their allies – that is, the *modes of participation*. Language and practices of 'sustainability', 'participation' and 'responsibility' have been adopted by multinational mining corporations. Standards for participation encoded at global scales cascade down through corporate structures to manage localised opposition to mining through *participatory mechanisms*.

This chapter analyses the contestations that have structured modes of participation in international institutions. It demonstrates and expands on the historical evolution of extractive accumulation to explain the emergence of corporate social responsibility (CSR) and global governance in the late 1990s and evolution as environmental social governance (ESG) up to today. It conceptualises governance and regulation as dynamic institutions produced through ongoing contestation between opposing interests by analysing the macro ideologies, context and relations within which participatory mechanisms are deployed, including shifts towards 'green', 'ethical' or 'sustainable' global capitalisms.

The first section explains how historical conflicts culminated in crises of legitimacy for the extractive industries in the 1990s and prompted the development of global private governance for the social and environmental dimensions of mining. International business associations, industry standards and governance mechanisms appropriated ideological fragments from their critics to reconstitute the legitimacy of mining corporations as responsible self-regulating actors. The International Council on Metals and Mining (ICMM) exemplifies this.

The second section considers how international organisations and development agencies – and the World Bank Group in particular – also underwent a crisis of legitimacy because of their financial support for controversial extractive development. This mirrored broader crises in development practice which prompted the 'social turn' in development practice and the rise of participatory development, which was copied into extractive industries.

The third section argues that trends towards corporate self-governance – private modes of participation – are expressed in increased responsibilities of corporations for community development, participation and sustainability. CSR, ESG, corporate community development and participatory environmental monitoring are an expression and expansion of corporate power used to manage conflict and create social conditions favourable to extractive capitalism. CSR and related participatory practices are not always mere greenwashing; rather they help to reshape the social relations of production and reproduction into configurations amenable to extractive accumulation. Together, these first three sections demonstrate and develop my argument that modes of participation and participatory mechanisms in mining involve a reassertion of corporate power in response to overlapping crises and challenges from below.

Of course, this is not a straightforward process of transformation and is contested at almost every step, not least by the decisions and actions of mining-affected communities. Thus, the exercise of corporate power and reactions to it from affected communities, state actors and civil society often produce unexpected outcomes.

The fourth and final section considers how mining critics and affected communities have responded to participatory mechanisms. There are well-documented examples of people affected by mining benefiting from deciding to embrace, co-opt, subvert, resist or build alternatives to corporate participation. But there is little existing literature explaining why and how communities affected by mining make strategic choices or what determines their successes and failures. I argue that, regardless of how they participate, groups will extract more benefits or more effectively resist if they are able to demonstrate power outside corporate and state-sponsored sites of participation – including through demonstrations, NGO campaigns and political and media strategies.

Crisis and the emergence of global governance

In the second half of the twentieth century, as exploration and resource extraction in remote areas increasingly became economically and technologically viable, the social and environmental dynamics of mining changed dramatically (Colley 2001; Dougherty 2016). The extraction of minerals and coal from remote areas, especially in developing countries, meant that small agrarian communities and Indigenous people became the principal groups affected by mining (Leifsen et al. 2017; Conde and Le Billon 2017; Filer and Le Meur 2017, 13). These changes led to new forms of conflict – forced relocations, land grabbing, collusion with corrupt regimes and militaries, environmental pollution and even civil war – which had become chronic by the 1990s (Evans et al. 2001).

In turn, significant controversies developed from local campaigns, jumping scales to attract global media attention. Non-governmental organisations rallied against the lack of regulation, transparency and accountability of mining companies in their overseas operations, especially when operating in authoritarian contexts (Szablowski 2007, 75–77; Bünte 2018). Infamous cases with global media attention include the 1996 execution of nine environmental activists in Nigeria, where Royal Dutch Shell was implicated (Hanlon 2008); the international campaign on blood diamonds (Fanthorpe and Gabelle 2013); civil war in Bougainville (Allen 2018); and the international NGO and labour movement campaigns against Rio Tinto (McSorley and Fowler 2001). Discourses on sustainability, human rights, corruption and environmental devastation framed global awareness of conflict, severely damaging the reputation of multinational miners and financiers, notably including the World Bank (Fox and Brown 2000; World Bank 2003).

Beyond reputational damage, several cases saw multinational miners sued by affected communities in their home jurisdiction.[1] This was famously demonstrated by Ok Tedi, traditional owners from Papua New Guinea, taking BHP to the Victorian Supreme Court in Australia (Filer and Macintyre 2006), Bouganvillian landowners suing Rio Tinto in the Los Angeles District Court (ACFOA 1995; Leith 2003; Allen 2018), and Indigenous claimants from West Papua suing Freeport-McMoRan in the New Orleans District Court (Regan 1998; Filer et al. 2008; see Kirsch 2014, 84–126 for an extended discussion of these international court cases). Building on their political advocacy with affected communities, international NGOs and coalitions launched campaigns to hold multinational miners operating abroad to the standards that apply in their home states (Bünte 2018, Chapter 4). Court cases and NGO campaigns together threatened to increase the regulatory burden on multinational miners. This internationalisation of resistance was game-changing for multinational miners in authoritarian countries who could no longer rely only on host governments, state-controlled media and militaries to control dissent. Furthermore, by 2002, the global mining sector was achieving a return on investment of only 4.67% (Kellow 2007, 115), and desperately needed to control any further threats to profitability.

Sustained negative publicity, NGO campaigns and political advocacy led to protracted crises of legitimacy for the global extractive industry (Danielson 2002, 7; Kirsch 2014, 159). Multinational miners were worried that recommendations of the United Nations Conference on Environment and Development Earth Summit in Rio de Janeiro 1992, if adopted, could pose a 'significant threat to [metals] markets' (Kellow 2007, 123). These crises of legitimacy threatened mining corporations' unregulated operations and the viability of significant ventures (Szablowski 2007, 77–82).[2]

The threat to profitability posed by community opposition is real. Franks et al. (2014, 7578) show that 'as a result of conflict, a major, world-class mining project with capital expenditure of between US$3 and US$5 billion was reported to suffer roughly US$20 million per week of delayed production in net present value terms', while cancellations of projects run into billions of dollars of lost capital. In a more recent Canadian study of 57 cases of extractive conflicts over more than 30 years, protesting communities stopped projects in 21% of cases, while another 17% resulted in new legislation and others resulted in the enforcement of existing regulations or triggered environmental assessment processes (Gobby et al. 2022, 4).

Multinational miners responded with dual strategies: the first was to establish a new international network of self-governance standards, partnerships and organisations (Hatcher 2014). The second was to relocalise and contain conflict through community development work, CSR and the participation of select local actors. Multinational miners pre-empted state intervention by establishing institutional guidelines and ideological legitimacy to manage the social and environmental impacts of mining. Together these constituted a new mode of participation, institutionalising guidelines and ideologies of representation for corporations to manage the multiscalar threats to their profitability.

An example is the International Cyanide Management Code,[3] developed as a partnership between the then International Council of Metals and Environment (ICME) and the United Nations Environment Program (UNEP) in May 2000. Three months earlier, at the Romanian Baia Mare mine owned by the Australian company Esmeralda, a tailings dam breached causing massive cyanide pollution to rivers across Romania, Hungary and Yugoslavia, killing fish and poisoning drinking water. The BBC called it 'the worst environmental disaster since the Chernobyl nuclear leak' (Batha 2000). Gold miners and cyanide manufacturers feared new stringent legislation would prove costly and so pre-empted this with the creation of a private voluntary code in partnership with the UNEP, to which Rio Tinto seconded staff (Burton 2001, 119–22). Although it is voluntary, as an industry-wide code it has benefits for medium and small gold mining companies which might not have the resources or experience to develop their own cyanide management procedures. The code relies on consultation with experts to establish its legitimacy, rather than with affected people.

For almost any aspect of the environmental and social dimensions of mining, there is a relevant international standard. All are voluntary, although each differs in terms of the actors involved, their political power, the problem being responded to, and the benefits conferred. While there are too many to consider in detail, Table 2.1 lists the most prominent. All confer legitimacy on members and some facilitate access to resources, such as finance, markets or technical guidance (on the Extractive Industry Transparency Initiative [EITI], see Bünte 2018). By providing guidelines which each actor can implement according to their own interpretation and interests, rather than providing hard regulations, this network of standards functions to mitigate environmental and social risk to corporations and sometimes state actors, investors and NGOs. This risk mitigation is about smoothing the process of extraction rather than preventing social and environmental harms (on the Equator Principles, see Wright 2012).

The Equator Principles demonstrate how voluntary adherence to standards can facilitate both social legitimacy and access to resources. The Principles are a set of guidelines adopted by financial institutions providing project finance with a total capital cost of US$10 million and over (Watchman et al. 2007). Project finance nominally governed by the Principles have accounted for up to 85% of global cross-border extractive project finance (Watchman et al. 2007, 95). Financial institutions which adopt the Principles place conditions on project developers that are often over and above the legislated requirements in host countries. These conditions include risk management plans for social and environmental risks, prior informed consultation in a culturally appropriate manner with affected communities, grievance processes, and public reporting of social and environmental impact assessments; in some cases there are also requirements to report greenhouse gas emissions ('The Equator Principles III' 2013). Thus, participation based on consultative ideologies of representation is being built into international capital markets.

The ICMM and its Ten Principles for Sustainable Development framework (ICMM 2023) is an important example because most of the largest multinational miners and national mining associations are members, it is influential in creating other standards, covers most areas of environmental and social impacts of mining, and provides a primary reference for how its members design community relations programs.[4]

A precursor to the ICMM, the Global Mining Initiative (GMI), was formed in 1998 by CEOs of eight of the largest multinational miners who recognised the industry's 'trust deficit' (Kellow 2007, 124) that could result in being 'legislated out of existence' (Dashwood 2013, 446). In 1999,

Table 2.1 Selected international standards and organisations

Standard	Organisation	Problem	Actors
ISO26000	ISO	Social responsibility	Corporations and associations via national organisations
Compliance Advisor Ombudsman	World Bank Group	Social and environmental conflict	Projects financed by IFC or insured by Multilateral Investment Guarantee Agency (MIGA); IFC and MIGA complainants.
International Cyanide Management Code	Established by United Nations Environment Program and International Council on Metals and the Environment	Environmental impacts of cyanide	Gold and silver mining companies, cyanide producers and transporters
The Extractive Industries Transparency Initiative	Established by Department for International Development (UK) (DFID), supported by IMF and World Bank	Corruption, transparency in state revenue	States Multinational corporations
The Voluntary Principles on Security and Human Rights	The Voluntary Principles Initiative	Human rights, violence	States, extractive corporations, NGOs
The Equator Principles	Independent, with IFC support	Environmental and social impacts of mining	Financial institutions
The Kimberley Process	United Nations	Conflict, war, diamonds	States, corporations, NGOs

(continued)

Table 2.1 (Cont.)

Standard	Organisation	Problem	Actors
The UN Global Compact	United Nations	Human rights, labour, environment and corruption	Corporations, NGOs, academia, business associations
Sustainable Development Framework Ten Principles	International Council on Metals and Mining	Environmental and social impacts of mining	Multinational mining corporations
The Rio Declaration	United Nations Conference on Environment and Development	Sustainable development	States
Global Reporting Initiative Guidelines	The Global Reporting Initiative	Sustainable reporting	Corporations, states, NGOs
OECD Guidelines on Multinational Enterprises	Organisation for Economic Co-operations and Development	Business ethics	States
Performance Standards on Environmental and Social Sustainability	International Finance Corporation (IFC)	Social and environmental sustainability	World Bank Group, IFC, mining corporations
Global Battery Alliance	World Economic Forum	'Critical minerals' used to manufacture lithium batteries	Mining companies, battery manufacturers, EV OEMs, NGOs International organisations

Sir Robert Wilson, then chairperson of Rio Tinto, framed the GMI as a response to crisis: 'Unless the major players in the global mining and minerals industry can present a convincing case that their activities are conducted in line with [sustainable development] principles ... their long term future is in jeopardy' (quoted in Evans et al. 2001, xvi–xvii). The GMI's two-year Mining, Minerals and Sustainable Development (MMSD) project investigated 'disputes concerning land tenure, environmental management, and relationships to communities' (Kirsch 2014, 168). Discourses and practices of sustainability and community development were appropriated through NGO cooperation. By attempting to overcome collective action problems of any one multinational corporation (MNC) going it alone, 'the MNCs formed a collective citizenship aiming to operate across multiple nation-states, strategically building political influence and the corporate reputation of mining companies [and] engineered reforms from above, via multi-stakeholder networks around CSR' (Phillips 2012, 172). The *collective* organisation of the companies is important, allowing them to claim that the *industry* is now self-regulated and hence that state regulation is unnecessary. The MMSD resulted in a four-step program for 'Supporting Sustainable Development in the Minerals Sector' (Danielson 2002, xxv): understanding sustainable development; creating organisational policies and management systems; achieving cooperation among those with similar interests; and building capacity for effective actions at all levels (Danielson 2002, xxv–xxxiv). Although the final report is devoid of any concrete recommendations for reform, it established a common language for sustainability and provided a base for proceeding initiatives. It created an ideological foundation of sustainable development to legitimise private development. The MMSD also began to embody consultative ideologies of representation. However, because the focus was on restoring the industry's international reputation, it was international NGOs rather than affected communities that participated.

The MMSD marked a shift in relationships between some NGOs and mining corporations. For NGOs which actively sought collaboration with MNCs, such as the World-Wide Fund for Nature (WWF), the MMSD presented an opportunity to influence corporate practices. For other NGOs, including the Australian Conservation Foundation (ACF) and Minerals Policy Institute (MPI), voluntary, market-based CSR was viewed as a threat to legal reform and strict regulation (Phillips 2012, 184–87). The MMSD attracted much criticism from critical activists, NGOs and academics for failing to provide significant improvements in outcomes, advocating voluntary standards and co-opting discourses of sustainability, human rights and poverty reduction (Kirsch 2014). Nevertheless, the MMSD began the process of reframing the mining sector's existing practices in terms of sustainability and inclusive economic growth.

Realising the need for ongoing legitimacy and profitability, the GMI prompted the existing International Council on Metals and the Environment to broaden its scope and reform as the ICMM in 2001 (ICMM n.d. 'Our History'). Adopted in 2003 and most recently refined in 2023, the ICMM requires that members commit to the Ten Principles, which include requirements to 'contribute to the social, economic and institutional development of host countries and communities' (2023, 9) and 'proactively engage key stakeholders on sustainable development challenges and opportunities in an open and transparent manner' (2023, 10) . The ICMM also harmonises the principles with other standards applicable to MNCs:

> To ensure their robustness, the principles have been benchmarked against leading international standards. These include: the Rio Declaration, the Global Reporting Initiative, the Global Compact, OECD Guidelines on Multinational Enterprises, World Bank Operational Guidelines, OECD Convention on Combating Bribery, ILO Conventions 98, 169, 176, and the Voluntary Principles on Security and Human Rights.
>
> (ICMM 2015, 3)

The principles borrow legitimacy from these other organisations and link them together as a network of self-governance arrangements. They commit members to develop and report on companywide and project-specific policies and procedures for environmental management, community development and stakeholder participation. The ICMM thus builds on the MMSD and extends consultation and participation as a problem-solving technique to people affected by mining.

The ICMM principles are voluntary, unenforceable, vague, focused on process, neglect measurable outcomes, and have little independent reporting or monitoring requirements, allowing great flexibility for individual corporations in their implementation. The same criticism can be applied to almost all self-governance standards (Vogel 2007, 164; Singh 2011). The voluntary nature and vagueness of the ICMM principles and other standards listed in Table 2.1 give individual mining corporations flexibility to create their own internal policy and guidelines. Each mining project will implement participatory mechanisms based on the participatory principles according to company policy and local conditions. This may result in the creation of consultative committees, community development funding, complaints mechanisms, cultural programs, and/or participatory environmental monitoring.

Having overcome threats to their legitimacy, multinational mining corporations emerged more powerful than ever. Their network of interconnected standards, policy and practices constitute a new mode of participation with consultative ideologies of representation and societal incorporation in corporate sites. However, mining corporations have not developed this mode of participation on their own; they are directly influenced by the ideologies and participatory development practices of international development organisations.

Development agencies and participatory development

Participatory development emerged following the rise in influence of neo-institutionalism[5] and the World Bank's 'social-development model' in the 1990s (for example, World Bank 2003; 2014; Fanthorpe and Gabelle 2013; Ali et al. 2017). In relation to extractive industries, the World Bank Group copied techniques of participatory development for use in extractive projects and influenced mining corporations to adopt them as a means of restoring legitimacy.[6] In 2001, following the Group's involvement in several controversial projects, the Bank declared a two-year moratorium on investment in extractive industries pending the completion of the independent *Extractive Industries Review* (World Bank 2003). The review concluded that the World Bank Group still has a significant role to play in extractive industry development, albeit with a renewed focus on contributing to 'poverty alleviation through sustainable development' by meeting the following conditions:

- pro-poor public and corporate governance, including proactive planning and management to maximize poverty alleviation through sustainable development;
- much more effective social and environmental policies; and
- respect for human rights.

(World Bank 2003, vii)

The review provided a new foundation for people affected by mining to participate in the planning, monitoring and implementation of environmental and social dimensions of mining. The World Bank Group adopted new standards for consultation and participation, revised policy and guidelines on social and environmental impacts of extractive industries, and renewed support for the Extractive Industries Transparency Initiative, the Voluntary Principles on Human Rights and Security, and internal grievance mechanisms (World Bank Group 2004). The report also recommended that Indigenous people affected by mining be afforded the right of free, prior and informed consent (FPIC); however, the Bank cynically adopted the FPIC acronym but changed it to free, prior and informed *consultation* (World Bank Group 2004). Support for extractive developments from the Group, including finance from the International Finance Corporation (IFC), were made conditional on extractive developments including certain kinds of participation by affected communities and NGOs (Szablowski 2007, 122–27; Hatcher 2014).

Grievance mechanisms are a prominent participatory mechanism through which agencies directly engage with local populations and work around state structures. They are a last defence at resolving grievances within international organisations before conflict escalates through more threatening avenues – such as court cases or international NGO campaigns (see Park 2014 on grievance mechanisms in the Asia Development Bank [ADB]). That is, they can contain the risk of reputational and ultimately financial damage to investors. Grievance mechanisms also shape the issues and actors who are deemed legitimate.

Fabiana Li (2015, 92–98) discusses how the Compliance Advisor Ombudsman (CAO), which handles grievances about projects financed by the IFC, both directly engages affected populations and 'scientises' issues. She argues that while the grievance process produced interesting scientific data, the technocratic framework meant that social, political and ethical dimensions of conflict were ignored. However, the data produced through investigations into grievances can be used by actors in other sites of political participation.

This is not to say that the CAO cannot be harnessed to extract concessions from mining corporations. Nomadic herders in Mongolia affected by Rio Tinto's Oyu Tolgoi mine used CAO mediation to secure 'commitments to improved environmental monitoring and management and compensation, as well as a number of initiatives to boost the economic sustainability of the herders' traditional livelihood' (Brueckner and Sinclair 2019, 115). The CAO itself was established in 2009 in response to international NGO campaigns against the IFC's involvement in controversial projects (Brueckner and Sinclair 2019, 115). The CAO internalises contestation to contain threats to the legitimacy of the IFC and its partners (see also MacDonald 2017).

The World Bank and other agencies' work is not limited to the projects they fund but also involves 'capacity-building' and reforming developing countries' legislation and regulations regarding extractive industries (Hatcher 2012; 2015, 328–30). Here the 'social development model' forms a basis for reform, which may require corporations to consult with affected communities on issues from environmental controls and monitoring, to compensation and endowment funds, to agreements about the provision of local jobs and so forth (Hatcher 2014). By placing the responsibility to consult on corporations, 'the environmental, social and human rights dimensions embedded in this new generation of mining regimes appear to have been, in practice, removed from the state's scrutiny' (Hatcher 2015, 437).

The World Bank Group's reform agenda facilitates corporate power while shielding mining corporations from social risk. The limited participation provided for in national mining codes leads Hatcher (2015, 323–24) to argue that 'the involvement of local communities translates into a renewed emphasis on sociopolitical risk management for capital and multilateral institutions rather than an opening of political space', reflecting 'a pressing need to rally certain segments of civil society and manage local resistance' (2015, 340).

In summary, the World Bank reformed its internal practices and influenced corporations and states to adopt frameworks for stakeholder participation in private-sector-led development. This amounts to the Bank and multinational corporations forging a new mode of participation based on technocratic problem-solving, consultative ideologies, societal incorporation, and corporate sites of participation. Ideological fragments from sustainability and participatory development practice were incorporated into neo-institutional ideologies of private-sector-led development to neutralise or co-opt critics. With this foundation, the World Bank Group was able to partially restore legitimacy for its involvement in the industry and contain risks to its investments without needing to fundamentally challenge the rationale for mining or the power structures surrounding corporate–community engagement. The next section considers the more material effects of CSR as a vehicle of corporate power.

Corporate social responsibility as corporate power

Most critical literature on ESG or CSR and power takes a Foucauldian, post-structuralist or constructivist approach (Welker 2014; Li 2015; Horowitz 2015).[7] In their scathing critique of 'social engineering of extraction' Virweijen and Dunlap (2021) argue that 'CSR is increasingly seen as a corporate method to pre-empt and neutralise criticism, without fundamental changes to corporate practices'. I agree with the first half of this assessment, but contend that CSR and other participatory mechanisms have affected material change to the relationships between corporations and communities. In this section, I argue that CSR is not merely the expression of an ethical imperative, corporate 'greenwashing', or a simple expression of corporate self-interest (O'Faircheallaigh 2008; Mzembe and Downs 2014; Guarneros-Meza 2022). It is a reassertion of corporate power deployed to shape the social relations of production and reproduction favourable to extractive accumulation.

In this view, CSR builds corporate power and influence over social and environmental issues (Elbra 2014; Welker 2014; Horowitz 2015).

While CSR programs might aim to build trust and legitimacy with the public, civil society, affected communities and state actors, the asymmetric power relations between them are reinforced. Hanlon makes the point that

> CSR represents a further embedding of capitalist social relations and a deeper opening up of social life to the dictates of the marketplace ... it is the result of a shift from a fordist to a post-fordist regime of accumulation at the heart of which is both an expansion and deepening of wage relations.
>
> (2008, 57)

This process amounts to a reorganisation of relationships and roles played by corporations, states and civil society driven by conflict over the extractive process. Through deploying fractions of their resources, mining corporations can influence key local actors and government decision makers.

For example, Freeport and Newcrest both provided 1% of their operating profit from their Grasburg and Gosowong mines for community development funds to villages surrounding their operations, providing health clinics, education and employment opportunities (Leith 2003; Newcrest 2011). Funds are distributed through local government councils, NGOs or community groups (Leith 2003). Such community development funds are often accompanied by agreements to guarantee local employment, provide education and training and relocation programs, or to protect biodiversity (Wanvik 2014). This helps to establish the legitimacy of large-scale mines and create local political, social and economic relations favourable to mining. The corresponding increase of community reliance on corporate generosity reinforces the role of the private sector in social life (Welker 2014; Elbra 2014).

Environmental and social impact assessments give corporations understandings of the risks to a specific development while community-based agreements, through the participation of community representatives, mitigate and control these risks (Barrow 2010). Impact assessments may involve the participation of people affected by mining or may simply be produced by experts. Either way, impact assessments provide the baseline of knowledge for negotiating community agreements, although usually only include those impacts deemed technically manageable (McKenna 2015, 145).[8]

The increase in corporate responsibility and power is not necessarily at the expense of state power, as corporations and state institutions often work in partnership as governance actors. For example, the Voluntary Principles on Security and Human Rights is a voluntary, consensus-based initiative that sets out principles for transparent, accountable and consultative corporate security policy in the oil, gas and minerals sectors. The Voluntary Principles reimagine corporate actors as active participants in the creation of human rights norms, conflict resolution and democratisation, rather than as simply owing obligations to adhere to local legislation (Guáqueta 2013). Signatories are expected to design security programs, using public and/or private security forces in consultation with local communities, governments and NGOs, in ways that promote human rights in line with international standards (Guáqueta 2013; Voluntary Principles Initiative 2022). Through the creation of the Voluntary Principles, corporate actors have become partners with states and NGOs in the process of designing security governance arrangements across local and global scales.

With corporations becoming more involved in community development programs, environmental monitoring, human rights governance, and stakeholder consultation, incentives are created for people affected by mining to engage with corporate actors. Leifsen et al. (2017, 1044) argue that 'new types of conflict arise which are often related to what constitute legitimate forms of information, knowledge, impacts and levels of compensation'. For example, compensation may be introduced to diffuse conflict but can itself become a source of conflict. Indeed, the main effect of CSR programs is to change conflict, rather than eliminate it (Li 2015; Jaskoski 2022). The subject of conflict is shifted from the impacts of mining to processes of consultation and development and the form of conflict from confrontational to collaborative. This amounts to a realignment of interests of people affected by mining to be less oppositional to corporate mining.

However, this process is not unidirectional. People affected by mining do not merely adopt corporate interests in response to patronage. Corporations must also make concessions and invest in community development in ways that are not directly reducible to the profit motive. Welker (2014, 1) shows how the community relations practices of Newmont at their ex-Batu Hijau copper mine evolved through a series of contestations with people affected by mining and other opportunists who learned how to pressure Newmont to provide 'development goods'. Thus, local CSR programs, like the global governance networks, evolve as corporate political strategies in relation to contestation and threat.

The major caveat I need to offer before continuing is that participatory mechanisms have not substantially replaced the kinds of violent, repressive strategies that have become infamous for their association with extractive industries. Indeed, Guarneros-Meza (2022, 5) refers to CSR and state repression as a Gramscian 'coercion and consensus' dialectic for maintaining hegemony in mining communities. The security arsenal available to corporations and states today is only limited by their budgets and vulnerability to public scrutiny. Police, military, private security, thugs, gangsters (*preman* in Indonesia), criminal courts and prisons all constitute violent means of containing conflict. Mechanisms of participation exist in the shadow of legitimate, illegitimate, legal and illegal deployable violence (Leith 2003;

Arellano-Yanguas 2011; Welker 2014). Indeed, they are both constituted against violence as the alternative and can provide cover for violent actions. To be sure, mining-affected communities may decide to participate in corporate programs if they feel there is an implicit or explicit threat of violence awaiting non-participation or resistance to mining.

The key contribution of the social reproduction approach to CSR is to uncover how participatory mechanisms are more than just consensus building, legitimising, or greenwashing. They create new social relations of reproduction through interventions into community livelihood strategies and the discipline of recalcitrant groups, resulting in either a convergence of corporate and community interests or crisis.

Contested strategies and reorganised conflict: embracing, co-opting, resisting, subverting and building alternatives

So far in this chapter, I have argued that modes of participation are the outcome of multinational corporations and international organisations responding to threats to extractive accumulation. Yet participatory mechanisms rarely operate in the way they were designed (Jaskoski 2020). People affected by mining embrace, co-opt, resist, subvert, disrupt, ignore or build alternatives to the participatory mechanisms designed by corporations, states and development agencies. They make strategic decisions based on their common sense understandings of the world and their capacity to resist or participate. It is the competing interests and power asymmetries between actors that produce diverse and often unpredicted outcomes, even in ostensibly similar situations.

The existing and growing literature on community reactions to participation describes the diverse reactions, options and outcomes of institutional configurations and community reactions. Excellent recent contributions have moved towards using mid-N data. Jaskoski (2022) and Gobby et al. (2022) examine the various permutations, options and outcomes of communities resisting mining or working through corporate participatory mechanisms like environmental impact assessments. One important conclusion of Jaskoski is that 'participatory institutions may streamline the approval of new mining and hydrocarbon development, by dividing communities and deterring them from trying to prevent extraction' (2022, 208).

The works of activists like Roger Moody (1992; 2007) have been particularly influential in connecting industry practices across time, people affected by mining, and NGOs to create global alliances. However, even activists with radical democratic, environmentalist and post-colonialist approaches frequently advocate for institutional reform as a response to conflict

(Lynch and Harwell 2002; Rushdi et al. 2021). Beyond normative arguments that community rights like free prior informed consent *should* exist, it is rare that activists or academics explain how communities assert or enforce their rights themselves. Social movement theorists provide detailed accounts of conflict and movement dynamics, but are often too fixated on the violence versus non-violence moral paradigm to assess the efficacy of communities' and activists' strategies (Wilson Becerril 2021; Kröger 2020).

By embracing participation, groups of people affected by mining can extract benefits from mining corporations. However, the extent of those benefits relies on the group's relative power, which often must be established through autonomous sites of participation. In Fabiana Li's (2015, 92–98) discussion of the World Bank's CAO, she describes how information discovered through technocratic participatory processes can be used by critics of projects in their public campaigning. O'Faircheallaigh (2008) argues that groups of traditional owners negotiating mining agreements secure more favourable outcomes where they have built alliances with NGOs and other groups. Herders affected by Rio Tinto's Oyu Tolgoi mine used CAO mediation to secure compensation, but only after public campaigning with international NGOs established their bargaining power (Brueckner and Sinclair 2019, 115). Horowitz (2008) argues that Indigenous groups in New Caledonia have reframed traditional cultural demands using the language of conservation to access development funding.

Participatory mechanisms may also be co-opted to serve purposes or groups which are unintended by the corporation. Welker's (2009, 144) research into Newmont Mining Corporation's CSR program at the Batu Hijau copper mine in Sumbawa argues that particular community leaders were able to manipulate community development programs by alternately showing opposition and support for the mine to extract 'patronage goods'. Arellano-Yanguas (2011) demonstrates how previously disinterested actors can capture rents intended as compensation when transparency initiatives alerted opportunists to the benefits of staging protests. Participatory mechanisms can thus create new demands by raising compensation as a prospect.

Participatory mechanisms can be subverted and brought into the service of interests opposed to mining. Shapiro (2010) documents how activists opposed to mountaintop removal in Appalachia subverted participatory consultative meetings. At one consultative meeting, local activists declined to address the corporate and state officials, literally turning their backs on the chair and instead addressing the public crowd with an impassioned speech (2010, 88–90). Participating in consultation allowed activists to meet with local supporters of mining and heal divisions among a community (Shapiro 2010, 137).

Of course, it remains an option for groups, especially groups critical of mining developments, to resist participation and continue to engage in more confrontational or autonomous forms of protest. This was the case in Kulon Progo (Chapter 6), where the Association of Shoreline Farmers (PPLP – *Paguyuban Petani Lahan Pantai*) in Kulon Progo, Yogyakarta, protested and disrupted company and government attempts to consult people affected by mining (JATAM 2009). This kind of confrontational response is calculated to head off co-optation and cost the corporation financially and reputationally. Participatory mechanisms also open new opportunities for resistance: groups critical of mining can use the shortcomings of CSR programs themselves as a point of criticism. These strategies are not mutually exclusive; groups of people affected by mining may switch between legal channels and militant confrontation, or any other strategy (Nem Singh and Camba 2016).

Finally, there are some recent examples of communities affected by mining creating their own participatory mechanisms, specifically in Indigenous-led governance and bottom-up participatory strategies (Baker and Westman 2018). For example, community assemblies can build power independent of the state and mining corporations (Torres-Wong and Jimenez-Sandoval 2022). In Australia, mechanisms such as Indigenous Land Use Agreements and Cultural Heritage Management Plans are recognising and responding to Indigenous traditional knowledge (Heiner et al. 2019; Bond and Kelly 2021). Both the construction of alternative community or Indigenous-led participation or incorporation of traditional knowledge into existing mechanisms has come as the result of long struggles over decolonisation.

While there is a wealth of literature exploring the various reactions of people affected by mining to participatory mechanisms, there is very little that explains why and how people affected by mining choose to participate or not. One notable exception is Conde and Le Billon (2017, 681) who, through systematic literature review, find that 'dependency towards mining companies, political marginalisation, and trust in institutions tend to reduce resistance likelihood. In contrast, large environmental impacts, lack of participation, extra-local alliances, and distrust towards state and extractive companies tend to increase resistance.' Fjellborg et al. (2022) echo some of those findings while also concluding that movements' *perceptions* of the openness of participatory mechanisms was just as important in determining the militancy of activists' reactions. Building on their emphasis on 'dependency', 'trust' and 'perceptions', I argue the *ideological receptivity* of affected groups to the consultative ideologies offered by participatory mechanisms is the best concept for understanding the reactions to participatory mechanisms.

Conclusion

In this chapter I have identified the major contestations, forces, crises and governance mechanisms that constitute modes of participation and shape participation between multinational mining corporations and people affected by mining. The contestations over impacts of mining, CSR, global governance, and national regulation are mutually constitutive. Overlapping global, national and company-specific crises of legitimacy drive the creation of global self-governance networks and the ideologies that constitute modes of participation for the social dimensions of mining. Language and practices of sustainability, participation and empowerment have been adopted by multinational mining corporations and combined with consultative ideologies of representation of corporate societal incorporation. This underlines the dynamic conflict management through new modes of participation.

Participatory CSR also drew from and influenced development practice and the neo-institutional ideological evolution of development agencies. The response of development agencies and multinational corporations also influenced reform of national regulation and policy on the social dimensions of mining. Intersecting processes, institutional arrangements and ideologies together lead to expanding corporate responsibilities and power in relation to the environmental and social dimensions of mining. In turn, as participatory mechanisms and strategies develop, this is changing the ways that people affected by mining engage and react to large-scale mining developments. As local conflicts change form and actors adopt new political and economic strategies vis-à-vis each other, this will drive further refinements or changes in modes of participation and the global and national governance regimes that constitute them.

The major contribution of this book is to explain the emergence of particular participatory mechanisms at particular times and places within the context of global extractive accumulation *and* to explain the reactions of affected people while taking their agency seriously. While this chapter has focused on the interaction between global governance and local participation, the next chapter fills in the national scale by examining the shifting balance of power in the political economy of extractivism in Indonesia since colonisation.

Notes

1 As opposed to the operating jurisdiction.
2 As introduced in Chapter 1, I use the term 'crisis of legitimacy' in the Gramscian sense, analogous to 'crisis of hegemony', to signify that a ruling class has lost

the consensus for their ideological leadership and risks being subjected to the regulation of other actors (Filippini 2017, 99). This is applicable to multinational mining corporations as a fraction of the global ruling class. Following crises, ruling classes need to re-establish control or risk facing a wider crisis resulting in their displacement (Gramsci 1971, Q13§23; 210–11).

3 The International Cyanide Management Code for the Manufacture, Transport, and Use of Cyanide in the Production of Gold.

4 As of 2023, ICMM had 25 members, 15 ranked in the top 40 global mining companies by market capitalisation (ICMM n.d. 'Our Members'; PwC 2023). ICMM members have headquarters across most major origins of mining capital – North America, South America, Europe, South Africa, Australia and Japan. Conspicuous by their absence are Chinese and Indian mining companies, which account for 11 of the 40 largest mining companies (PwC 2023).

5 Neo-institutionalism increased in influence following decreasing legitimacy of the deregulation agenda of the 'Washington consensus' in the 1990s. This led to the so-called 'post-Washington consensus', typified by the World Bank Group's 'social turn' and 'good governance' agenda (Doornbos 2001; Hatcher 2014; Carroll and Jarvis 2015). The World Bank Group's 'social-development model' entailed a renewed focus on poverty reduction along with social and environmental concerns (Hatcher 2015, 323).

6 'Participatory mechanisms' in mining borrow heavily from earlier lessons in 'participatory development' by international organisations like the World Bank (White 1996; Cooke and Kothari 2001, 5; Leal 2007; Guggenheim 2006). Likewise, the critical literature on participation in mining builds on critiques of participatory development which argue, for example, participatory techniques are employed 'as a technical method of project work rather than as a political methodology of empowerment' (Hickey and Mohan 2005, 242).

7 Here, I use corporate social responsibility as an umbrella term for a range of mostly corporate practices including community relations, sustainable community development programs, 'social license to operate', negotiating benefits with communities and environmental and social impact assessments (O'Faircheallaigh and Ali 2008; Osburg and Schmidpeter 2013; McKenna 2015).

8 Impact assessment procedures have evolved from narrow considerations of environmental impacts towards holistic assessments including cultural change, economic inequality, gender, health, human rights and governance, and from considering only what is required by law to complying with international standards, to assessments tailored for specific projects (Bice 2016, 91; McKenna 2015, 145; Sinclair et al. 2022).

3

Contesting extractivism in Indonesia

Extractivism is a core strategy of the most powerful economic and political actors in Indonesia. Expanding extractive industries[1] – along with 'downstreaming' onshore processing – has been central to successive governments' developmentalist agendas. Meanwhile, the root causes of many social conflicts can be traced to extractive industries' land grabbing and the broader social and environmental impacts of extraction. This chapter identifies and analyses the actors, interests, contestations and resistances that drive the evolving governance of social and environmental impacts of mining. By doing so it serves two objectives:

1. Understanding the political economy of extractivism in Indonesia *in and of itself*. This is important for communities and activists crafting counter-hegemonic strategies. The political economy of Indonesian extractivism then forms the context for the three case studies in the following chapters.
2. Developing Indonesia as a case study of the ways that international and domestic actors' strategies create institutions to sustain extractive accumulation.

The first section of this chapter reviews recent contributions to the literature on extractivism as a political-economic strategy and ideology of national development prioritising mineral export and processing over environmental protection and human rights, placing Indonesia in a global comparative context. As at the global scale, participation is a key strategy to undermine resistance to extractivism. While multinational mining corporations and state actors often contest the spoils of mining, their interests largely coincide in relation to the social impacts of mining. That is why, despite huge variations in regime type, there are patterns of corporate participation undermining resistance.

The rest of the chapter analyses the political economy of mining in Indonesia, divided across four historical periods: The historical foundations of extractive accumulation in the colonial, early independence and New

Order periods; the early *reformasi* period; the rise of resource nationalism; and authoritarian and green developmentalism.[2] These periods, along with the dominant actors and ideologies are summarised in Table 3.3.

I argue that powerful state institutions, including the office of the president and the Ministry of Energy and Mineral Resources, domestic conglomerates and foreign capital, have remained dominant since the New Order regime. However, responsibility for managing the social and environmental impacts of mining has shifted from state institutions to mining corporations – most noticeably since the withdrawal of the military from politics. Following massive popular mobilisations in 1998, the *reformasi* period saw a significant increase in opportunities for people affected by mining to pursue their interests through democratic institutions, international alliances, media freedom, courts and corporate participatory mechanisms. However, since 2019, many state-sponsored sites of participation have been closed. This can result in increasing levels of violent conflict or people affected by mining turning further towards corporate and international sites of participation. The potential for rising conflict and crises is increasing as Indonesia seeks to capitalise on new 'energy transition mineral' supply chains for low carbon technologies – especially nickel.

Extractivism and participation

'Extractivism' is a descriptive and conceptual term used to criticise governments' development strategies that place the extraction and export of natural resources at the centre of politics, economics and ideologies of national development.[3] Derivative terms like 'new-extractivism' or 'neo-extractivism' and 'progressive neo-extractivism' gained popularity in the late 2000s, with the so called 'pink-tide' of 'post-neoliberal' states in South America that coincided with the global commodity boom. Revenue from extractive industries helped progressive governments break with the neoliberal imposition of a small state and fund ambitious social programs (Rivera Andía and Vindal Ødegaard 2019, 14). However, funding broad-based welfare and progressive policy agendas with accelerated extraction of raw minerals required the repression or co-opting of Indigenous communities, environmentalists and other social movements, generating new conflicts, contradictions and resistance within society (Veltmeyer and Petras 2014; Rivera Andía and Vindal Ødegaard 2019).

Extractivism more generally has been used as a critique of similar development models of governments from across the political spectrum in Africa (Ayelazuno 2014; Mentan 2018), Asia (Kröger 2020) and North America (Gobby et al. 2022). Once entrenched in the logic of national development, extractivism can become an ideology of development, a rationale for state action and continued privileging of multinational mining companies (Kröger 2020, 5).

Contradictions between states' (sometimes progressive) developmentalist agendas, the repression and co-optation of social movements, and close relationships with multinational mining corporations and international organisations requires a careful and responsive balance of governance arrangements. Kröger's (2020, 7) contribution to the literature on extractivism is that 'the regulation of extractive investments arises not only from government strategies but also from the comparative strength and strategies of resistance groups and their relations to state and corporations'. Others have gone further, to argue that practices of resistance are *necessary* to transform current extractivist logics within dominant governance structures (Gobby et al. 2022). Indeed, resistance the world over has led to the emergence of environmental and social impact assessment, corporate social responsibility and community development practices being required in law – constituting a new set of participatory political technologies mandated by states but managed by corporations (Leiva 2019, 141).

Patterns of national regulations across regimes and regions

For all the attention on global governance, the major source of regulation of social and environmental impacts of mining remains domestic states. Since the early 2000s, an increasing number of jurisdictions around the world *require* mining corporations to practice corporate social responsibility (CSR) and offer community development programs. Yet laws and regulations are most often too vague or lack enforcement mechanisms, effectively leaving corporations to self-regulate social and environmental impacts (Rosser and Edwin 2010; Devi and Prayogo 2013; Li 2015). For example, Guinea's 2011 mining code was the result of massive social struggles for justice. This code introduced transparency, accountability and obligations to conduct social and environmental impact assessments. However, the most onerous and ambitious requirements were reversed in 2013 (Campbell and Hatcher 2019). Similar patterns have been documented across resource-rich countries in Southeast Asia and the Global South (Hatcher 2020, 12).

Breslin and Nesadurai (2018) argue that despite the common depiction of Southeast Asian states jealously guarding their sovereignty, forms of private governance operate across issues where states have left 'governance gaps' in areas such as sustainable forestry, labour standards and maritime safety. Private and public-private forms of governance emerge at political scales where it suits intersections of interests between powerful state and non-state actors (Bünte 2018). Hatcher (2020) traces the World Bank's successful efforts to reform and liberalise the mining laws of Southeast Asian states throughout the 1990s. The results were extremely favourable investment environments for multinationals with limited avenues to redress environmental and social grievances within individual countries. Instead, participatory mechanisms of the corporations and international finance institutions themselves effectively took over governance of the social and environmental impacts of mining (see also Hatcher 2015).

The transfer of responsibility for governance of social and environmental dimensions of mining to corporations does not represent an increase in corporate power vis-à-vis states but is the result of an intersection of interests between dominant actors within powerful state institutions, multinational mining corporations and domestic capital. The priority is to smooth conflict, undermine resistance, and facilitate industrial development or export industries based on extraction. Indonesia is no exception to such extractivist strategies. To understand the specific social and economic relations shaping conflict, we need a deeper dive into the history of Indonesian extractivism.

Extractivism in Indonesia

From 2010 until July 2023, mining comprised 25.7% of total exports and 7.1% of GDP (Bank Indonesia 2023b; 2023a).[4] From 2016 to 2020, mining contributed 5.6% to state revenue, while oil and gas contributed a further 6.1% (EITI Indonesia 2022). Mining therefore retains a significant position in the 'commanding heights' of the economy, just behind oil and gas in terms of its contribution to economic development, government revenue and foreign exchange reserves.

Figures 3.1 and 3.2 show the changing contributions of metal mining, refining, coal, and oil and gas to exports and GDP over the last ten years. What is remarkable is that the decline in value of oil and gas exports has almost been replaced by coal and intermediate and refined metals. This could be the result of resource nationalist strategies. Whatever the cause, it shows the vital and increasing role of mining within the Indonesian national economy.

On the other side of the ledger, the Consortium for Agrarian Reform (KPA) reported 1,769 cases of land conflict from 2014 to 2018, resulting in 41 fatalities, 51 non-fatal shootings, 940 arrests, and 541 other instances of violence (KPA 2019).[5] Specifically in relation to mining in 2021, KPA reported 30 separate conflicts over 155,168ha of land affecting 161,136 families (KPA 2022, 8). That is, despite the rise of CSR and participation, violent conflict and land disputes remain chronic. To understand the current relationships shaping extractive conflicts and participation in Indonesia, a historical account of extractivism follows.

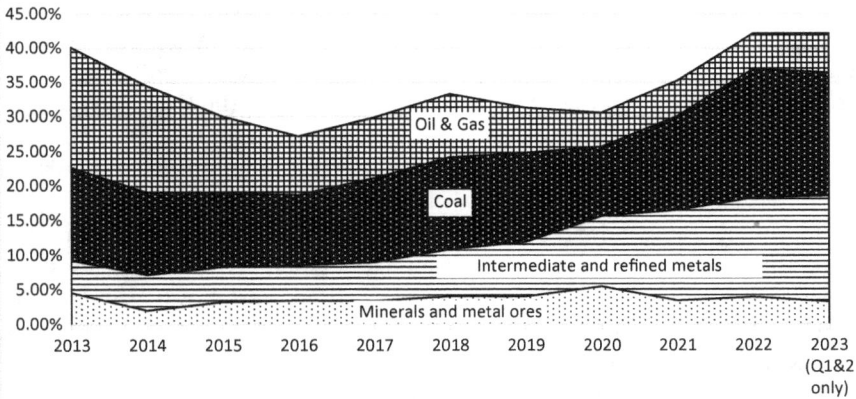

Figure 3.1 The contribution of mining, smelting and oil and gas to Indonesia's exports.

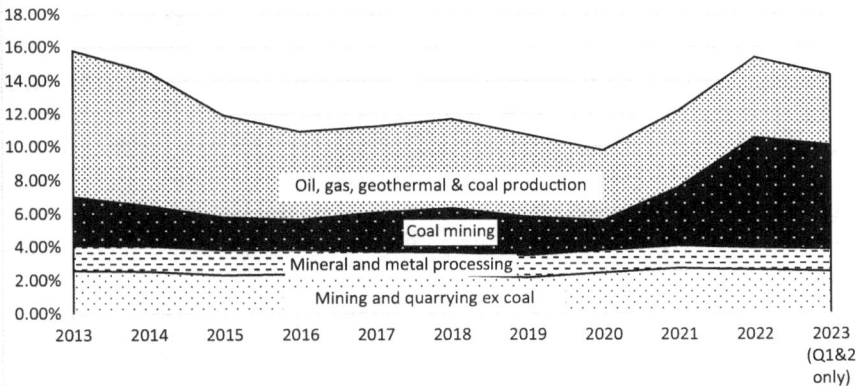

Figure 3.2 The contribution of mining and oil and gas to Indonesia's GDP, 2012–22.

The colonial and New Order foundations of extractivism

Extractivism has played a key role in the development of Indonesia's economy and foreign relations, as well as shaping conflict between large capital, labour, peasants and Indigenous people since at least the 1600s. The VOC (Dutch East India Company) and the colonial state established and placed European capital at the helm of the 'structural relations of extraction' (Tilley 2021, 7). Two of the world's major extractive corporations were established as royal trading companies during the colonial period. Billiton (later to merge with Australian Broken Hill Proprietary Company to form BHP) and Royal Dutch Petroleum Company (later merging with the Shell Transport and Trading Company to form Royal Dutch Shell) channelled profits from the extraction of tin and oil in Sumatra to the Dutch royal family and other European investors (Zanden and Marks 2012, 84–88). Such large-scale industry became symbolic in nationalist aspirations and hubs of organised labour.

Following independence,[6] during the 1950s and 1960s, the Indonesian state, through the military, nationalised many Dutch assets, replacing some foreign investors with military men (Meckelburg 2019, 68; Zanden and Marks 2012, 149). This created the foundation for a military-supported domestic oligarchy to emerge after 1965. Factions of military officers formed alliances with international capital against domestic opposition, including communists. For example, declassified memos show Shell managers were aware of and cooperated in the arrest of over 600 union organisers and workers linked to oil refineries in Palembang during just the first month of the 1965–66 genocide (Green 1965).

During the New Order years (1965–98), alliances developed between multinational mining companies, national and provincial politicians, military and civil administrators and emerging domestic conglomerates (Winanti and Diprose 2020). Indonesia's oligarchy[7] evolved during the New Order regime as Soeharto maintained political power through vast patronage networks financed by oil, other centralised extractive industries, and export-import licencing. Domestic business required foreign capital and corporate resources to drive development in the mining sector (Robison 2009, 115). Mining, along with oil and forestry, provided 'major sources of foreign exchange earnings and state revenues' (Robison 2009, 217). Mining also supplied domestic demand for aluminium and steel processing, which were important resources along with coal and oil, for the New Order's industrialisation strategy (Robison 2009, 181). Mineral exports and domestic processing became a key source of wealth and power for the domestic oligarchy incubated during the New Order regime while the state bureaucracy tightly controlled business through export and import licencing. Of course, the New Order regime's most infamous function was to 'suppress the active and mobilised lower class groups in villages, plantations, towns and cities using mass violence, incarceration, intimidation and constant monitoring by village officials and the military' (Meckelburg 2019, 69).

The Indonesian Foreign Investment Law No. 1/1967 and Basic Provisions of Mining Law No. 11/1967, with its contract of work (CoW) system, created a stable legislative framework for foreign investment. Foreign mining companies were required to accept local business partners and in return foreign capital was protected by the New Order's centralised economic system.

Land acquisition and community relations were handled by domestic business partners, the central government or the military (Leith 2003).

This relationship is best demonstrated by Freeport-McMoRan which was, until 2018, majority owner of Grasberg, the world's largest gold and copper mine, in West Papua. The mining operation is notorious for its financial and political links with the military, human rights violations, dispossession of Indigenous people from land, clashes with organised labour and toxic waste (Bachriadi 1998; Leith 2003). Freeport was the first foreign company to sign a contract with Soeharto's regime, within months of the dictator taking power and while the Indonesian mass violence was still occurring, and quickly became the largest single source of tax revenue while providing foreign legitimacy for the Indonesian government (Leith 2003, 3).

At the other end of the archipelago in Aceh, another separatist conflict involved a huge resources project. The Free Aceh Movement (GAM) formed in the 1970s at the same time as the world's most productive gas fields were being developed by Mobil and Bechtel (Aspinall 2007). While this conflict was not *caused* by the gas-field development, it became a symbol of local grievances and an opportunity for the movement to disrupt resource flows (Robinson 1998; Harker 2003). Some of the earliest actions by GAM were raids on gaswork sites.

In the 1990s, the extractive industries in Indonesia suffered a decline in legitimacy in parallel with global crises in the sector. The secrecy surrounding the relationship between Freeport and the military was shattered by the Australian Council for Overseas Aid's (ACFOA) report 'Trouble at Freeport' (1995), which accused military officers and Freeport security of murder, torture and intimidation. This was followed by several other reports and international media coverage. Some of the traditional owners of the Freeport concession, with the support of WALHI (Friends of the Earth Indonesia), launched legal action against Freeport in the USA in 1996. While the court case failed, it did succeed in garnering extensive publicity of the mine and creating negotiating power for the traditional owners with Freeport. In 2001, villagers in Aceh, supported by the International Labor Rights Fund (ILRF), took their case against ExxonMobil to the US courts. Exxon was accused of complicity in, indeed direct financial support of, human rights violations perpetrated by a military unit that was contracted to protect their operations (Harker 2003). Again, the case was dismissed, but succeeded in raising the profile of accusations against Exxon and the military. This internationalisation, or *jumping scales*, of resistance through legal action was game changing because multinational miners could no longer rely only on a close and secretive relationship with Soeharto and the military to control resistance.

These and other incidents threatened the balance in the relation-ship between Soeharto, domestic oligarchs and foreign mining capital as it became increasingly costly to violently supress opposition to resource extraction. Following international pressure in the late 1980s and 1990s, the Indonesian government began to construct a regulatory framework to manage the social and environmental effects of mining: from 1986 compa-nies were required to submit environmental impact assessments, and in 1990 the Environmental Impact Management Agency (BEPEAL) was formed to regulate and enforce environmental laws, even though under-resourced and ineffective. Presidential Decree No. 55/1993 required MNCs to negotiate directly with landowners (Leith 2003, 43). Soeharto enacted this decree because negotiations with landowners had become too risky and 'messy' and government wanted to transfer this risk to corporations (Leith 2003, 43). So, even before the fall of the New Order government, responsibility for the social and environmenal impacts of mining was being transferred from the central government and military to corporations.

By the late 1990s, the New Order regime was facing multiple crises[8] that would eventually bring it down and usher in *reformasi*. As more infor-mation surfaced about the role of foreign capital, development agencies and foreign governments sustaining Soeharto's regime and turning a blind eye to human rights abuses, their legitimacy as responsible actors was also brought into question (Leith 2003, 33–34; Guggenheim 2006, 121). This shows how multiple crises may spread and combine to produce far-reaching consequences.

The reformasi *era*

The immediate aftermath of the Soeharto's fall in 1998 saw a wave of popu-lar organising and land occupations (Meckelburg 2019, 78). However, oligarchs and business conglomerates retained their pre-eminent position within Indonesian political economy, maintaining close ties between politi-cians, bureaucrats and business, even as centres of politics and administra-tion devolved to provincial and regency levels (Robison and Hadiz 2004; Hadiz 2010).[9] Perhaps the most terrifying indicator of the continued dom-inance of oligarchy in extractives was the Lapindo disaster (Symon 2007; Tapsell 2012; Drake 2012).

In May 2006, volcanic mud started flowing from a gas exploration drill site near Sidorajo, East Java. It is estimated that 90 million cubic metres of mud erupted, displacing approximately 40,000 people (Tingay 2015). The operating company was jointly owned by the Bakrie family and Santos Ltd. Aburizal Bakrie, through his business empire, was one of the most powerful of the New Order's oligarchs. Bakrie was a government minister from 2004 to 2009 and chairperson of the Golkar Party 2009–14 (Tapsell 2012). Santos, an Australian oil and gas company, owned an 18% share in Lapindo until selling out in 2008, while denying responsibility for the disaster. Compensation to victims was deadlocked until 2015 when the Indonesian government provided compensation to tens of thousands of victims on behalf of Bakrie Group (Drake 2016, 6). Despite the absence of the military in this case, oligarchs, their political and bureaucratic allies, and multinational corporations (MNCs) demonstrated their political power that enabled them to avoid legal sanction.

While domestic conglomerates controlled by oligarchs and mutinational corporations remain dominant in the mining industry, decentralisation and reform opened up space for opponents to organise. Law No. 4/2009 on Mineral and Coal Mining designated responsibility to issue licences and raise taxes to the regency, provincial and national governments, depending on the size of the mine (Devi and Prayogo 2013). Law No. 32/2009 on Environmental Protection and Management and Government Regulation No. 27/2012 on Environmental Permits required mining companies to produce environmental impact assessments and environmental monitoring and management plans before they received environmental licenses from the appropriate level of government (PwC 2015).

Perhaps most significant for people affected by mining is that democratisation and decentralisation also resulted in demilitarisation,[10] alongside a proliferation of fora and methods for communities and NGOs to express grievances (Erb 2016). Demilitarisation was a key turning point in the Kelian case (Chapter 4). Media were also less restricted (Tapsell 2012). In Buyat Bay, WALHI supported a local campaign against tailings dumping in the sea which resulted in a civil case against Newmont Mining and the arrest of the mine's president director (Symon 2007). This case indicates that space for NGO campaigning increased. The criminal case was dismissed while the civil case was settled for US$30 million ('Newmont, Indonesia Settle Pollution Lawsuit' 2006).

Hadiz (2010, 144) argues that 'the main benefit of democratisation for marginalised and formally repressed social groups is that they can now organise more freely'. On this point, there is substantial agreement with Aspinall (2013), who points to fragmented labour activism and new opportunities for electoral populism emerging in the post-authoritarian period. Despite the continued dominance of oligarchy in national politics, subaltern groups have been able to fight and often win battles – farm by farm, village by village or regency by regency – through flexible alliances, selective militancy, and informal linkages with formal politics. The point is that a range of state-sponsored sites of participation opened up to contain conflicts that spilt over from 1998. However, various communities, activists and NGOs were actually able to use participatory mechanisms to achieve material benefits.

Reflecting global trends as well as domestic processes of decentralisation and democratisation, 2007–18 saw more regulations for mining corporations requiring CSR and community development, summarised in Table 3.1. Also reflecting global trends, requirements are vague and effectively voluntary (Mahy 2011a, 71–75).

While each of these laws opened opportunities and provided principles which communities, activists and NGOs could use to support their claims, their social and environmental provisions were so vague and unenforceable that they did not function as strong legal limits on corporate power. Instead of legally enforceable limits and sanctions, they created participatory avenues for social actors to negotiate claims. The effect was to keep activists, advocates and community organisers fragmented across issues and scales defined by separate participatory mechanisms with mining corporations self-regulating in relation to social and environmental impacts.

Resource nationalism from 2014

In contrast to social and environmental regulation, various state agencies exert considerable authority over licencing, taxation, down-stream development requirements and export controls (Warburton 2016). Industry groups

Table 3.1 Examples of laws and regulations requiring participatory CSR

Article 74 of **Law No. 40/2007** on Limited Liability Corporations and Articles 95 and 108–9 of the Mineral and Coal Mining **Law No. 4/2009**	Required corporations in natural resources to implement CSR programs from a dedicated budget, in consultation with local government and community. However, the budget, purpose and sanctions for noncompliance were not specified, nor were the consultation mechanisms (Waagstein 2011).
The Environmental Protection and Management **Law No. 30/2009**	Enshrined 'rights to a safe and healthy environment' which had been 'instrumental as a right claim for local communities as well as environmental NGOs' (Wardana 2022, 238).
Ministry of Energy and Mineral Resources **Regulation** (*permen*) **No. 25/2018** on Mineral and Coal Mining Business	Specifies that community development activities must proceed in accordance with work plans approved by the provincial government.

were apparently surprised when, in January 2014, the government confirmed plans to implement several 'resource nationalist'[11] measures contained in the 2009 Mining Law relating to divestment and export tariffs (Engineering & Mining Journal 2014). These included domestic ownership requirements, export tariffs and bans on selected raw minerals (Winanti and Diprose 2020). These measures were all based on the idea that 'the people', not 'foreigners', should be the primary beneficiaries of the country's resources.

It is important to note that the government's resource nationalism since 2014 is just one pillar of a border 'new developmentalism' in Indonesia – an ideology where economic development justifies 'greater state intervention in the market to stimulate economic growth, direct industrial upgrading, and ensuring economic redistribution' (Syukri 2024, 2; Warburton 2019). While the roots of new developmentalism can be seen earlier, new developmentalism became identified with Joko Widodo's presidency (2014–24). In this context, the resource sector, resource nationalism and extractivism have become central to the government's legitimacy and aspirations.

Since 2014, the central government has implemented an increasingly resource nationalist regulatory agenda. Progressive export bans and rates of duties are aimed at stimulating downstream processing of minerals (smelter construction) and capturing a greater share of value in Indonesia through increased government revenue, domestic linkages, employment and local procurement (PwC 2018). For example, as of January 2020, nickel ore export was banned and instead must be refined[12] before export (PwC 2022, 21);[13] exporting unrefined bauxite was restricted by quotas and permitting from June 2023 (Ghifari 2023); and copper, tin, iron, lead, zinc and manganese ores must meet minimum concentrations prior to export (PwC 2022, 137–42). Nickel concentrates and bauxite bans are notable given their role in lithium-ion battery manufacture, an objective of the government's developmentalist and industrialisation strategies.[14]

The balance of power between domestic conglomerates, governments and MNCs continues to shift. Under Government Regulation No. 1/2017 and Ministerial Regulation No. 9/2017, foreign mining companies are expected to divest 51% of their ownership of resources projects to domestic partners (PwC 2018). These divestment requirements have led the largest foreign-owned mines to be sold to domestic conglomerates. For instance, Newmont sold its remaining US$1.3 billion stake in the Batu Hijau copper mine to PT Amman Mineral Internasional in 2016 (Schonhardt and Hufford 2016), while in March 2020, Newcrest sold its Gosowong mine (Chapter 5) for US$90 million rather than divesting 51% (Brown 2020). Unlike Newmont and Newcrest entirely selling out of Indonesia, Freeport-McMoRan retained just under 49% ownership of its gigantic Grasberg mine in West Papua. Even so, the acquisition of 51.23% of the mine by

state-owned enterprises[15] was a major achievement of resource nationalist policy, taking back control of natural resources for the state (Winanti
and Diprose 2020). These sales represent a fundamental restructuring of the
ownership of Indonesia's largest mines. Oligarchs' domestic conglomerates
have graduated from local partners facilitating foreign capital to controlling
managers of the largest operating mines, while MNCs have sold out. Of
course, there is significant overlap between national political and corporate
elites, so the deployment of state power in favour of domestic conglomerates is not surprising. Resource nationalism has rebalanced power between
domestic and international corporations, while achieving nothing for the
rights of people affected by mining or their allies.

Why is it that the resource nationalist agenda has produced no benefits
for 'the people' in whose name it is enacted? Rosser and Edwin (2010) argue
that, although interest groups had managed to organise and pass CSR provisions in Law No. 40/2007, implementing regulations has been blocked
by coalitions of MNCs and domestic capitalists with connections to the
Indonesian presidency and cabinet. This is consistent with later research
showing that domestic capitalists were instrumental in ensuring the non-
implementation and watering down of CSR provisions (Warburton 2014;
Aspinall 2015). The comparison of CSR with resource nationalism shows
that the lack of CSR regulation and enforcement is not simply a matter of
state capacity or power, as state actors clearly have the power to enforce
regulation when it is in their interests. In relation to the social and environmental impacts of mining, the interests of MNCs, oligarchs and state
actors align to smooth conflict and capital accumulation through extraction, affecting what Szablowski refers to as a 'selective absence of the state'
(2007, 27). In fact, it is more accurate to say that state actors are siding or
overlapping with corporate interests against people affected by mining.

The 'authoritarian' turn

The re-election of President Joko Widodo (Jokowi) for a second term over
the populist ex-military challenger Probowo Subianto in May 2019 was
hailed by liberal commentators as a victory for 'pluralism' in Indonesia
(Power and Warburton 2020). However, soon after winning the election, and
inviting main opposition elements to join the government in cabinet and key
ministries, the executive embarked on an ambitious reform agenda designed
to 'simplify, cut and prune regulatory obstacles' (Joko Widodo, quoted in
Nursyamsi et al. 2019). Those 'regulatory obstacles' were any obstacles to
investment, business operations and profit such as anti-corruption initiatives, transparent decision making, uncertainty in licences, land-rights activists, human rights and environmental protection.

The so-called 'Omnibus Law on Job Creation' was central to this strategy. It actually amended 79 different legislative instruments (Wardana 2022). In addition to the Omnibus Law, several other significant pieces of legislation were announced in 2019. Table 3.2 summarises the most important of these, highlighting their pro-business functions and the dates when they were eventually passed.

Journalists, activists and academics have rightly lamented these reforms as the latest moves towards 'democratic regression' or 'backsliding' in Indonesia (Setiawan 2022; Chamas et al. 2022; Warburton and Power 2020). But democratic regression is not surprising when understood as an exercise of oligarchic power against threats to their capital accumulation. As each of the case studies in the next three chapters shows, communities of people affected by mining, activists and NGOs had been using every avenue available to resist extractive land grabbing or secure benefits for themselves. Even though resistance was fragmented and sporadic, it still represented a threat to the primacy of extractive accumulation. Acknowledging this, Jokowi's 'authoritarian turn' can then be seen as the latest move in an ongoing struggle over development. Ironically, it was the announcement of Jokowi's legislative agenda in 2019 that united previously fragmented oppositional groups in the largest and most widespread protests in Indonesia since the overthrow of Soeharto (Nursyamsi et al. 2019).

In August 2019, a massive 'Papuan Lives Matter' wave of protests erupted across Papua province and Indonesia in response to ongoing racist harassment and violence towards Papuan people.[16] These protesters were joined by another wave of civil society actors, furious at the passage of laws defanging the Corruption Eradication Commission (KPK) in September. Then, as more details emerged about Jokowi's Omnibus Law, Papuans, civil-society groups and solidarity activists were joined by huge groups of workers' unions, organised peasants, feminists, LGBT activists, and masses of high school and university students to form the biggest, most diverse and united counterhegemonic bloc since 1998. Massive street protests brought activity in Jakarta to a standstill as demonstrators blockaded parliament during the final sitting weeks of 2019, delaying passage of the Omnibus Law, the mining law and the new criminal code despite severe repression from police and university and school authorities (Setijadi 2021).

But when parliament returned in 2020, the COVID-19 pandemic changed everything. Jokowi took advantage of social restrictions in place to pass laws while opposition groups were isolating at home (Setijadi 2021; Wardana 2022). In June 2020, during the initial and strict lockdowns of the pandemic, Law No. 3/2020 on Mineral and Coal Mining was passed by a parliamentary chamber convened via video link. The massive Covid-induced economic recession intensified the already desperate pursuit of

Table 3.2 Selection of authoritarian-developmentalist laws passed 2019–22

Law	Date Passed	Function
19/2019 on the Corruption Eradication Commission (KPK)	17 October 2019	• Independence of the commission removed in favour of reporting to the executive. • KPK employees become public servants. • New oversight board appointed by president and legislature (Power 2020).
3/2020 on Mineral and Coal Mining	10 June 2020	• Recentralises mining licencing under national government ministry. • Guarantees no changes to mining licences once granted or to spatial planning once an area has been designated as a mining zone. • New criminal offence of 'hindering or disturbing' mining operations with up to one year jail (Wardana 2021; Harsono 2020).
11/2020 on Job Creation Omnibus Law As amended by Government Regulation in Lieu of Law No. 2/2022	5 October 2020	• Amends 70+ existing laws. • Abolishes minimum wage setting. • Reduces severance pay. • Reduces corporate taxation. • Reduces requirements for environmental impact assessment (Setijadi 2021; Wardana 2022; JATAM 2020).
1/2023 New Criminal Code (KUHP)	December 2022	• Ban on sex outside of marriage and providing contraception. • Criminalisation of LGBT. • Ten-year sentence for Marxist-Leninist organising. • Reintroduces law against insulting the president, state institutions or *pancasila* (Indonesia's official ideology). • Reduces legal liability of corporations and decreases sanctions in the Environmental Protection and Management law (Chamas et al. 2022).

'development' at all costs; Jokowi himself was mindful of maintaining a legacy of development despite setbacks due to the pandemic (Setijadi 2021).

In August and September 2020, shocked by the opportunism of the government, protesters returned to the streets to attempt to block parliament again, but were met with ferocious violence from police (Nursyamsi et al. 2019). After the Omnibus Law passed in early October, protests intensified. It is worth briefly looking at why activists and students were so strongly opposed to Jokowi's legislative agenda, using the two examples most pertinent to mining.

The amendments to the mineral and coal mining law consolidated the power shift back towards large corporations, both domestic conglomerates and multinationals. In expert testimony to a judicial review, Agung Wardana (2021) outlines three features of the law that contradict peoples' right to a clean and safe environment. First, the new law recentralises regulation and licencing of mining to the national over provincial governments. Second, it guarantees that no government will make changes to mining areas or license conditions after licences are granted. Finally, and most concerningly, the law provides for a new crime of 'hindering or disturbing' mining operations with a penalty of up to one year in jail or Rp100 million.[17] There have already been many cases of landowners and environmental activists being jailed and fined under this provision (Wardana 2021). The aim of the law reform, as with the other laws amended by the omnibus legislation, was to ease the requirements of doing business and provide more security to capital investment, and were welcomed by business and investors (PwC 2022, 8). Meanwhile, the amendments failed to specify further implementing regulations on required community development programs (Harsono 2020). This again highlights the power of corporate miners and state actors over NGOs and affected communities in the regulatory and legislative process.

One of the 79 acts that was amended by the Omnibus Law was Law No. 32 of 2009 on Protection and Management of the Environment. Provisions for conducting environmental impact assessments (AMDAL) in the original 2009 law had been significantly revised in 2012, with increased public participation, review mechanisms and access to justice, and increasing participatory mechanisms for communities and NGOs (Wardana 2022, 245). The 2020 revision reversed these improvements. Environmental NGOs are now excluded from participation, and mechanisms for administrative appeal are severely restricted.

In the successive amendments to the environment and mining laws we can see a trend of increasing (regulatory) requirements and participatory opportunities for communities and civil society actors from the 2000s until 2017 and then a reversal of these gains since 2019.

'Green' developmentalism

Since 2019, simultaneous with the pandemic and 'democratic regression', there has been a burst of activity, investment and strategic jostling over the boom in minerals for electric vehicle (EV) and battery production. Indonesia has a significant supply of 'energy transition minerals', including nickel, bauxite, tin and copper – required for lithium-ion batteries and EVs, growing industrial capacity in refining minerals and auto manufacture, and one of the world's largest consumer markets.[18] The government has ambitions to connect the dots with an integrated battery and EV manufacturing sector (Huber 2022; Veza et al. 2022). This involves continued downstreaming (*hilirisasi*) of nickel smelting to create more refined nickel products, cathodes, batteries and feed EV industries as well as attracting foreign capital. Newly formed state-owned enterprise (SOE) Indonesia Battery Corp (IBC) will oversee the construction of an EV battery plant with Korea's LG, while Hyundai is constructing an EV plant near Jakarta. CATL, BYD, Toyota and Honda are also investing in the sector (Huber 2022).

As with the resource nationalism described above, the primary beneficiaries of the new green developmentalism will be large SOEs like IBC and domestic conglomerates owned by oligarchic families. Conglomerates like the Bakrie & Brothers Group can even use the 'green' technology behind their industrial strategy to rehabilitate their reputations and reposition themselves to profit from the climate emergency (Freischlad 2022; Wijaya and Sinclair 2024).

The major threat to this strategy is social and environmental conflict. As with the multiscalar conflicts and crises of legitimacy described in the previous chapter, social and environmental threats to extractive accumulation and green developmentalism in Indonesia are both local and global. The most pressing ethical issue in the global battery supply chain is replacing cobalt mined with forced labour or funding armed warlords, as some mines in the Democratic Republic of the Congo (DRC) are, and technological improvements in batteries are reducing the proportion of cobalt to nickel required in batteries.[19] Indonesian nickel is perceived as more ethical than DRC cobalt, but Indonesia must compete with Australia and North America for ethical mining and low-carbon refining (Digges and Brown 2021). Indonesian nickel mining and refining is plagued by environmental pollution, poor labour standards, land conflict and energy-intensive refining powered by coal (Morse 2021; Rushdi et al. 2021).

MNCs like Tesla, BMW and VW, along with international organisations like the EU and World Economic Forum, are already creating new global standards for ethical management of EV and battery supply chains (for example, IRMA 2018; GBA 2022). Perhaps dismayed at recent legislative reforms, Indonesian activists are already challenging the social legitimacy of OEMs like Tesla for purchasing nickel from Central Sulawesi and North Maluku (for example, JATAM 2022). If domestic channels for redressing grievances remain closed, the kinds of crises of legitimacy that jump to international scales could emerge again, sparking a new cycle of crises and reform.

Conclusions

Table 3.3 summarises the approximate historical periods identified in this chapter, showing the broad shifts in dominant actors (roughly in order) within the political economy of extractivism, the resultant regulatory-ideological agenda, the most common sites of participation for affected communities, and which eras the case studies in the following chapters fit into. The point is to provide a reference for understanding the shifting opportunities for affected communities to resist or participate in relation to extractive industries. For example, in Kelian (Chapter 4), activists' fortunes changed dramatically following the fall of the New Order regime, the withdrawal of the military and democratisation. The biggest caveat to offer for this chapter is that the constellations of political and economic interests, regulations and contestations vary markedly by province, just as they have varied over time. While that was too much detail to fit into this chapter, the provincial dynamics of North Maluku, East Kalimantan and Yogyakarta are described in the following case study chapters to illustrate the crucial importance of analysing dynamic variations in political economies.

In the political economy of extractivism in Indonesia, the fundamental oligarchic structure has remained remarkably consistent since the New Order regime. The three-way alliance between domestic conglomerates, central government and MNCs remains dominant in structuring formal and informal institutions, even as the balance of power and responsibilities between these groups shifted. Responsibility for the social and environmental impacts of mining has gradually and increasingly shifted from governments to corporations, while the central government has reasserted its authority over licencing and revenue raising. The most significant challenges to domestic oligarchy and multinational miners have come from well-organised and well-connected communities of resistance. Following the recent turn away from provisions in national legislation for participatory community development and environmental management and towards increasing avenues for international contestation of legitimacy in green supply chains, opportunities for resistance shift again. The next three chapters turn towards local-scale social relations of production and reproduction,

Table 3.3 Historical foundations of Indonesian extractivism

Era	Dominant actors	Regulatory agenda	Sites of participation	Case studies
Colonial 1600s–1940	Dutch Corporations Colonial administration Other MNCs	Colonial extraction		
Independence 1945–65	National government Military Communist party and associated mass organisations	Nationalisation	Populist and democratic state-sponsored	
New Order 1966–98	National government Military oligarchs MNCs Domestic conglomerates	Developmentalist	State and ruling party-sponsored	Kelian (Chapter 4)
Reformasi 1999–2014	MNCs Domestic conglomerates National, provincial and regency governments	Decentralisation	Democratic and consultative state-sponsored Consultative corporate-sponsored	Kelian (Chapter 4) Gosowong (Chapter 5) Kulon Progo (Chapter 6)
New-developmentalism 2014–19	Domestic conglomerates National and provincial governments MNCs	Resource nationalism	Democratic and consultative state-sponsored Consultative corporate-sponsored	Gosowong (Chapter 5) Kulon Progo (Chapter 6)
Neo-authoritarian and green developmentalism 2019–?	Domestic conglomerates National government MNCs OEMs and battery manufacturers Chinese capital	Resource nationalism and 'green' developmentalism	Corporate and international organisation-sponsored sites of participation	

including common sense understandings of the world, to understand the variation.

What does the case of Indonesia tell us about emerging patterns and directions of global extractive accumulation? Like most developing countries, the extractive sector in Indonesia is dominated by MNCs, domestic capital and bureaucratic institutions, each wanting to maximise their share of extractive revenue. This coincidence of interests results in limited regulation and minimal enforcement of the social and environmental dimensions of mining. Indeed, trends of reducing the regulatory burden on mining capital also prevail in developed countries with significant domestic mining oligarchies such as Australia, the USA and Canada. However, even given the dominant alliance of oligarchs, politicians and MNCs in Indonesian extractives, the outcomes of participation and resistance vary widely. Even when left-wing populist governments have been elected (for example, Ecuador, Venezuela), the reliance of state revenue on extractives means only slight concessions are won.

Only sustained widespread resistance can challenge the alliance between foreign capital, domestic oligarchs and entrenched bureaucracies at the national and international scales. Corporations and governments continue to use both repression and participation to undermine, divide and co-opt resistance movements. Globalising supply chains for green technologies like electric vehicles and emergent governance mechanisms provide new opportunities to contest the social and environmental impacts of mining on international scales.

Notes

1 'Extractive industries' in Indonesia include oil and gas, palm oil, and plantation agriculture, among others. This chapter focuses principally on large-scale corporate mineral and coal mining. It does not provide a detailed account of the legal requirements and regulation of mining in Indonesia – such accounts exist elsewhere (PwC 2022; Setiawan 2022).

2 This is definitely not an attempt at categorical historical periodisation, but a heuristic for the purpose of developing the argument in this chapter based on identified patterns.

3 Extractivism as critique shares some assumptions with dependency theory, problematising the reliance of states on extraction of low-value-added commodities and exploitation by multinational corporations and international organisations (Rivera Andía and Vindal Ødegaard 2019, 15).

4 Mining products for export consisted of copper ore, nickel ore, bauxite, non-monetary gold and other mining products, plus 'base metal products' (which includes intermediate and refined metals), as classified by Bank Indonesia

(2023a). If oil and gas is included, this figure rises to 36.4% of exports and 16.2% of GDP. For GDP mining-related activities, included here are 'coal and lignite mining', 'metal ore mining', 'other mining and quarrying', 'processing of basic metals' and 'manufacture of other non-metallic mineral products' (Bank Indonesia 2023b).

5 These figures are a decrease on previous years – in 2013 alone, the KPA reported 369 land conflicts, 29 fatalities, 30 shootings, 130 other instances of violence and 239 arrests (Nugraha 2013). These reports include conflict around plantations, infrastructure, mining, forestry and other agrarian conflict. These figures surely underestimate the prevalence of violence as they rely on communities or NGOs reporting to the KPA.

6 Independence was declared in 1945 and the Dutch were finally expelled in 1949.

7 According to Hadiz and Robison (2013, 38), oligarchy is a political economic system 'defined by an increasing fusion of wealth and politico-bureaucratic power, articulated in the relationships and interminglings between the leading families of business and those of politics and the bureaucracy as they became enmeshed directly in the ownership and control of capital'.

8 Student opposition, rebellious peasants and workers, the Asian Financial Crisis, and key oligarchical allies abandoning the Soeharto family culminated in an organic crisis that saw Soeharto resign in May 1998.

9 Hadiz and Robison (2013, 38) demonstrate how, following political decentralisation and democratisation, Indonesia's oligarchs adopted new strategies for maintaining their dominant political and economic power: 'For example, oligarchic power in Indonesia now more distinctly accommodates members of the growing apparatus of administration and politics at the local level. Many of these local members have successfully reinvented themselves as parliamentarians and political party leaders and forged new kinds of alliances with local business interests, leaders of mass organizations old and new, and, sometimes, even with military or police commands.'

10 Although the military retreated from its explicit political role, in most places the domestic security role has been assumed by the police. Without the independent financial base like the military, the police may be even more susceptible to rent-seeking and hiring out their services to corporations (Baker 2013). It is still common practice for mining corporations to employ *Brimob* (mobile brigade – paramilitary/anti-riot police) units to protect their assets.

11 'Resource nationalism' is an ideological fragment; there are certainly many different manifestations and scales of resource nationalism, from state led to versions that privilege private domestic capital (see Koch and Perreault 2019).

12 Must be refined into matte of at least 70% ferronickel, nickel pig iron or other alloys.

13 Unrefined nickel exports were previously banned in 2014 but the ban was relaxed in 2017.

14 While some point to this as a resurgence of the developmentalist state, it is at least an 'altered developmentalism', combining marketisation with nationalism (Gellert 2019).

15 Of the 51.2% owned by SOEs, 52.5% is owned by PT Indonesia Asahan Aluminium (Inalum) and 47.5% by PT Indonesia Papua Metal and Mineral. Papua Metal and Mineral is, in turn, 60% owned by Inalum, 28% by the Papuan Provincial Government and 12% by the Mimika regional government (Winanti and Diprose 2020, 1540). This means that the government closest to the landowners and people most affected by the mine ultimately own just 2.92% of the mine.

16 'The West Papua Uprising swept across 23 towns in West Papua, 17 cities in Indonesia, and 3 cities overseas during the period of 19 August to 30 September 2019' (Koman 2020, 7).

17 Approximately AU$9,585 as of December 2022.

18 Indonesia is the world's largest nickel producer, and having successfully secured the construction of smelters domestically through resource nationalist policies discussed above, is well placed to pursue further downstream industrialisation.

19 Until recently, most battery cathodes were nickel-manganese-cobalt oxide (NMC) with 10–20% cobalt and 60–70% nickel. New NMCA batteries can reduce cobalt to 5% of the cathode material. The quest continues to produce reliable and safe cobalt-free lithium-ion batteries.

4

Violence and participation at Rio Tinto's Kelian mine

At the turn of the millennium, Rio Tinto's Kelian gold mine was ground zero for new modes of participation in the extractive industries. It is an excellent example of corporate social responsibility (CSR) rhetoric masking dispossession and conflict. Participatory mechanisms were developed in response to localised blockades, international campaigning and global governance. With them, Rio Tinto undermined local and international alliances opposed to mining while securing support from others less directly affected. Not only was Rio Tinto successful in securing social conditions until the gold was exhausted, but they now hold the mine up as a leading example of sustainable and participatory mine closure, to be emulated around the world (Rio Tinto 2015).

The Kelian open-pit gold mine in West Kutai, East Kalimantan (Fig. 4.1), produced windfall profits[1] for Rio Tinto and brought the multinational into conflict with 4,000 small-scale alluvial gold miners who were violently evicted from 1985 to 1992. Conflict that began in the area surrounding the mine site 'jumped scales' in 1998 when local organisers forged national and international alliances with NGOs, directly threatening Rio's already besieged international reputation as a responsible miner. To regain its legitimacy and forestall government intervention, Rio turned to participatory mechanisms and global governance standards as an alternative to violent repression. The lifespan of the mine (1985–2005) gives valuable insights into why one of the world's largest mining companies, Rio Tinto, helped craft new global standards – incorporating new modes of participation – at the turn of the millennium and how these were implemented as participatory mechanisms on the ground. Likewise, the early 2000s were a crucial time for the emergence of participatory development and 'sustainable capitalism'. For these reasons, this chapter presents a 'critical case' in the development of participation as a conflict management strategy in the extractive industries.

Unlike the cases of Gosowong and Kulon Progo (Chapters 5 and 6), conflict between Rio Tinto's Indonesian subsidiary, PT Kelian Equatorial

Mining (KEM),[2] and affected communities began during the authoritarian New Order regime in Indonesia and before the widespread uptake of participatory mechanisms in the extractive sector. It provides an example of participatory mechanisms being implemented in response to an activist campaign once Rio Tinto could no longer rely exclusively on violence to repress local opposition. KEM's participatory mechanisms included a village support program, negotiations over compensation, negotiations about human rights abuses, participatory mine closure planning, and a community advice committee. Particular actors were included on specific issues according to KEM's need to contain conflict, enhance their legitimacy and mobilise community resources. However, some aspects of this have produced ongoing conflicts over the nature of participation. Why conflicts had specific manifestations and how they were contained and sustained is understood as a result of clashing modes of production and reproduction and the ideologies that support them.

This chapter proceeds in six parts. The first describes the history, geography and economy of Kelian River small-scale mining settlements from the 1940s. The social relations of production and reproduction that developed around small-scale gold mining and subsistence agriculture left a legacy of social solidarity and independent ideologies that would later support organised resistance to industrial mining. The second section describes the genesis of conflict from 1985: primitive accumulation (land grabbing) took the form of violent evictions of small-scale mining communities, initial compensation payments, and human rights abuses committed by military, police and KEM employees. Violence and human rights abuses were not only committed during evictions but also to repress ongoing opposition to the mine. Violence also took a distinct gendered dimension. This highlights the *ongoing* conflict produced by extractive dispossession. The third section bridges the themes of violence and participation. I argue that through geographically differentiated patterns of violence and CSR, KEM created a geography of participation that secured broad legitimacy in the Kutai Regency and contained conflict to a few remote villages. This strategy proved successful in creating social relations favourable to extraction until the end of the New Order regime in 1998.

The next three sections analyse waves of conflict and participation between people affected by mining, national and international NGOs, KEM and Rio Tinto. The first lasted from 1997 to 1998, beginning when nascent activism, through national and international networks, mobilised an international reputational threat to Rio Tinto and ending with Rio Tinto International ordering KEM to negotiate with representatives of people affected by mining. The second wave, 1998–2003, concerns the relocalisation of conflict and negotiations between newly formed activist organisation

Lembaga Kesejateraan Masyarakat Tambang dan Lingkungan (LKMTL; Council for Environment and Mining Communities Prosperity) and KEM. In addition to the international campaign, LKMTL capitalised on new political opportunities available following *reformasi*[3] including increased space for human rights discourse and the decreased power of the Indonesian military. The second wave finished with the negotiation of a Rp60 billion (approximately AU$11.4 million) compensation payment for victims of human rights abuses in 2001. The final wave involved a proactive approach by Rio Tinto, which collaborated with the World Bank to create a participatory mine closure plan in 2000. The participatory management of the ex-mine site as a protected forest continued through the involvement of NGOs and a community advisory forum until at least 2023. This was one of the World Bank's first attempts to apply principles of participatory development to the private sector.

These three waves of conflict and participation show how Rio Tinto increasingly turned to participatory mechanisms to contain risky forms of conflict generated by extractive dispossession. The motivation was to align the interests of people affected by mining with their own and change forms of engagement from confrontational to collaborative. In this, the participatory mechanisms were somewhat successful. Enough ideological common ground was found between KEM's corporatised consultative ideologies of representation and the human rights-based left-nationalist ideologies of activists that negotiations could proceed, although not always smoothly. Potential opposition by indirectly affected villages was neutralised through community development programs and employment. Nevertheless, conflicts over the forms of participation – who could participate, when, on what issues – continues, both within the participatory mechanisms and outside.

Rio Tinto implemented participatory strategies in Kelian, just like it did at a global scale in response to material and ideological threats to profitability (Chapter 2). These are not ethical additions of an enlightened multinational corporation – although some employees are surely motivated by ethical conduct – but the hard-headed calculations to smooth the accumulation of capital through extraction. The implication is that groups of people affected by mining and their NGO allies obtain concessions and compensation by mobilising threats to corporate profitability – not appealing to corporations' 'responsibility'.

Gold and peoples' mining: roots of resistance

Alluvial gold was first discovered by locals in the late 1930s in an upstream area of the Kelian River (Hopes 2004c, 23). The closest settlement was the

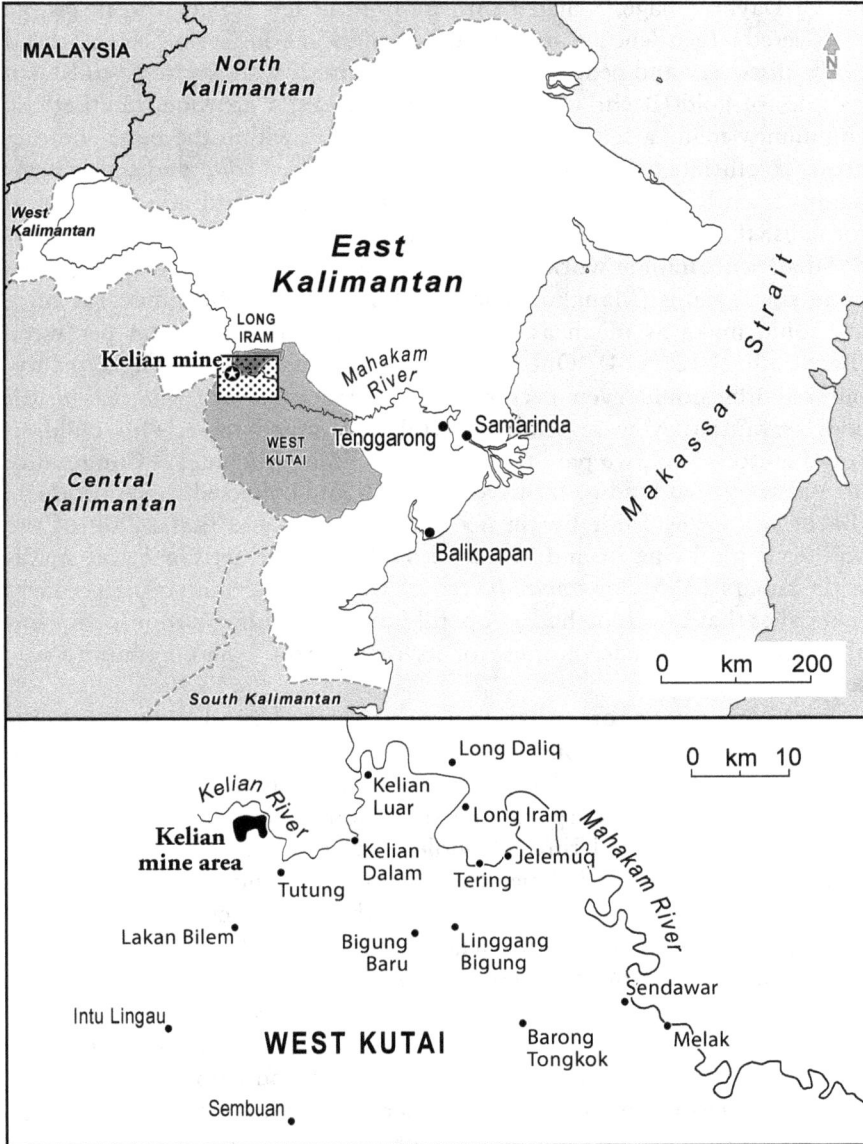

Figure 4.1 East Kalimantan and the Kelian area, showing selected towns and villages.

Bahau Dayak village, Kelian Luar.[4] In 1948, a few Kayan Dayak people discovered larger deposits and sold it to traders in Long Iram.[5] News spread of the discovery and people from across Indonesia were attracted to Kelian by tales of gold (Bachriadi 1998, 166). In 1949, a growing, multi-ethnic community made a settlement a Loa Tepu (now within the mine contract area). To officiate this, they held a festival and invited *adat*[6] and government figures from Kelian, Long Daliq, Long Iram, Bigung and other villages to formalise the settlement (Bachriadi 1998, 167).

Small-scale mining work was carried out by individuals, family groups or in small teams (Mangkoedilaga et al. 2000). In good times, the miners could make as much as Rp100,000 (AU$68) per person per week (Bachriadi 2012, 174). One ex-miner said they made 'enough, plenty, our children could even become police officers, *cemat* [district head], civil servant, they were schooled while we mined there. Our children could go to school, we paid the fees from mining [income]'.[7] Community members opened land to farm,[8] caught fish and collected forest products (Bachriadi 1998, 168). By the 1970s, it is estimated that 2,000 of the 4,000 people living in and around Loa Tepu were artisanal and small-scale miners (ASM) or *penambang rakyat* (peoples' miners). Ex-miners remember that Loa Tepu had a hopeful future, providing not only cash but also subsistence needs. Because of its remoteness,[9] the community was self-organising. [10]

Strong histories of organisation, especially if independent from government and big capital, along with control of land, ideology and alliance structures, are the factors that I argue enable a community to either engage effectively in or resist corporate participation. Although their control of land was later severed through violent evictions, in Loa Tepu, small-scale miners developed independent organisation and ideology based on the relations of production of gold and the reproduction of social life through subsistence agriculture legitimised through Dayak *adat*. Indeed, the organisation of their (heterogeneous) villages and work teams, with social solidarity and profit-sharing arrangements, closely resembles what Lahiri-Dutt (2018) refers to as 'extractive peasants'.[11] That means their relations of production, subsistence, social reproduction and common sense more closely resemble smallholder farmers than larger-scale mining. Experiences of organisation, labour-intensive work, social solidarity and a shared fate meant that the evictees did not simply disperse when faced with a threat. Rather, experiences in organising productive activities and daily life translated into the ability to organise collectively against threats.

Rio Tinto, corporate mining and the genesis of conflict

The genesis of conflict between KEM and small-scale miners was the act of dispossession – of enclosure – by Rio Tinto and government actors. This must be understood within the political economy of East Kalimantan, which has been dominated by extractive industries since the colonial era. This was especially true of Kutai Regency, where income from extractives pushed government revenue to more than double other regencies in the province by 1998, before Kutai was split into three regencies in 1999 (Casson 2001, 9). Government finance, campaign funding and patronage systems were dependent on revenue from extraction, producing collusive relationships between politicians, bureaucrats and corporations (Anugrah 2019). The extractive political economy of East Kalimantan, combined with the authoritarian regime in Indonesia, left little room for oppositional politics (Mahy 2011a; Maimunah and Agustiorini 2020).

Corporate engineers first arrived in 1975 to conduct surveys for Rio Tinto[12] (Bachriadi 1998, 168). At first, residents were happy, because the engineers needed assistance, and they paid cash. There was no significant conflict during the exploration phase. Yet, looking back, one ex-small-scale miner told me that was the moment when they lost their freedom: 'Before Rio Tinto arrived, the community was still free.'[13]

In 1985, KEM signed a contract of work (CoW)[14] with the Indonesian government to exploit the primary gold deposit (Mangkoedilaga et al. 2000). In addition to the mining area, KEM also needed to construct a 69km road and port facilities at Jelemuq on the Mahakam River where 24 families lost their land (Bachriadi 1998, 176; Atkinson 1998, 28). From this point, relations with the small-scale miners changed dramatically.

There are vastly different and conflicting accounts of land acquisition, the compensation process and human rights violations that occurred up to 1992. My purpose here is not to determine the truth of these historical matters but to explain the genesis of conflict between small-scale miners and KEM. Grievances over evictions morphed into conflict about compensation which manifested as demonstrations throughout the 1990s and international campaigning from 1997.

The Long Iram district government formed a land acquisition team (*Tim Pembebasan Lahan*), which would distribute some compensation or 'moving money' (*uang pindah*) and convince residents to move. In January 1982, the *cemat* (district head) of Long Iram ordered the small-scale miners to close operations (Mangkoedilaga et al. 2000, 23). KEM sent security guards to deliver eviction notices. Ex-miners recounted, 'They said if you like it or not, you have to move from here, they also said the government has ordered it.'[15] The government did not recognise their *adat* rights.

Indeed, the land acquisition process was not conducted with the consent of, or even in consultation with, landholders, but was negotiated between the district government and KEM. Conflicts with landholders over land acquisition were resolved in KEM's favour as a result of then president director of KEM Alan Hawke's 'extensive local contacts and, in particular with the *Bupati* [regent] and *Panglima* [five star general] in Balikpapan' (Davis 2004, 39). From the beginning, KEM developed close relations and mutual interests with local government officials. Such lack of consultation, let alone negotiation or consent, resulted in disagreements about compensation, residents refusing to move and violent evictions.

Community Aid Abroad (Australia) (CAA, now Oxfam Australia) investigations from 1998 to 2003 report that compensation for land of AU$130 to AU$650 (Rp200,000–1 million) per household was promised to evictees (Atkinson 1998, 26–28; Kennedy 2001; Nyompe 2003). Researcher Bachriadi (1998, 177) reports that the Long Iram district head set compensation at Rp200,000 (AU$136) per hectare, but that many landowners expected Rp5–10 million (AU$3,410–6,821).[16] Furthermore, while a number of residents reportedly received compensation between Rp400,000 and Rp2.5 million (AU$273–$1,705) per family, many others did not accept this offer and held out for fairer compensation (Bachriadi 1998, 180). One group of ex-small-scale miners told me that each family made Rp100,000 (AU$68.21) per person in 1990.[17] According to Bachriadi (1998, 177), many of the residents did not perceive such amounts of money as compensation but as 'moving money' (*uang pindah*) to cover costs associated with moving, far short of being able to replace lost land, buildings and crops, let alone livelihoods.

KEM community relations staff could not tell me how much compensation was paid, but stated that everything was clear and settled according to the laws and regulations of Indonesia and that they had recognised 444 families as landholders:

> They received compensation depending on the size of their land and building. We offered them two hectares of land [in Tutung], but they rejected that, they preferred to take cash. We built them houses, some just took money if they wanted to go back to their original village. It was already clear. [Only] after 1998, they started to demand more.[18]

KEM management considered the issue fairly settled, while affected people felt cheated.

Bachriadi (1998, 171) reported that residents of Loa Tepu were promised replacement facilities in Tutung, a new settlement being built by the company outside the mining area. According to Tutung residents, KEM promised to build houses, two hectares of land each, clean water facilities, sanitation facilities and electricity. However, all that was provided was a cleared plot of land 15 by 25 metres and a clean water supply.[19] Another ex-resident recalled that when it came time to move, construction of houses in Tutung was not finished and that in some cases KEM only provided tents.[20]

By 1990, the mining area was under corporate control.[21] Residents who refused compensation or refused to move until compensation was paid or replacement houses built were subjected to intimidation and violence from the land acquisition team, KEM security, military and police.[22] These events are catalogued in many sources, most reliably in the report of the independent fact-finding team (Mangkoedilaga et al. 2000) convened by Komnas HAM (the National Commission on Human Rights).[23]

Residents resisting eviction were arrested, their houses and gardens were burnt and their possessions destroyed, or they were shot[24] (Kennedy 2001). Between 1982 and 1990, more than 500 houses and cottages were burnt (Mangkoedilaga et al. 2000, 24–25).[25]

Two ex-small-scale miners described how hopeless they felt as they were forced to move to Tutung:

> Although the community is right, they are always made wrong. If we insisted [on our rights], the iron hand will come. That is the problem and that is why all kinds of violence short of bombings were used ... we were just like a herd of cows that was pushed into a barn together.[26]

And

> I was arrested and twice was sent to Tenggarong. Before PT KEM enclosed [the land] I strongly defended it, I did not want to move, I did not want to receive compensation. They were offering 20 million rupiah. For us that is small, in three days we would make that much from mining. So, to receive compensation, we were forced, it must be received through the violence of *Brimob*, police. If I wanted to or not, we couldn't stand it any longer. Because that was a previous age, rather violent.[27]

One of the last remaining families in the mining area was Pak Daniel Paras's. On 20 December 1991, KEM security and *Brimob*[28] officers ordered them out. He refused because he had not received compensation or a replacement home in Tutung, as had been agreed to (Mangkoedilaga et al. 2000, 29–30). He and his four children were eating breakfast when *Brimob* officers opened fire on their house. Officers then entered, ransacked their house and forced them out. According to Bachriadi's research (1998, 184), when seven houses on Gunung Runcing (an agricultural area within the mining contract area) were destroyed, their occupants only received taxi money of Rp40,000 each for river taxis to transport their possessions.

This kind of blatant violence was the norm for land grabbing by multi-national corporations in the 1980s. Soon, however, enough pressure would mount on corporations like Rio Tinto that they were forced to find new, more amenable strategies for undermining resistance and smoothing extractive accumulation.

Of course, these events were traumatic; one ex-resident of Loa Tepu told me that he witnessed beatings and 'too much violence'.[29] He believes the violence was ordered by KEM:

> Well, it is like this, for example there's an order to use violence from the people at the top ... that is the reason they [the police] feel legitimised in using forceful violence ... PT KEM was protected by the state which abandoned its people unprotected.[30]

Small-scale miners were cleared out and production began in 1992.[31] The violent evictions, reframed as human rights violations, would haunt KEM through the 1990s and find international audiences in 1997. Miners moved to either Kelian Dalam,[32] Tutung, or returned to their family's origin.[33]

Each location developed different patterns of participation and manifestations of conflict. The initial act of dispossession totally disrupted the livelihoods of evictees who needed to find and construct new sources of subsistence, production and social reproduction. The strategies adopted by evictees resulted in differentiated dynamics between KEM and communities in each location. I will describe these patterns now, before showing how KEM attempted to contain manifestations of conflict and create more stable social relations.

Manifestations of conflict post-eviction

In Tutung, where most of the evictees were moved, most opened land for gardening or rubber plantations. A few of the well-connected residents secured contracts or employment with KEM to provide transport, construction or security services. The company contracted builders for the school, mosque, police station and government offices in Tutung.[34] Others engaged in informal and precarious work.

Many of the 444 evicted families stayed in Tutung while they struggled to obtain the compensation they believed they were entitled to. In the words of one ex-resident of Tutung:

> There has not been justice. For the community, we wanted just livelihoods. Try to open land, two hectares to farm. That was the promise – to make two hectares of land, we could live like that. Houses were also promised but that didn't happen. Whoever was working ... just built their own houses in Tutung, there wasn't any built by the company. We had to pay for it all ourselves.[35]

Up to 200 protests, demonstrations and blockades over evictions and compensation had been held by the end of 1992; most were met with strong repression by police, military and company security (Nyompe 2003). The demonstrations built in intensity until 24 December 1992, when over 400 people marched from Tutung to the gates of KEM and blocked the road for seven days. Local police and military forces, acting in close coop-eration with and supported by KEM security, responded by arresting 15 people. None of the arrests followed legal process (Mangkoedilaga et al. 2000, 14–19). One of the arrested leaders, Edward Tarung, died in custody[36] (Mangkoedilaga et al. 2000, 19–21). This demoralised and broke organised resistance but did not end the searing resentment felt by evictees.

Many evictees who had moved to Kelian Dalam continued to pan for gold further downstream in the Kelian River, however: '[We made] only enough to eat every day, just enough to eat, we could die too, it was dif-ficult. There is only a tiny amount of gold.'[37] Down river, they could only make Rp87,000 (AU$59) per person per week in good times, which became increasingly less frequent.

Some small-scale miners saw that it could be more profitable to repro-cess the waste rock and tailings of KEM (*ngerebok*). They had to enter the mining location at night. KEM considered this theft and if people were caught, they were sent to the police station in Tenggarong or shot at by KEM security and *Brimob* officers hired by KEM (Bachriadi 1998, 186).[38] In 1995, one person died after being chased into the Namuk tailings dam (Mangkoedilaga et al. 2000, 34). At least two other people were shot when they were caught (Bachriadi 1998, 187).

Before KEM began operating, residents of Kelian Dalam used the river water to wash, catch fish, bathe and for drinking.[39] After KEM began oper-ating, residents reported the river water would cause itching and rashes on their bodies (Bachriadi 1998, 189). In 1991, five residents died after bathing in the river. After this, the community used the river water with limitations; they stopped drinking the water and washing at certain times of the day.

KEM was aware of these risks. Their 1990 environmental assessment (AMDAL) stated that:

> High concentrations of sulphide and sulphur dioxide originating from waste rock will produce changes in the soil and through erosion and washing will increase the content of sulphur compounds in Bayak River and Nakan River [subsidiaries of Kelian River] … Liquid waste, especially which overflows from the dam if still containing cyanide can react with the heavy metals and has synergistic characteristics, that is to result in compounds becoming more poi-sonous. These compounds do not just affect the water quality, but also water

vegetation and if absorbed by aquatic animals can enter the food chain, this
can create sub-lethal and dangerous conditions.

(cited in Bachriadi 1998, 191)

This was before the mining industry adopted standards of consultation.[40]
Kelian Dalam residents were not even warned, let alone given an opportunity to participate in decision making or environmental monitoring.

Until 1998, the relationship between evictees and KEM remained confrontational. Between 1986 and 1998, KEM had progressively paid
compensation to 4,509 people for lost land and possessions, totalling
Rp7,750,409,929 (approximately AU$4.5 million at average exchange
rates) (KEM 2007). Beyond this, there was little incentive for Rio Tinto to
address the concerns of people affected by their practices until the formation of LKMTL and the struggle jumped to national and international scales
(Nyompe 2003).

Forms of production, subsistence and reproduction adopted by evictees
continued to bring them into conflict with KEM, either through protest
activity or trespassing. KEM's strategy of repression through violence with
limited compensation further exacerbated these tensions until they found
expression after 1998. Another major factor determining both the impacts
of violence and later participation was gender.[41]

Gendered and sexualised violence

In much of the literature about the impacts of mining, women are depicted
as being disproportionately victimised.[42] A more recent angle of feminist
enquiry seeks to 'step beyond ... current discourses of victimhood' (Lahiri-
Dutt 2012, 203) by emphasising the agency and roles of women in mining
and mining communities.[43] In Gosowong and Kulon Progo (Chapters 5 and
6), there are examples of how gendered divisions of labour and relations of
social reproduction both determine and are changed by forms of participation and activism. However, in the case of Kelian, women and gender non-
conforming evictees were disproportionately disempowered by extractive
dispossession. There was little opportunity to reverse this through participation or resistance.

Company security, police and the military all used gendered violence and
sexual harassment as part of the evictions of the mining communities up
to 1992. This culture persisted during the operations of the mine, as many
women complained of sexual harassment and violence by KEM employees.
The Komnas HAM report finds that out of 21 reported cases, there were 17
cases of 'sexual harassment, rape, and sexual relations under psychological
pressure [that] deserve further investigation' (Mangkoedilaga et al. 2000,

35). In 16 of these cases the perpetrator was an employee of KEM (the general manager of KEM was responsible for six of these), and at least four of the victims were girls under 16 years old.[44] Only one of the perpetrators ever faced sanctions from his employer and there was a culture of ignoring, denying and supporting perpetrators at KEM (Mangkoedilaga et al. 2000, 35).

The gendered patterns of violence established during the original act of primitive accumulation continued during the mine's operation, serving to further silence women. Although KEM set up a Harassment Team to accommodate complaints in 1995 (Rachmayana 2004, 182), ex-KEM managers remain dismissive of claims of sexual harassment or sexual assault. One explained that

> KEM employees were mostly Indonesian [not local] and ex-pats. There was successful relationships and marriages. There were [cases of pregnancy] but [the woman] already had a family. Forced, not possible, different religions, not possible. Mixed. There were successes and failures. Sexual harassment? Most of the cases are failed relationships, not sexual harassment. It was solved in the *adat* way. Maybe before construction, I don't know about that. There were many contractors for construction.[45]

Even more so than victims of other kinds of human rights abuses, victims of sexual violence were silenced through the repressive measures of KEM and security forces and through shame in their own communities (Rachmayana 2004, 182) – where patriarchal common sense prevailed. It would not be until after *reformasi* that these issues began to be taken seriously, and even then the women survivors would not negotiate directly with KEM, but would have their voice represented through layers of NGOs.

Community Aid Abroad (CAA) investigations linked changes in gender relations – and other social transformations – to the economic impacts of the mine. Inequality grew between households and between men and women as 'the cost of basic necessities led to more traditional subsistence and cooperative economic activities being regarded as inferior to having a job at the mine' (Atkinson 1998, 35). The influx of male workers from across Indonesia and abroad led to large-scale prostitution near Jelemuq (Atkinson 1998, 36). As employment, both in mining and downstream services (with some exceptions such as sex work, truck driving, and cleaning services) is skewed towards men,[46] women and their economic contributions are devalued along with the decreasing status of communal production, their lower status within new systems of production, and the gendered division between production and social reproduction.

Economic development and employment patterns dramatically exacerbated gendered inequality. As corporate mining and wage labour replaced more communal village-based profit-sharing production and subsistence, forms of social reproduction required to sustain production also rapidly changed. These changes, stemming from the act of extractive dispossession, led to a separation of productive from reproductive activities and a commodification of labour power (Federici 2004, 74). The commodification of labour included the commodification of sexual labour and women's bodies, and violence against women and girls. This disempowerment is also reflected later in the lack of women participating in negotiations and consultations, despite being disproportionately affected. By the mid-1990s, a new mode of extractive accumulation encompassing new forms of social reproduction was emerging.

The geography of conflict and participation

KEM's engagement with people affected by mining was not limited to evictees. They also established CSR programs for the 27 villages in the area to the south of the mine. These programs included a village support program, the Rio Tinto Foundation and agricultural college, employment opportunities and a ranger program. This section argues that there were four distinct geo-economic areas with different patterns of conflict and participation. Each of KEM's CSR programs were also interventions into local political and economic relations – which became more dependent on the company and more integrated into market capitalism. This differentiation enabled KEM to secure broad legitimacy in West Kutai Regency while containing serious challenges to remote areas.

The first geo-economic area is the two villages closest to the mine site – Tutung and Kelian Dalam. As discussed above, they make up the bulk of evictees and victims of human rights abuses. Residents of these villages were consequently the most enthusiastic supporters of LKMTL, with obvious interests in compensation.

The second geographical area is the five Dayak agricultural villages slightly further away. Being shifting cultivators only occasionally engaging in alluvial gold mining, they were less directly affected by industrial mining. Because of their proximity to the mine site and claims to traditional custodianship of the forests, these villages, in addition to Tutung and Kelian Dalam, had direct interests in how the forest is managed. These five villages – Kelian Luar, Lakan Bilem,[47] Batu Apui, Sembuan and Intu Lingau plus Kelian Dalam (Mine Closure Steering Committee 2002, 2) – would be wiped out if either of the dams at the mine failed. Therefore, their interests were the good management of the mining infrastructure and forests while obtaining some benefits from Rio Tinto, including compensation for pollution.

These five villages did receive some benefits from KEM's village support program, Rio Tinto Foundation, employment and ranger program (detailed below). These villagers seem to have rarely engaged with any kind of activism or politics outside their villages and were more or less passive recipients of CSR. Village heads and *adat* figures from these villages also participated in KEM's community advisory committee (*Komite Penasehat Masyarakat*, KPM), detailed below.

The third area consists of villagers further down the Mahakam River, Long Iram and Tering in particular, which was the multicultural trading post for gold and other forest products. This group was politically astute and managed to secure some compensation from Rio Tinto through protest action loosely connected with LKMTL. Their participation was conducted through negotiations with government officials during protests.

The final geographical area is the largest and least directly affected by the mine, consisting of the 27 villages which KEM defined as 'local', including all the villages mentioned above. Residents of these villages were prioritised for employment, were eligible to attend the agricultural school and could apply for assistance from KEM's village support program.

Taking this geographical view helps show how KEM maintained a good or neutral reputation in Kutai by giving small benefits to those who suffered negligible impacts. The isolation of victims within West Kutai led LKMTL to seek support outside the regency. KEM used different modes of participation for LKMTL and others who were able to mobilise political power. KEM's community relations employees also speak differently about their village support and CSR programs, which they are proud of, and the compensation process which they view as a nuisance manipulated by NGOs.

KEM's village support program, established in 1992, invited representatives, usually village officials,[48] from 27 villages to bring proposals for funding to KEM's community relations department. Villages received money and equipment to cement village roads, renovate schools, build village government offices, mosques and churches, provide water sanitation, establish health clinics, support celebrations, and provide rice during droughts.[49] The program both mitigated negative effects of mining – for example by providing water sanitation where rivers were no longer clean – and provided additional benefits. From 2000, the program changed focus to sustainable development. KEM established a consultative group which focused on sustainable economic development such as support for agriculture, fisheries and livestock.[50] For example, in Lakan Bilem, in 2005, KEM helped establish a cacao plantation by purchasing enough seed to plant 70 hectares.[51] As it was village officials – supposedly in consultation with other villagers – who presented proposals and negotiated projects, the village support program utilised and cemented existing village hierarchies and patronage networks. That is, KEM's emerging consultative ideology of participation fitted well with and piggybacked on the existing mode of village governance.

The Rio Tinto Foundation was established in 1995 to build public infrastructure in Tutung and an agricultural college in Liggang Bigung. With funding from AusAID, the foundation provided rice to drought-stricken farmers in 1997–98 and established public health programs (Bua 2004, 127). Local people were hired to construct the buildings. Children from the 27 villages can attend the agricultural college for free and graduates may receive scholarships to continue their education, while the majority find employment in palm oil plantations.[52] The agricultural school aims to change patterns of agriculture by teaching the younger generations about fertiliser, sedentary farming, plantation work and cash cropping – as opposed to traditional methods of shifting cultivation.

KEM's village support program and the Rio Tinto foundation involved limited participation compared with the negotiations and mine closure planning that were developed later in response to activist campaigning. However, education, infrastructure development and employment facilitated modest changes in the local political economy. Through community development programs and the agricultural college, villages were encouraged to change from shifting cultivation for subsistence to sedentary agriculture producing for market. Their relations of production became more integrated with capital, state and the company. Sedentary, marketised production is less threatening to mining than subsistence shifting cultivation, as it is predictable and creates more compliant subjects. Through these early CSR programs, KEM was able to distribute relatively few resources to a large number of people and thereby secure legitimacy in Kutai. The patron-client relationship also ensured little opposition from village elites who reinforced their political and social positions through participation and community development programs. Meanwhile, confrontational conflict over justice, human rights and compensation was contained to a small group of people mostly in Kelian Dalam and Tutung – until the conflict took on national and international dimensions.

Jumping-scales – the internationalisation of conflict

The power to force KEM to negotiate came from LKMTL's success in rescaling conflicts about compensation. The human rights-influenced left-nationalist ideology of LKMTL activists made a strong foundation for collaboration with international NGOs. Indeed, these two factors – ideology and alliance structures – are two of the factors I argue determine the ability of people affected by mining to participate in corporate mechanisms or to reject them.

As described above, before 1998, demonstrations and efforts to obtain compensation and justice by the ex-small-scale miners met severe repression. The activists needed a new strategy to pursue their claims. Pak Pius Nyompe, whose mother's land at Jelemuq was acquired without compensation by KEM, had previous experience advocating for land rights in cases along the Mahakam River.[53] Pak Pius became involved in the Kelian case in 1997, advocating with residents of Tutung and Tering (Hopes 2004b, 178). LKMTL was established by Pak Pius and 13 other representatives of the evictees in July 1998; before that it was informally known as 'the group of 14'.[54]

While LKMTL had no political program other than obtaining compensation for victims, they had an ideological foundation based squarely in human rights, citizenship and human dignity. One of the 14 representatives explained that he was a member of PNI (*Partai Nasional Indonesia*; Indonesian Nationalist Party) in Sumatra before the 1965 genocide, while another was a member of PRD (*Partai Rakyat Demokrasi*; Democratic Peoples' Party) before 1998.[55] This indicates that LKMTL leaders were influenced by ideas of left-nationalism, if not socialism, that emphasise the rights of citizens to share in the benefits of national development. This political tradition is grounded in the dignity of the common people (*rakyat*) struggling for land and justice. While the adherents of left-nationalist ideology among the peoples' miners were limited to a few activists with previous experience of political struggle, it resonated with many of the small-scale miners struggling for land, livelihoods and dignity, helping to translate their experience into ideas and action. The elements of this ideology that focus on human rights, justice and human dignity also provided common ground for later networking with NGOs and provided the basis of negotiations with KEM.

Around 1995, issues of human rights abuses and environmental destruction were taken up by several regional and national NGOs including JATAM (*Jaringan Advokasi Tambang*; Mining Advocacy Network) and WALHI (*Wahana Lingkungan Hidup Indonesia*; Friends of the Earth Indonesia).[56] Through working relationships between JATAM and CAA activists, field trips were arranged for Australian activists to visit the Kelian area in September 1997, make a short documentary film and begin reporting on the issues, reaching international English-speaking audiences (Macdonald and Ross 2002, 37).

These visits to Kelian coincided with the beginning of CAA's campaign to create a mining ombudsman which would hold Australian-based mining companies operating abroad to Australian standards.[57] In January 1998,

CAA funded a month-long Australian tour for five activists representing communities affected by the Kelian mine, including Pak Pius Nyompe. Pak Pius spoke at events organised by CAA, unions and other activist organisations and organised a protest at the Melbourne home of 'one of the prominent board members of Rio Tinto'.[58]

Meanwhile, Rio Tinto had become the target of a multinational campaign when the Construction, Forestry, Mining and Energy Union (CFMEU) in Australia created a coalition with other labour, environmental and human rights organisations impacted by or struggling against Rio Tinto (McSorley and Fowler 2001; International Longshore and Warehouse Union 2010; Manheim 2001, 127). The network produced the 'Tainted Titan' report (ICEM 1997), along with a short film documenting Rio Tinto's past controversies and then current industrial relations battle with the CFMEU (CFMEU Mining and Energy Division 1998). Rio Tinto refused to address the report or the network as a whole and instead singled out particular groups to engage in negotiations (McSorley and Fowler 2001).

The CAA tour culminated in Rio Tinto executives in Melbourne meeting with Pak Pius and receiving a list of grievances.[59] At that meeting, one executive reportedly stated, 'We are working totally within Indonesian laws and procedures.'[60] In the eyes of Pak Pius and CAA, such a statement only underscored that the law in Indonesia was inadequate in protecting human rights, rhetorically strengthening CAA's campaign to hold companies to Australian standards when operating overseas. Rio Tinto executives ordered KEM to negotiate.

Soon after Pak Pius returned to Indonesia he was approached by the head of Rio Tinto Indonesia and PT KEM:

> They asked about all the problems that we were campaigning about in Australia, so that we can sit down together and solve them ... I asked for three months ... because I have to go village to village in order to collect [information from] people and victims. So at the beginning of May, with *reformasi* approaching, we arranged the demands of the people to present it in Jakarta. Eighteen people went to Jakarta.[61]

Yet, they felt that KEM was not serious about negotiations.[62] So, in May 1998, Pak Pius attended Rio Tinto's AGM in London and met with more Rio Tinto executives (Atkinson et al. 2001, 15). The sustained international pressure led Rio Tinto London executives to order KEM to negotiate again. Through informal alliances with NGOs, the local group was able to 'jump scales', turning a local conflict into an international one, where more resources and allies were available and Rio Tinto's legitimacy was vulnerable. The temporary alliance was easy ideologically as the liberal human rights focus of the NGOs fitted well with the grievance and justice focus of LKMTL.

As described in the Chapter 2, in the late 1990s Rio Tinto was adopting new strategies towards international criticism, courting critics instead of attempting to silence them. Rio Tinto also worked to relocalise conflict, ordering KEM to negotiate and solve grievances with LKMTL to mitigate further damage that could be done by the international network. This was part of the then emerging mode of participation being formalised through global standards, legitimised through consultative ideologies as a problem-solving strategy.

Contesting power within and around negotiations

Following Pak Pius's return from London, a series of meetings between KEM, community representatives and JATAM were arranged. In June 1998, KEM agreed to pay Rp10 million (AU$1,632)[63] to each of the 444 evicted families and continue negotiations about other grievances (Phillips 2001, 189; Atkinson et al. 2001, 15). According to KEM community relations staff, this amount was trivial: '4.44 billion rupiah. For KEM it was a small amount, so we just paid.'[64] Each of the families donated one-tenth of their compensation to formalise a new local organisation, LKMTL, and continue campaigning (Atkinson et al. 2001, 15).

Negotiations over human rights violations, environmental pollution and other effects of mining were more complicated. Who would be paid how much compensation, and when, was the outcome of each side (KEM and LKMTL) employing various strategies to contest each other's power, within and outside negotiations.

To be sure, the 444 evicted families were not the only people affected by loss of land, livelihoods, resources and human rights abuse. Before KEM began operations, many of the local Dayak people would move back and forth between the mining area and other villages or were living in Kelian Dalam (outside the contract area) and were not captured within the 444 families, even though gold contributed to their livelihoods.[65] LKMTL recruited these people along with anyone claiming to have suffered negative impacts; after initial screening, LKMTL registered 5,026 legitimate claimants.[66]

Negotiations over compensation through 1998 and 1999 were fraught; both LKTML and WALHI at times boycotted meetings (Lynch and Harwell 2002; Nyompe 2003, 4). CAA activists recall their frustration:

In mid-1999 the company's approach changed. In violation of the previous agreement with the community, a government official was introduced into the negotiating process. The company also began a separate negotiation process with another group (called Team Murni), which supposedly represented the community, but which did not have the formal mandate of LKMTL. This

caused considerable anger and frustration, leading to a breakdown in the
negotiations, to communities blocking the mine road and to subsequent arrests
by the police.

(Atkinson et al. 2001, 15; see also Lynch and Harwell 2002;

Nyompe 2003, 4)

The negotiation process had been a way of working out who had the power
to force compromise. Pak Pius appreciated this: '[When negotiations were
breaking down] I begun to mobilise the masses to create pressure. Always
demonstrating until they agreed to sit and negotiate.'[67] An agreement
between KEM and LKMTL was reached on 11–12 January 1999 to invite
an independent investigation into human rights violations led by Komnas
HAM (Mangkoedilaga et al. 2000, 7; Atkinson et al. 2001, 14–15). Bringing
in independent experts was a way to facilitate compromise.

Although international pressure had forced KEM to begin negotiations,
LKMTL had to bring more pressure to bear on KEM to resolve outstanding
grievances. LKMTL mobilised power outside official negotiations – through
demonstrations, reports on human rights violations, and continued international campaigning. The fall of the New Order regime was vital to the success of LKMTL. From May 1998, there was a feeling of 'euphoria because of
reformasi, so that the community dared to demonstrate'.[68] In the context of
reformasi, the military became hesitant to crack down. This new political situation meant there was more space both for LKMTL to demonstrate locally
and for national NGOs to speak out, as with the Komnas HAM report.

From 1998 to 2000, demonstrations blocked the access road to the mine
more than ten times.[69] In April and May 2000, LKMTL supporters, frus-
trated with the slow process of negotiations, set up roadblocks between
the port and the mine. The blockade lasted over 40 days. The prolonged
blockade and lack of supplies forced KEM to halt production, evacuate
workers, and declare *force majeure* on contracts for the delivery of gold.[70]
KEM estimated that the blockade cost at least US$12.5 million in lost rev-
enue (Casson 2001, 13). Police and military reinforcements were dispatched
to repress the demonstration. Desperately wanting to avoid violence and
international publicity, KEM agreed to LKMTL's framework for continued
negotiations, ending the blockade and the need for military intervention.[71]

The results of the investigation into human rights violations, released
in early 2000, lent legitimacy to LKMTL's position. The report found evidence supporting claims of human rights violations. It recommended further
investigation of accusations followed by negotiation of compensation *and*
prosecution by Indonesian courts (Mangkoedilaga et al. 2000). Results of
the investigation spread quickly among national and international NGOs
and media, damaging Rio Tinto's international reputation (Muhammad
et al. 2005, 153).

Rio has since acknowledged human rights violations occurred, including

> the ill-treatment of persons during the relocation of settlers in the mine area by
> Kelian Equatorial Mining security personnel and police officers, including the
> eviction of artisanal miners and the destruction of their living places and work-
> ing equipment, causing loss of livelihoods. Some claims involved allegations
> of serious physical abuse by security forces carrying out the relocation. The
> ill-treatment of protesters by company security personnel and police, includ-
> ing cruel and degrading treatment during arrest and detention following dem-
> onstrations against Kelian Equatorial Mining. Sexual harassment and sexual
> abuse of women by Kelian Equatorial Mining employees.
>
> (Kemp et al. 2013, 82)

Despite a 'public expression of regret' (Kemp et al. 2013, 81), no party
involved ever faced court. JATAM was critical of this as a bad precedent in
Indonesia:

> Although Komnas HAM found evidence of a number of human rights viola-
> tions in 1999–2000, in fact this case has never been investigated, just evapo-
> rated. If the government was serious about this problem, they must drag the
> groups violating human rights to court.
>
> (Muhammad et al. 2005, ix)

Instead, Rio provided compensation without admitting guilt.

Negotiations throughout 2000 were beset by conflicts over who had
the rights to participate, the appropriate 'solutions' to human rights violations, and power struggles within the negotiation process. CAA criticised
the process:

> The company attempted to resolve the human rights issue by organising a
> traditional reconciliation ceremony instead of more formal legal action. In
> October 2000, WALHI – the organisation which had been facilitating the
> negotiations – withdrew in frustration at the company's attitude.
>
> (Atkinson et al. 2001, 15)

With both local demonstrations threatening production and the human
rights report attracting international attention, Rio Tinto needed damage
control. In March 2001, following further negotiations, KEM announced a
Rp60 billion compensation package (AU$11.1 million) for victims, without
admitting guilt or liability (Nurcahyana et al. 2008; Macdonald and Ross
2003, 51).

The decision to avoid formal legal proceedings was in the interests of
both KEM and LKMTL. The activists had no faith in the justice system
and pointed to close links between government and KEM. For example,
then *bupati* (regent) Thomas Ismael (2006–16) was transportation manager
for KEM 1990–2000. Given KEM was the largest single taxpayer in West

Kutai, this structural and personal relationship was interpreted as evidence they would not get a fair hearing.[72] KEM employees stated compensation over litigation was more in keeping with Dayak *adat* practices, but of course this also limited their exposure to negative publicity. Although Komnas HAM and JATAM favoured legal processes to achieve justice, other parties favoured direct negotiation with the company, legitimised through *adat* as an ideology and material offers of cash.

Gendered participation

While the NGOs highlighted gendered sexual violence as the most shocking of human rights violations to escalate their campaign, LKMTL leaders were all men. LKMTL approached some women, including victims of violence, to help identify and collect the stories of other victims of sexual harassment and violence, but none took leadership roles.[73]

After the investigation into human rights abuses, Komnas Perempuan (The National Commission on Violence Against Women) acted as an intermediary between LKMTL, KEM and (alleged) victims of sexual violence to negotiate compensation. Activists from *Asosiasi Perempuan Untuk Keadilan* (Association of Women for Justice; APIK) accompanied women during the validation process.[74] Negotiation for compensation supposedly followed *adat* custom: 'meetings were held, attended by the complainants, Komnas HAM as mediator, complainants' lawyers, LKMTL and several Heads of Traditional Law' (Rachmayana 2004, 182). This was strictly about paying compensation for allegations, not establishing the validity of claims.

This shows how not only the impacts of mining, but also participation is structured along gendered lines. Although gendered violence was a critical part of the narrative of human rights abuses, women and gender non-conforming people consistently had less access to resources and opportunities than their male counterparts, reflecting the subordination of reproductive to productive labour. Their participation in corporate processes was mediated through an extra layer of NGO representation.

This section demonstrates that after a mechanism for negotiations was established, following the initial international pressure the alliances brought on Rio Tinto, they became a site for continued contestation over the interests of multiple parties. Like political institutions in general, participatory mechanisms do not *resolve* conflicts, rather they become terrain for new kinds of contestation. In this case, to break deadlocks within the negotiations, LKMTL mobilised several forms of power outside corporate sites of participation – demonstrations, international networking, the independent report on human rights and the assistance of women's NGOs. These non-institutional modes of participation allowed LKMTL to develop and demonstrate its bargaining power within negotiations. While there was tension between the corporate consultative ideology of Rio Tinto and the human rights, left-nationalist ideologies of LKMTL, there was eventually enough receptivity around interpretations of *adat* to make agreements. Some ideological common ground could be found, supported of course by cash compensation.

Mine closure and forest protection

In 1998, KEM began planning for mine closure, set for 2003. At that time, Indonesia did not have significant regulations for mine closure. The World Bank, also in the process of developing social policy for its investments in the extractive sector, advised that a 'trilateral process of consultation and problem solving, involving mining companies, governments, and communities, is required for a mine to be closed successfully' (World Bank and International Finance Corporation 2002, v).

The World Bank advised KEM on how to establish a participatory committee, which stakeholders to invite, and how decisions should be made.[75] The committee operated from 2001 to 2003, with a mandate to address five matters:

1. Rehabilitation of the tailings dam, waste rock dam and mine pit;
2. The creation of a protected forest;
3. Transformation of the buildings, plant and infrastructure into a wetlands 'biofilter';
4. Transferring some assets to local government and communities;
5. Finalising the Rp60 billion compensation payout.

Stakeholders included local activists, regency and provincial government, *adat* representatives, academics from the Institute of Technology Bandung, and representatives from KEM and Rio Tinto.[76]

In public documents, Rio Tinto (Everingham et al. 2016, 136–37) described the mine closure planning process as representative of 'Kelian Equatorial Mining, Rio Tinto, the surrounding community, and the district, provincial and central governments' and that 'key decisions on all aspects of mine closure were to be made by consensus ... or if a decision could not be reached by consensus, then working groups were tasked with reconsidering the options and presenting them at the next meeting'. Rio's corporate documents present a picture of harmonious participation. Indeed, Rio Tinto (2015, 10) boasts that it 'received the Indonesian Government's "Caring Company Forest Reclamation Award" for rehabilitation at the Kelian mine site'.

In contrast, Nyompe (2003), describes how LKMTL and WALHI withdrew from participation in the Mine Closure Steering Committee (MCSC) and working groups because of serious disagreements about both mine closure plans and outstanding compensation for past abuses:

> Our opinion was always cut, they would never listen to our problems ... [The] MCSC [Mine Closure Steering Committee] is formulistic, there were no opportunities to ask questions or submit input. WALHI attended the first meeting, their question was cut off and they had no opportunity to ask questions, so they withdrew and did not participate again.[77]

Even according to KEM staff who participated in the committee, negotiations were not straightforward:

> I have to say that the process was not easy ... political, we cannot avoid that. ... the local NGO has other interests – they had a hidden agenda, sometimes they are a bit political. They walked out and then come back again. So complicated at that time.[78]

Interviews with KEM employees contradict the notion that 'consensus' was the basis of decision making, stating that controversial issues were tightly controlled by the chair, oppositional views were not admitted for discussion, and votes were taken when there was disagreement.[79]

The MCSC was a site where multiple interests clashed and usually were resolved in the company's favour. For example, LKMTL and WALHI wanted to use the forum to ensure issues of compensation were resolved before the company closed; some other members were interested in opportunities to mine again.

After KEM concluded mining-related activities, the contract area was turned into a 6,670ha protected forest. A new corporation, *PT Hutan Lindung Kelian Lestari* (Sustainable Kelian Protected Forest Limited; HLKL) was set up to rehabilitate and manage the forest in 2006.[80] Its status as a protected forest precludes mining, fishing or returning to the area.

As part of the effort to protect the forest, HLKL set up a ranger program and participatory community advisory committee (*Komite Penasehat Masyarakat*; KPM). The KPM comprised village officials or *adat* heads from each village. The ostensible aim of this group was to

> provide advice on cultural issues and advise on how to operate. So how the forest can be watched for long, not against the cultural values. ... It is such a good thing, we can get input on community and cultural issues and also get information if there is any intruder from the village to our area. They can help us with that.[81]

The above and below quotes demonstrate how the KPM was designed from the beginning to serve two functions: officially to provide cultural advice about forest management and second to police villagers who might illegally enter the protected forest area. According to various village officials:

> KEM also gives advice, socialisation, that [our villagers] cannot enter the protected area. That is all. Dam Namuk will flood Sembuang (Lakan Bilem); Dam Nakan will flood Kelian Dalam and Luar. It would wipe out this village. At the beginning they asked about how to manage the forest ... how to respect the land and traditions. Our advice was to restore the forest to its original condition and preserve the streams and small rivers.[82]

> KPM is mostly just about hearing about the impacts of people disturbing the KEM area. They just want to talk about the problems of people entering the KEM area, not about the school. They just tell us after there is a violation, just to give us advice not to let our community enter the restricted area.[83]

Clearly, the KPM, enabled by consultative ideologies of representation, was a way for KEM to utilise the participation of village heads to solve the 'problem' of trespassing. Of course, the forest is not only guarded by rangers and village officials, who may have split loyalties, but also by police and military personnel hired by HLKL:

> I was in the forest with a friend, we were cooking rice. And all of a sudden someone came and screamed 'Don't run!' He was shooting. He was shooting upward and then he shot me, it hit me but the third and the fourth bullet didn't hit me. They wear uniform, *Brimob*. I don't know exactly but I know his commandant's name was [redacted]. I was cleaning my gold mining tools. We were far deep in the forest, so we took some time to cook. It was after the closure of PT KEM operation.[84]

However, the KPM was disbanded after a few years because the HLKL managers thought that members of the advisory committee were 'pushing their own agendas'[85] as some of the members of the community advisory group were apparently involved in illegal mining – 'They were too ... naughty.'[86]

Participants agreed to participate because they thought they would be consulted on a wider range of issues, yet when the limitations of this became clear, the consultative mechanism fell apart. The KPM produced opportunities for each actor to pursue their own interests – this participatory mechanism was co-opted to various ends and consequentially disbanded when it failed to serve the function intended by HLKL. This final attempt at participation in the Kelian area neatly demonstrates how the original land grab is still – 35 years later – disrupting the lives of people affected by the mine and still requires constant rebalancing of violence and participation to manage the conflicting interests generated through changing modes of production and social relations of reproduction – when these are threatening to extractive accumulation – even well after the extraction of gold has ceased.

Conclusion

The life of the Kelian mine (1985–2004) corresponds to the critical time when the global mining industry was responding to crises of legitimacy, developing new standards of global governance and experimenting with participatory mechanisms. Indeed, the MCSC at Kelian was a testing ground for the new social approach of the World Bank and Rio Tinto. This case offers windows into three different phases of community participation in extractive accumulation – through how Rio Tinto has attempted to undermine resistance of people affected by mining: first, the absence of participatory mechanisms that prevailed until 1998, when Rio Tinto relied on violence and repression to counter opposition and charity to secure legitimacy; second, participation as a direct response to pressure from critics was beset by conflict both within and outside corporate-controlled processes; finally, in the MCSC and KPM, more proactive and systematic participatory mechanisms that we expect from contemporary multinational mining corporations.

It is clear here how risks to international reputation (the CAA campaign), disruption of local operations (LKMTL blockades), and domestic liability (Komnas HAM), combine with international governance (World Bank guidance and international standards) to determine when, why, how, and the degree to which Rio Tinto implemented participatory mechanisms. Although influenced by nascent global standards, participation, particularly negotiations over compensation, was a direct response to challenges and threats resulting from the original act of primitive accumulation. In this case, participatory mechanisms were an attempt by the company to change patterns of local conflict from confrontational to collaborative and respond to international campaigns by presenting as a good global citizen, within the mode of participation which was taking form at the global scale in organisations like the World Bank and ICMM (Chapter 3).

Rio Tinto employed two distinct scalar strategies: first to globalise the issues through the formation of new global governance standards and second to relocalise the issue by engaging LKMTL directly and cutting out their international allies. A methodological focus on only global governance mechanisms, only localised conflicts or only conflicts within state institutions would fail to appreciate how conflicts at one scale are affected by, and can become entangled with, conflicts across other scales.

In this way, through consultative participation, Rio Tinto has managed to limit compensation payments, avoid legal proceedings, and maintain territorial control over their site. This shows how multiscalar conflicts entangle to produce changes in corporate strategies and a limited exchange of interests between people affected by mining and the corporation.

LKMTL's main source of power before 1998 was its international and national alliances. Experiences of organisation and solidarity remembered from the time of small-scale mining carried over into resistance through the 1990s and provided a base from which LKMTL could build alliances following *reformasi*. Because this was a campaign focused on obtaining compensation (in lieu of justice) for past abuses, it was easily incorporated into a human rights framework. Negotiations for compensation for human rights violations, although a compromise on their preference for justice, fitted well with both LKMTL's 'common sense' understanding of themselves as victims entitled to redress and the liberal human rights ideologies of NGO allies and therefore smoothed collaboration across cultural and language barriers. Multinational mining corporations have also been forced to incorporate some elements of human rights discourse into their ideological framework. The greatest weakness of LKMTL and the communities in Tutung and Kelian Dalam is their lack of resources and land, which of course had been destroyed by the evictions. Those community members who did gain control of land or other resources were embedded within corporate or state hierarchies, and evictees developed divergent interests.

Given the lack of resources and divergent interests, the organisational ability and ideological coherence of LKMTL members was remarkably resilient. The legacy of small-scale mining was a sense of solidarity through shared fate, organisational experience and the belief they had been wronged and were entitled to justice. This legacy was not overcome by the new modes of large-scale corporate gold production, despite some attempts by KEM to provide development goods, education and employment. While KEM espoused trickle-down economics and believed in their civilising mission, LKMTL believed in human rights and justice. Conflict between KEM and the people affected by mining, then, while primarily a conflict over land and resulting from changing modes of production, was also a conflict between competing ideologies sustained by relationships of social reproduction.

Notes

1 Up to 400,000 ounces of gold a year were produced from 1991 to 2005 (Darling 1995; Kemp et al. 2013; Everingham et al. 2016; Atkinson 1998).

2 The mine was operated by PT KEM, 90% owned by Conzinc Riotinto of Australia (CRA) and 10% by Indonesian company PT Harita Jayaraya. In 1995, CRA merged with its parent company, UK-based Rio Tinto – Zinc Corporation (RTZ) in 1995 to form dual-listed Rio Tinto Group, known as Rio Tinto Limited in Australia and Rio Tinto Plc in the UK. For simplicity, I refer to all these related companies as Rio Tinto or simply Rio unless a distinction is necessary.

3 The democratisation and decentralisation reforms that followed the resignation of authoritarian President Soeharto in May 1998.

4 Located where the Kelian River flows into the Mahakam River, then called Long Kelian, the village was settled in 1818 by forest people who took up shifting cultivation alongside collecting forest products for subsistence and trade; this included small amounts of gold. Village secretary, West Kutai, interview with the author, 11 August 2017.

5 Long Iram is a town located downriver on the Mahakam that was established by Banjarese traders in the late nineteenth century as a trading post for forest products destined for the Kutai Kingdom. In 1902 the Dutch stationed a military company there, wresting control of the trade from the upper Mahakam from the Kutai Sultanate (Magenda 1991).

6 Traditional or Indigenous systems of law, culture, norms and institutions.

7 Ex-small-scale miner, interview with the author, Long Iram, 8 May 2017.

8 Like their claims to gold deposits, forest gardens had no formal tenure. Tenure may have been recognised under traditional *adat* law; however, formal certification by central government agencies was impossible, especially as the evolution of forestry laws in Indonesia progressively outlawed shifting cultivation (Peluso et al. 2008).

9 Loa Tepu is 40km upriver from the district capital, Long Iram, which is, in turn, approximately 330km upriver from the then regency capital Tenggarong.

10 Ex-small-scale miners, group interview with the author, Kelian Dalam, 10 August 2017.

11 In Indonesian, miners used the term '*tambang rakyat*' (peoples' mining) which connotes social solidarity, self-organisation and the absence of big capital.

12 The then Indonesian subsidiary of Rio Tinto was PT Rio Tinto Bethlehem Indonesia.

13 Ex-small-scale miners, group interview with the author, Kelian Dalam, 10 August 2017.

14 CoW No. B-06/Pres/1/1985 to exploit 286,233 hectares (Bachriadi 1998, 161).

15 Ex-small-scale miners, group interview with the author, Kelian Dalam, 10 August 2017; also, ex-small-scale miner, Tutung, interview with the author, 9 August 2017.

16 Approximate, at 1990 average exchange rate.

17 Ex-small-scale miners, group interview with the author, Kelian Dalam, 10 August 2017.

18 Ex-community relations manager, PT KEM, interview with the author, 8 August 2017.

19 Village head, West Kutai, interview with the author, 8 December 2018.

20 Ex-small-scale miner, interview with the author, Long Iram, 8 May 2017.

21 Ex-small-scale miners, group interview with the author, Kelian Dalam, 10 August 2017.

22 KEM also directly employed both active and retired police and military officers, blurring the distinction between KEM and state security forces (Mangkoedilaga et al. 2000, 26).

23 The Komnas HAM report is the result of a one-year investigation by a fact-finding team, consisting of representatives from Komnas HAM, LIPI (Indonesian Institute of Sciences) and TRK (Volunteer Team for Humanity), assisted by LKMTL and KEM. The investigation was the result of an agreement between LKMTL, KEM and other NGOs on 11–12 January 1999 to invite an independent team to investigate claims of human rights violations (Mangkoedilaga et al. 2000, 7). The investigation was designed as a first step in getting closer to the truth (*'lebih mendekati kebenaran'*) (Mangkoedilaga et al. 2000, 6) and provides a basis for further investigation within the formal justice system. Given that further investigation never occurred, this report is the most reliable source available.

24 Ex-small-scale miners, group interview with the author, Kelian Dalam, 10 August 2017.

25 Some of these were abandoned, some were temporary shelters (*pondok*), and some were the homes of small-scale miners that KEM wanted to leave the area.

26 Ex-small-scale miner, interview with the author, Tutung, 9 August 2017.

27 Ex-small-scale miner, interview with the author, Long Iram, 8 May 2017.

28 Mobile Brigade, paramilitary and anti-riot police.

29 Ex-small-scale miner, interview with the author, Tutung, 9 August 2017.

30 Ex-small-scale miner, interview with the author, Tutung, 9 August 2017.

31 Ex-community relations manager, PT KEM, interview with the author, 8 August 2017.

32 Kelian Dalam is a village downstream from KEM's contract area on the Kelian River.

33 Ex-small-scale miners, group interview with the author, Kelian Dalam, 10 August 2017.

34 Ex-small-scale miner, interview with the author, Long Iram, 8 May 2017.

35 Ex-small-scale miner, interview with the author, Long Iram, 8 May 2017.

36 LKMTL activist, interview with the author, 7 December 2018.

37 Ex-small-scale miner, interview with the author, Long Iram, 8 May 2017.

38 Ex-small-scale miners, group interview with the author, Kelian Dalam, 10 August 2017.

39 Ex-small-scale miners, group interview with the author, Kelian Dalam, 10 August 2017.

40 See Chapter 4.

41 While all violence has a gendered dimension and is not limited to sexual assault or harassment, in this case, sexual violence became a major problem for KEM and a major component of human rights-based campaigning after 1998.

42 For example, an AMAN (*Aliansi Masyarakat Adat Nusantara*; Archipelagic Indigenous Peoples' Alliance) leader gave the example of how environmental pollution can have gendered dimensions if women are collecting water, washing and cooking with it, but also with that kind of awareness, women can fight harder for their land. Interview with the author, Jakarta, 25 August 2016. See also Atkinson (1998, 67).

43 For a more detailed discussion of gendered legacies of mining, victimisation and agency, see Sinclair (2021).
44 The report also finds that most of the cases did not involve physical violence but misuse of authority, economic power (especially in promising employment or threatening continued employment) or manipulation.
45 Ex-community relations manager, KEM, interview with the author, 8 August 2017.
46 Notwithstanding KEM's affirmative action employment policy, especially regarding haul truck drivers (Hopes 2004a, 48).
47 Lakan Bilem became a village in 2005; before it was a hamlet within Sembuang Village.
48 Under the New Order regime, village heads were elected, but candidates were vetted by the state Golkar Party. After 1998, the restriction to Golkar-approved candidates was removed. Other village officials, including village secretary, were appointed by the village head in consultation with the district head (Aspinall and Rohman 2017).
49 Village head, West Kutai, interview with the author, 11 August 2017; village head, West Kutai, interview with the author, 12 August 2017; ex-small-scale miners, group interview with the author, Kelian Dalam, 10 August 2017.
50 Ex-community relations manager, KEM, interview with the author, 8 August 2017.
51 Village head, West Kutai, interview with the author, 12 August 2017.
52 Rio Tinto Foundation officer, interview with the author, 4 December 2018.
53 Pius Nyompe, LKMTL, interview with the author, 10 October 2016.
54 In 1997, Pak Pius had gathered 14 representatives, all men, each from a different ethnic group, by going house to house to find local organisers. Pius Nyompe, LKMTL, interview with the author, 10 October 2016.
55 PNI, led by President Soekarno, was the dominant political party before 1965. It was a left-wing party of national liberation. Thousands of members of PNI's left faction were murdered along with communists in the 1965–66 genocide. PRD was an anti-authoritarian socialist party active in the campaign to overthrow the dictator Soeharto in the 1990s. LKMTL activist, interview with the author, 7 December 2018.
56 Pius Nyompe, LKMTL, interview with the author, 10 October 2016.
57 This followed the successful action in the Victorian Supreme Court against BHP over its Ok Tedi mine in 1996 (Slater and Gordon 2018); see Chapter 4.
58 Jeff Atkinson, personal communication, 14 January 2019.
59 Putih Jaji activist, interview with the author, 10 October 2016.
60 Putih Jaji activist, interview with the author, 10 October 2016.
61 Pius Nyompe, LKMTL, interview with the author, 14 April 2017.
62 Pius Nyompe, LKMTL, interview with the author, 14 April 2017.
63 Approximate at 30 June 1999 exchange rates.
64 Ex-community relations manager, KEM, interview with the author, 8 August 2017.

65 Ex-small-scale miners, group interview with the author, Kelian Dalam, 10 August 2017.

66 Ex-community relations manager, KEM, interview with the author, 8 August 2017.

67 Pius Nyompe, LKMTL, interview with the author, 14 April 2017.

68 Pius Nyompe, LKMTL, interview with the author, 14 April 2017.

69 Community relations manager, KEM, interview with the author, 8 August 2017.

70 Community Aid Abroad. 2002. 'Rio Tinto's Kelian Gold Mine, Indonesia'. Unpublished timeline.

71 Anthropologist and consultant to KEM, interview with the author, 7 August 2017.

72 After Kutai Regency was split into three regencies in 1999, PT KEM was the single largest taxpayer in West Kutai (Casson 2001, 11), granting it significant structural power.

73 Pius Nyompe, LKMTL, interview with the author, 14 April 2017.

74 Pius Nyompe, LKMTL, interview with the author, 14 April 2017.

75 Manager of community relations, KEM, interview with the author, 17 May 2017.

76 Manager of community relations, KEM, interview with the author, 17 May 2017; also Mine Closure Steering Committee (2003).

77 Pius Nyompe, LKMTL, interview with the author, 10 October 2016.

78 Manager of community relations, KEM and HLKL, interview with the author, 17 May 2017.

79 Ex-community relations manager, KEM, and HLKHL site manager, interview with the author, 8 August 2017.

80 Pius Nyompe, LKMTL, interview with the author, 10 October 2016.

81 Manager of community relations, KEM, interview with the author, 17 May 2017.

82 Village head, West Kutai, interview with the author, 11 August 2017.

83 Village head, Lakan Bilem, interview with the author, 12 August 2017.

84 Ex-small-scale gold miner, interview with the author, 9 August 2017.

85 Manager of community relations, KEM, interview with the author, 17 May 2017.

86 Ex-community relations manager, KEM, and HLKHL site manager, interview with the author, 8 August 2017.

5

Participation, gold and governance
in Gosowong

The Gosowong gold mine in North Halmahera (Fig. 5.1) was the most significant Indonesian mine managed by an Australian corporation.[1] Until March 2020, Newcrest Mining Limited owned 75% of the operating company PT Nusa Halmahera Minerals (NHM), while 25% was owned by the Indonesian state's consolidated mining company PT Aneka Tambang (Newcrest 2016).[2] Gold production began in 1999, around the time that international governance mechanisms for the social and environmental dimensions of mining were first being developed. The participatory mechanisms implemented by NHM have evolved in response to international standards *and* conflict with people affected by mining.

Newcrest was a member of or signatory to many of the international organisations and standards governing the environmental and social dimensions of mining. These include the Minerals Council of Australia's (MCA) 'Enduring Value Framework'; the International Council on Mining and Metals' (ICMM) 'Ten Principles of Sustainable Development';[3] the 'Voluntary Principles on Security and Human Rights'; 'The Extractive Industries Transparency Initiative (EITI)'; and the 'International Cyanide Management Code' (Newcrest 2015, 12); and in November 2017 Newcrest was admitted as the 25th member of the ICMM (Eames 2017). These standards committed Newcrest to implementing participatory consultative mechanisms with affected people, forming the foundation for Newcrest's more detailed internal sustainability and community relations policies (Newcrest 2017). Of the three cases in my research, it most strongly embodies international standards, presenting a typical case of contemporary participatory community relations implemented by a multinational miner.

In previous chapters, I have argued that participatory mechanisms are enacted by mining companies for two purposes: first, to contain multiscalar conflict; second, to facilitate changes in the social relations of production and reproduction in the area surrounding the mine. The puzzling aspect in this case is the prevalence of violent conflict and public demonstrations which surrounded the mine from 1999 until around 2005, after which reports of violence, grievances and conflict all but ceased. Contestation persisted, but it was less visible. Conflict shifted from public and political to private negotiation, and fewer national NGOs advocated about the case. Although the forms of participation were rather typical, the case could be seen as a rare successful *implementation* of participation to reduce violent and threatening manifestations of conflict, and therefore deserves detailed investigation.

This chapter examines the roots of contestation, generated by extractive accumulation disrupting historically constituted social, political and economic relations. Analysis of how these contestations have been reshaped through participation over 20 years of mining is divided into six sections. The first gives some historical background on the political economy of North Halmahera up until the establishment of the mine, arguing that through centuries of colonialism and capitalist development, local political economic relations have developed in a far more hierarchical pattern compared to the other two case studies in this book. Second, mere months after gold was first produced, violent conflict broke out between Kao people (Indigenous, majority Christian) and Makian (transmigrants, Muslim). In fact, the new mine was an indirect trigger for this conflict, which engulfed North Maluku province in 1999 and 2000. Likewise, the community development programs of NHM helped to restore peace in the post-conflict period. The third section details how in the post-conflict period, contestation around the mine turned from one supposedly centred on religion and ethnicity to environmental and cultural concerns. A broad multi-ethnic alliance formed to confront NHM about various grievances. Activism turned national in 2003 when NGO WALHI (*Wahana Lingkungan Hidup Indonesia*; Friends of the Earth Indonesia) North Maluku, together with national allies, took action in the constitutional court attempting to block NHM from opening a new underground mine – Toguraci – within a protected forest (d'Hondt 2010). Local demonstrations against the expansion turned violent and one protester was killed by police.

The fourth section turns to look at NHM's response to these conflicts. The company increased the size of community development contributions almost tenfold from 2004 to 2007, when NHM began contributing 1% of revenues to its community development and empowerment program, climbing to US$4 million in 2010 (d'Hondt et al. 2010, 10; Newcrest 2010). In addition to the village support program, the 1% fund also financed larger economic development projects in partnership with business, and district and regency governments which worked to facilitate changes in relations of production in North Halmahera. In 2007, the United Nations Development Programme established the Legal Empowerment and Assistance for the Disadvantaged (UNDP-LEAD) program in North Maluku (UNDP 2008). Together, these participatory

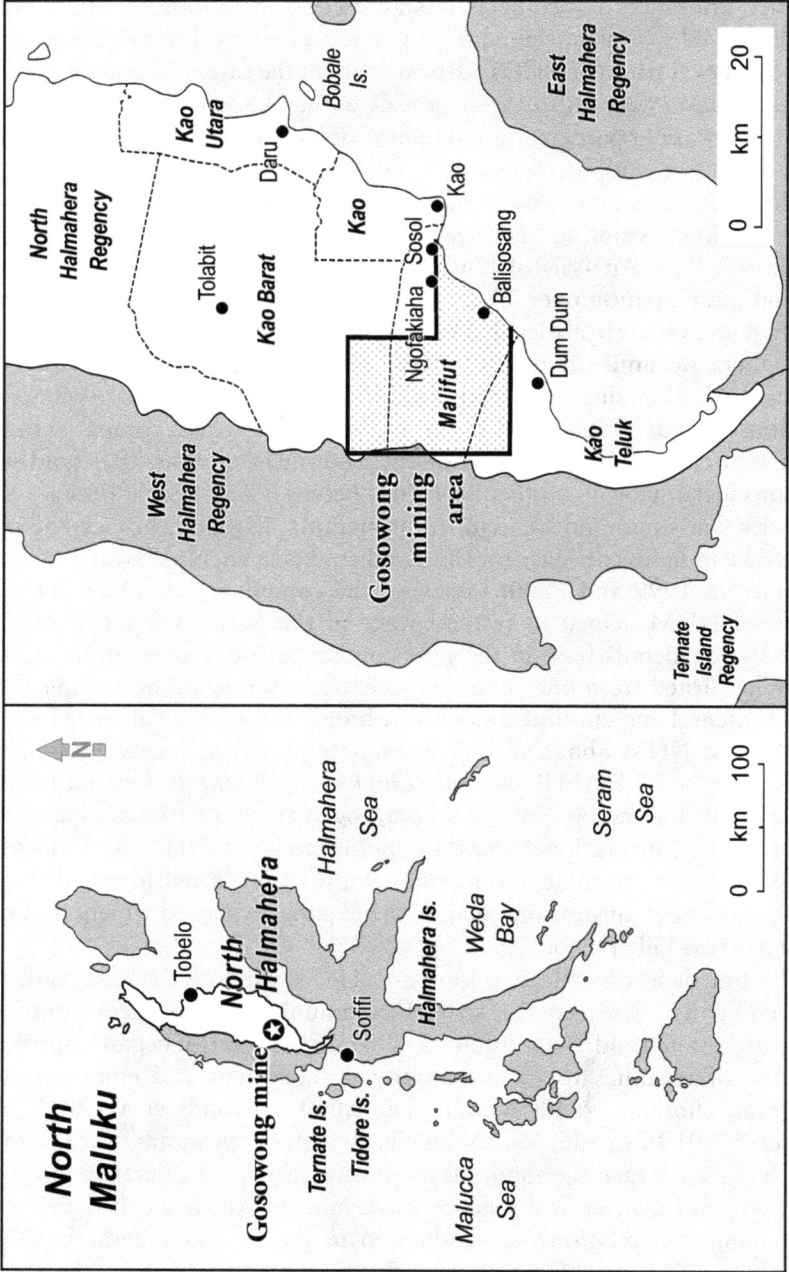

Figure 5.1 North Halmahera showing the five affected districts.

mechanisms helped depoliticise conflict. Villagers affected by mining still organised protests, but these now focused on process and forms of participation, rather than direct opposition and the effects of mining. The fifth section examines the rise of *adat* (Indigenous custom, law or tradition) as an ideological and organising framework. A new *bupati* (regent) ran a successful campaign to extract a greater share of revenue from NHM between 2005 and 2010, drawing on Indigenous identity and alliances through national NGO AMAN (*Aliansi Masyarakat Adat Nusantara*; Alliance of Indigenous Communities of the Archipelago). AMAN activist Ibu Afrida's story demonstrates how *adat*, or indigeneity, continues to be a robust ideological framework and incorporated gender equity as a key organising tool. The sixth section finishes the chapter by juxtaposing a participatory mechanism that NHM did not implement – participatory environmental monitoring – to highlight the power of NHM to define the agenda of who can participate on what issues, when.

Through the evolution of conflict, various people affected by mining, along with opportunists not affected by mining, have formed various alliances to place demands on and extract resources from NHM. These alliances are more cross-class than in my other two cases. They are also more fluid, as they are based on multiple interests which may only coincide for short periods. The outcome of this is that people living closest to the mine, the most affected by pollution and the loss of customary forests, have relied on shifting alliances with more powerful actors. Together, these events reveal a model example of how a mining company has been able to both manage conflict and facilitate changes in economic relations through participation. Through economic development programs, NHM has positioned itself within existing and new relations of production aligned with the interests of provincial and regency elites. Through the 1% fund, the range of grievances expressed has changed from environmental pollution and rights violations to transparency.

Political economies: cloves to gold

The history of North Halmahera, from at least the fifteenth century, has been characterised by waves of outsiders imposing political power and economic interests on the Indigenous people. Sultans, colonialists and corporations were attracted by North Halmahera's natural resources: cloves, nutmeg, exotic birds, copra, fish, timber, and gold. To extract these resources, the exploiters established forms of political rule: sultanates, colonial administrations, and the republic. These forms of rule developed corresponding relations of production and reproduction. Patron–client relations, trading networks, settlements, missionaries, plantations, wage labour, transmigration and mining enclaves have all enabled the extraction of natural resources from North Halmahera and dramatically changed the lives of its Indigenous peoples (Duncan 2003; Topatimasang 2016).

Roem Topatismasang (2016, 48–61) and his team of anthropologists argue that there have been three significant waves of penetration affecting the economy and political structures of Indigenous people[4] in North Halmahera. First was 'co-optation' by the Ternate sultanate[5] and Dutch East India Company (VOC), driven by attempts to monopolise the spice trade, which peaked in the eighteenth century (Brown 2003, 33). The second was the entrance of Protestant missionaries, who helped 'settle' semi-nomadic Indigenous people through conversion and on coconut plantations and cattle farms. The third wave was the resettlement programs of the Republic of Indonesia in the 1960s, which aimed to 'civilise and advance' people still living semi-nomadically in forested areas. This resettlement coincided with the opening of forests and natural resources for exploitation. Little or no compensation was given to resettled forest people following the enclosure of their communal forests (Duncan 2013, 41).

A new monopoly in clove trading was established in 1989 by the Clove Market Control Board (*Badan Pengendalian Pemasaran Cengkeh*; BPPC) run by Tommy Soeharto (Topatimasang 2016, 24–25). Transmigration programs resettled mostly Javanese peasants in the interior of North Halmahera, while other land was 'freed' for timber concessions and plantation agriculture, creating resentment from those disadvantaged (Duncan 2013, 41). Not far behind logging and plantations was a wave of systematic exploration for minerals beginning in the mid-1980s. These waves of penetration always met resistance, in some places more than others, resulting in an uneven geography of development.

The result of this was the development of a two-speed economy. On one side there are tightly controlled hierarchical patron–client systems of production, finance and distribution for national and international markets. Local people bear the brunt of disadvantage in the form of environmental deterioration and loss of traditional land (Duncan 2013, 42). Some cash from these activities (unevenly) trickles down to local managerial, working and peasant classes which finances the import of rice, consumer goods and construction material. On the other side, just as persistent, the subsistence economy provides basic needs of local people and is still embedded in complex relationships of reciprocity and *adat*.[6] Therefore, village elites and those who aspire to 'middle-class' lifestyles became dependent on and deeply integrated into relations of production controlled and managed by corporations and governments in Tobelo, Ternate, Amsterdam, Jakarta, Melbourne and elsewhere. Ideologically, this pattern of development left a patchwork – a 'syncretic historical residue' (Rupert 2006, 93) of *adat*, feudalism, Protestant and Islamic religious beliefs, nationalism and modernisation. The differentiated common sense of the group structures the way that people affected by Newcrest's gold mine have made claims to community development, employment and damages.

The most recent wave of changing capital formations and systems of rule began when Newcrest and NHM commenced operations in 1997, and with 350 employees, became the largest employer in North Halmahera (Wilson 2008, 36, 56). The land acquired by NHM was a forested area and although some Indigenous people had still been foraging in the forest until it was enclosed by NHM,[7] it contained no agricultural[8] or residential areas. Therefore, unlike the other two case studies in this book, this act of primitive accumulation had negligible impact on pre-existing local modes of production. The impacts on relations of production and reproduction would come later, when pollution disrupted river-based livelihoods. The major impact of primitive accumulation was environmental and cultural. This is reflected in the manifest forms of conflict, which were mostly about confronting NHM over pollution, disrespect of traditional and sacred sites, and receiving a fair share of the benefits of resource extraction. Only months after production began, mass violence erupted in the area immediately surrounding the mine and spread across North Maluku to Tobelo, Ternate and Tidore.

Elite-directed mass violence

In 1999 and 2000, North Maluku was engulfed in mass violence. This is popularly thought to have been an ethnoreligious conflict that began between transmigrant Makian Muslims and Indigenous, majority-Christian Kao that turned into generalised violence between Muslims and Christians in Kao, Tobelo, Ternate and across North Maluku. However, most rigorous scholarship points to intra-elite conflict over state revenue, political office and natural resources during the decentralisation of Indonesian politics as the immediate cause of conflict (Wilson 2008; Smith 2009; d'Hondt et al. 2010; Barron et al. 2012; cf. Duncan 2013). Likewise, everyone I interviewed in North Halmahera emphasised that while religion was a major fault line, the conflict was about land, decentralisation, and elite contestation.[9]

Back in 1975, the Maluku provincial government had forcibly relocated the entire population of Makian Island to the southern part of what was then Kecematan (district) Kao because of the risk to Makian Island of volcanic eruptions. The Makian and Kao ethnic communities (and other transmigrant communities) lived as neighbours without any serious incidents but with very low levels of integration, little clarity about the status of land ownership, and growing tension along religious, ethnic and economic lines

(Wilson 2008; Smith 2009; Usman 2016). That lack of clarity about land ownership proved to be a problem during the decentralisation process.

North Maluku province split from Maluku in October 1999. However, it was the creation of new Kecematan Malifut in the southern half of the old Kecematan Kao[10] that sparked raids and reprisals between villages. Depending on how the borders were drawn, one of these districts would include the Gosowong mine within its administrative boundaries (see Fig. 5.1). Local political figures assumed the local government would have more opportunities to extract rent, including by insisting on local employment. Political elites motivated by perceived windfall benefits of decentralisation, including, but not limited to, potential revenues from mining, used the underlying tensions between Kao and Makian people to their advantage. Fear was used to mobilise ordinary people in service of elite positioning. Throughout 1999 several people died, and 10,000 people fled their homes.

The violence quickly spread west to Ternate and north through Tobelo, as politicians there fanned the flames of Christian and Muslim rivalry as part of campaigns to be elected as North Maluku's first governor. It is estimated that during 1999 and 2000, around 3,500 people lost their lives (d'Hondt et al. 2010). The violent conflict ended when local military units were reinforced by troops sent from Jakarta in July 2000 (Wilson 2008).

Barron et al. (2012) argue that the peace established in North Maluku was more durable than that in Central Maluku (Ambon) because elites did not find violence profitable and other revenue streams became available that removed incentives for continued 'ethnic conflict'. While they do not mention the mine in their book, one crucial revenue stream was community development funding and employment by NHM. Indeed, until mine closure, NHM has and will provide development funding to 83 villages across five districts – a much broader area than is directly affected by mining – in order to avoid further conflict based on perceived ethnic favouritism.[11] Thus NHM indirectly and unintentionally played a role in both triggering conflict and restoring peace.

Alliances and grievances

Following the end of mass violence in North Maluku, new grievances from people affected by the mine surfaced. Complaints such as pollution levels, disrespect of *adat*, exploitation of resources, and lack of compensation combined with perceived opportunities for development funding, which saw local farmers, fishers, villagers, ex-employees, small-scale miners, officials from all levels of government, and NGO activists join forces in protest.

Importantly, this alliance was multi-ethnic and cross-religious (d'Hondt et al. 2010, 19–25). Not surprisingly, over time, different sections of this fluid alliance have broken off as they have benefited from their demands being met.

Talking about their involvement with the NHM case from 2003, an AMAN activist told me that

> aside from having problems with the community, land that is used by NHM has not been paid for, chemicals spill into the river, polluting the river that is used by local people for their daily needs. In the wet season, the rivers overflow into gardens; you can see the plants dying, tomatoes and chillies dying from those chemicals, cyanide and mercury[12] ... In 2011 a waste disposal pipe burst ... Before NHM came, they could eat, drink and earn income from fishing.[13]

Motivated by these grievances, protesters occupied the mine site, blocked roads and held demonstrations. Of course, these grievances are directly related to the mine – either to resentment over the initial land grab or the environmental impacts of mining and processing gold with cyanide. People affected by mining sought redress for the initial and ongoing impacts of primitive accumulation. Conflict and confrontation developed in several different directions, influenced by organisational and ideological alliances, especially the environmentalism of WALHI and pan-*adat* of AMAN.

Mining in protected forests

Protest and opposition to Newcrest's mining peaked when they announced plans to establish a new underground mine – Toguraci – a few kilometres away from the existing open pit but within the boundaries of a protected forest. Locals objected because Toguraci is a customary sacred place and a protected forest. Semi-nomadic 'Forest Tobelo' and villagers living close to the forest had still been foraging and hunting there until it was enclosed by NHM.[14] Demonstrations escalated until 'operations were suspended from October to December 2003 while the mine was occupied by illegal miners' (Newcrest 2012, 25). When Newcrest says 'illegal miners', they are actually referring to heterogeneous groups of people, consisting of small-scale miners, other locals, village officials and NGO supporters. The characterisation was used to delegitimise opposition and justify payments to Indonesian police, including *Brimob*,[15] to provide security (d'Hondt 2010; Newcrest 2012; 2015).

In January 2004, one group of protesters, trying to access a traditional forest area near Toguraci, was caught and beaten by *Brimob* officers with rifle butts and sticks, with one protester executed on the spot. Others allege they were interrogated in Newcrest offices and transported by a Newcrest helicopter to jail (Hamby 2016). Newcrest (2012, 144) denies that, but does not deny that it paid *Brimob* to provide security.

Forestry Law No. 41/1999 had made mining illegal in protected forests. This law was an obstacle to NHM's development of Toguraci. An explosive investigation by Chris Hamby provided evidence that executives from Newcrest mining threatened to take the Indonesian government to arbitration under investor–state dispute settlement provisions in trade agreements:

> [A former NHM executive] had delivered the company's 'message to the government' during a meeting with mining ministry officials, he recalled. 'If we cannot mine in this area,' he remembered telling them, 'we will wash our hands [of] Indonesia and go to international arbitration.' The message was clear: Indonesia would be sued, perhaps for hundreds of millions of dollars.
>
> (Syahrir AB, quoted in Hamby 2016)

Together with similar threats from other multinational mining companies, Hamby argues, this resulted in exemptions to the ban on mining in protected forests. In March 2004, President Megawati issued a decree allowing 13 exemptions to the Forestry Law (including Toguraci) and the national parliament passed Law No. 19/2004 amending the 1999 Forestry Law to allow companies to continue mining in protected forests if contracts of work were signed before 1999, thus limiting potential liability under investor–state dispute settlement clauses (Down to Earth 2004; 2005; d'Hondt 2010).

Local activists lead by WALHI North Maluku joined forces with groups from other locations facing similar proposals to form the National Coalition Against Mining in Protected Areas. The coalition launched action in the Constitutional Court to challenge the presidential declaration and Law No. 19/2004. The court eventually found that six of the mines should not have been given exemptions and upheld the other seven, including Toguraci. D'Hondt (2010) further reports that NGOs decided against appealing the decision as further legal action would have been too costly and uncertain.

With further legal avenues ruled out and protesters being beaten and killed by *Brimob*, options for directly confronting Newcrest were running out. There was a dramatic decrease in protest activity and especially in media and NGO reporting. The demoralisation of opposition is an obvious explanation for this, with one activist stating: 'Since [the protester was killed] there hasn't been any struggle, only NGOs that struggle in the name of the people, but it is limited.'[16] What is less obvious is how conflict changed as new alliances formed around different sets of interests, particularly community development and *adat*. People affected by mining were ready to turn to participation and engagement just as NHM was prepared to expand its participatory programs.

NHM's participatory mechanisms

Newcrest and NHM had to respond to mounting tensions surrounding the mine. The risk of international media attention on human rights abuses and environmental pollution posed a risk to its reputation, even if it avoided legal sanction. The demonstrations themselves posed a clear risk for the profitability of its operations. To be sure, Newcrest had a choice in how to respond. Continuing to rely on *Brimob*'s violence and existing community development programs was not a good option. Instead, NHM developed new participatory mechanisms to undermine opposition and set the agenda, defining legitimate actors and issues.

The option that Newcrest and NHM chose was to dramatically increase community development funding, with a tenfold increase from 2004 to 2007 through a new 1% fund. This fund took 1% of profit before tax, depreciation and amelioration and distributed it through village teams for community development programs. By 2011, Newcrest was contributing AU$22.5 million through its community development and empowerment (CDE) programs (Newcrest 2011). The 1% fund was divided into a village support program and a sustainable economic development program. The village support program was further divided into educational support, including scholarships; support for health programs; and infrastructure and social activities. Aside from the 1% fund, NHM also agreed to a new regional development contribution to provincial and regency governments and reached agreements with other community groups.

Participatory village support program

From 1997 until 2006, CSR funding was administered directly by NHM, villagers could make proposals, and NHM's CSR staff would allocate funding on a case-by-case basis. The 1% fund's first full year was 2007. Not only did the amount of funding increase, but the 1% fund provided more certainty and an ability to plan longer-term community development projects. To administer and allocate the funding, a three-person team was established in each village.[17] According to NHM's village team guidelines, the village teams should be appointed by village consultative assemblies (*musyawarah desa*) and NHM recommends that the village team should be made up of people outside the village government structure; however, NHM does not attempt to enforce these guidelines.[18] In all of the six villages across four districts where I met members of the village team, the village head (*kepala desa*) was the chairperson of the village team and other members were officials serving the village government, like the village consultative body (*Badan Permusyawaratan Desa*; BPD).[19] The village teams were responsible for creating proposals in consultation with residents, village officials, *adat* and religious figures, and district officials[20] before presenting them to NHM's CDE manager for approval. Village teams have mostly used the funding to supplement existing village government expenditure. The money has been used to build roads, fences, churches, mosques and teacher accommodation; purchase seed, equipment for farming, and livestock; pay building and land tax; and subsidise rice.[21]

Under Indonesia's Village Law No. 6/2014, village heads are elected by residents every six years while other village officials are appointed by the *kepala desa* in consultation with the *cemat* (Salim et al. 2017, 10; Meckelburg 2021). The law remains vague on how members of the BPD are appointed, and variation exists across villages: in some they are elected, in others they are appointed by the *kepala desa* and in others appointed by the BPD. The *musyawarah desa* is an annual citizens' assembly where villagers are consulted on village administration and development priorities. Some villages have developed robust participatory governance practices, while in others deliberation and consultation exist only on paper (Syukri 2024). In practice, this means that political power in the village is centred around the *kepala desa* who retains final decision-making authority over the village government's budget. Indeed, Aspinal and Rohman (2017) show that elections for *kepala desa* are characterised by money politics, and victors gain access to patronage networks and state resources, including the *dana desa* (village fund).[22] Village governance, then, mixes democratic and consultative ideologies of representation to legitimise the allocation of development funding.

This mode of participation in village governance fits neatly with NHM's consultative ideologies of representation and provides a ready-made institutional and ideological structure through which NHM's village support program is distributed. By default, the program is managed by existing powerholders within the village government and reinforces the status quo of political relationships and patronage within villages. In villages with good democratic practices and relatively equal distribution of funding, the 1% fund is also likely to be distributed fairly. Where villages suffer from higher levels of corruption, gendered, religious or ethnic inequality, and projects favour elite interests, this money will also reinforce these patterns. For example, during a visit to one village, two coconut farmers, who were not government officials, said that they made suggestions at the *musyawarah desa* to assist with farming but decisions about what to propose to NHM were made by the village team. The farmers were hesitant to offer opinions beyond simply describing the process – they seemed to accept the situation as default, or part of the received common sense understanding of village politics.[23]

The implementation of the 1% fund changed how conflict was expressed, which actors were involved, and the issues they raised. The privileging of village officials within the fund makes them less likely to support NGOs who advocate for their villagers which could potentially jeopardise funding and therefore patronage resources. Thus, a vital link between people affected by mining and potential allies was removed. NHM had effectively taken control of the agenda. Indeed, d'Hondt's (2010) research reports that this new structure of community development has directed grievances away from NHM and towards villagers who influence the distribution of funding. That is, the structure of conflict changed from disparate groups of people collectively voicing protests against NHM into intercommunity disputes between the administrators and beneficiaries of CDE funding and those who miss out.

All the participants I interviewed who were involved in administering the 1% fund reported two major grievances: the transparency and the efficiency of the funding process. By a lack of transparency, village officials mean that the village teams merely receive a sum of money but have no way to check if it is actually 1% of revenue from mining. By efficiency, respondents meant that the approval process can be too slow to respond to evolving development needs, or proposals are not assessed holistically.[24] One example given to me was that, when a village team proposed to establish an aquafarm, NHM agreed. However the equipment sourced by NHM was incomplete and not accompanied by training, so the project did not go ahead and the whole amount was wasted.[25] That is, grievances are technical and process orientated. There are other grievances, such as low numbers of locals employed in the mine, continued concern about pollution, and resentment that the 1% fund is framed as community development rather than compensation for lost resources and violations of *adat*. However, these grievances have moved into the background and are used more as justifications for demanding greater community contributions rather than issues to advocate about.

Demonstrations continued after 2007, although were less frequent, and organised at the local level by villagers and district or village governments, as opposed to NGOs. These demonstrations also changed their objectives, focusing on the efficiency and transparency of the 1% fund.[26] Tensions over the administration of the 1% fund culminated in April 2015 when demonstrators blocked the road and all deliveries from the port every day between 6 am and 6 pm for a month.[27] These demonstrations pressured NHM into making a series of changes to the way the 1% fund is delivered.

By 2015, NHM management had also recognised problems with the transparency and accountability of the program. From their point of view, because NHM's funding was filtered through subdistrict government and village teams, they were not receiving acknowledgement for their contribution and their reputation was suffering. Reporting on projects funded through the 1% fund was minimal, and management could not evaluate the effectiveness of the various projects. The lack of accountability also presented a risk under Newcrest's new anti-bribery and corruption policy.[28] Thus both sides recognised transparency, accountability and efficiency as problems, yet had different ideas about what these terms meant and how to solve them.

In 2015 NHM replaced their CSR team and hired consultants to redesign how the 1% was to be delivered and evaluated.[29] Following this, the 1% was given as a dedicated budget to the village teams, case-by-case proposals no longer needed to be presented to NHM for assessment, and the district governments no longer distributed funds to villages or received a cut. Instead, village teams proposed yearly budgets for approval by NHM and produced annual accountability reports.[30]

Following those changes, there is now more scope for village teams to plan long-term projects. It has also increased the significance of annual village consultative assemblies (*musyawarah desa*) in determining the strategies for CDE funding. This is the same village assembly that discusses the village fund (*dana desa*) from the central government. The teams and village governments attempt to align the 1% fund and *dana desa* as much as possible. Their view is that this supports existing projects and consolidates community development efforts.[31] The new system addressed NHM's concerns about transparency and accountability and addressed some village concerns about efficiency, but did not address village concerns about transparency. NHM, in implementing its participatory community development funding, piggybacked on the existing mode of participation in village governance, producing a de facto hybrid state-corporate site of participation. This simplified NHM's task by fitting into existing political relationships but also cemented pre-existing hierarchies within villages.

In December 2016, the Ministry of Energy and Mineral Resources issued Regulation (*permen*) No. 41/2016 on Community Development and Empowerment for Mineral and Coal Mining Business Activities. This regulation provides for the implementation of provisions in Law No. 40/2007 on Limited Liability Corporations and Law No. 4/2009 on Mineral and Coal Mining requiring all corporations involved in the resources sector to develop and implement community development programs with a dedicated budget (see Chapter 3). The new regulation specified which communities count as 'local' and what kinds of development could be classified as sustainable community development. It also specified that community development programs must be designed in consultation with affected community representatives and the provincial government. For NHM, this meant that they began to divert a portion of the 1% fund from village teams into new sustainable development programs which were designed in consultation with the provincial government officials not villages.[32] It also meant that village teams had to only use their community development funding for sustainable development programs. This excluded the use of the 1% fund from paying tax, subsidising rice and many cultural and religious activities. These changes triggered demonstrations against NHM in December 2017.[33] However, Regulation No. 41/2016 was withdrawn by Ministry of Energy and Mineral Resources Regulation No. 25/2018 on Mineral and Coal Mining Business, which simply specifies that community development activities must proceed in accordance with work plans approved by the provincial government.

While it is evident that the dramatic decrease in reports of conflict coincided with a tenfold increase in community development funding from NHM, the question becomes *how* this community development funding reshaped and managed conflict. My fieldwork revealed that conflicts persisted, but they have changed from conflicts over the effects of mining to conflicts over the distribution of benefits. Conflicts over funding are contained within the established politics of village governance. I have also shown how the participatory village support program – part of NHM's 1% fund – has controlled the definition of legitimate grievances, who can advocate for them and on what terms they will be settled. The 1% was the dominant mechanism bringing about a depoliticisation of conflict. However, there were also other significant mechanisms from the UNDP, regency government and NHM's sustainable economic development program.

Sustainable economic development and social relations

NHM also coordinated sustainable economic development projects with the 1% fund, but separate from the village support program, through three streams: education, health, and economic development. The education and health streams worked with the provincial government departments to build and refurbish schools, community health centres and a hospital in Kao. The economic development stream included two cassava factories, a tapioca flour factory and corn, cassava and sago plantations managed in partnership with the agricultural department of North Halmahera, *kecematan* governments, local business partners and NGOs (PT Nusa Halmahera Minerals 2015). It was focused on creating long-term ventures that could survive after the mine eventually closes and was further divided into training programs and increased support for factories and plantations.[34] While the village support program was successful in containing conflict within village structures, the economic development stream was directed at changing local modes of production under the frame of 'sustainable development.'

In addition to the plantations established under the program, NHM has a local purchasing scheme to buy produce for processing in the factories and for use at the mine.[35] In two villages we visited in Kao Barat, both had experience with selling NHM agricultural produce. The first is a Kao village where a majority are coconut farmers. In attempts to establish wider cassava gardens, NHM provided fertiliser and bought the cassava. However, they only paid Rp200 per kilo. The farmers interviewed found this a laughable proposition, as they could get higher prices for cassava selling it to traders, while coconut production is more profitable again. They did not continue in the program.[36] The second village was a transmigrant village of Javanese people who opened rice fields. While NHM also has a program for buying rice and although the price they offered was fair, their terms were prohibitive. NHM wanted to sign a contract to take delivery of two tons of rice each and every fortnight. The farmers were scared to commit because production is not stable year-round and NHM was not flexible. They were also reluctant to continue selling rice to NHM because payments for deliveries took between one and two months to process.[37] NHM's purchasing program did not fit with relations of production centring on smallholder agriculture; they required more hierarchically organised and centrally managed relations of production.

Through these sustainable economic development programs, NHM created (or revived) systems of production based on medium to large-scale production, wage labour, and capitalist managerialism. They invested in plantations and factories while treating smallholders with contempt. The managers of the plantations and factories are regency government departments, local businesses and NGOs whom NHM wants to keep close. The workers are then also kept dependent on local elites and NHM's patronage. These hierarchical, capitalist relations of production are much more favourable to mining than, for example, smallholder or collective farming, as they provide more predictable local produce and a more compliant population.

What is immediately striking about this sustainable economic development is the similarity with the Dutch East India Company and the New Order's economic policy for Halmahera. Both encouraged cash-cropping plantations owned and managed by local elites while labourers were at the bottom of a strict hierarchy from Jakarta (or Amsterdam) at the top, through sultanates and provincial governments, plantation managers and village governments. Thus, NHM's program utilises and built upon established economic hierarchies and capitalist ideologies of modernisation, reinforcing existing systems of economic power and patronage. These changes helped break up cross-class resistance and left people affected by mining more likely to engage with the corporation.

UNDP-LEAD

The United Nations Development Programme's Legal Empowerment and Assistance for the Disadvantaged project (UNDP-LEAD) was a human rights-based approach to legal empowerment and access to formal and informal justice. It operated from 2007 to 2009 in three provinces, with North Halmahera as the pilot. A primary focus of the program is support- ing informal legal processes such as mediation and arbitration. The project operated through making grants to NGOs and university-based institutions which would, in turn, provide education, advocacy and otherwise assist dis- advantaged people to improve their access to justice. One of the priority areas was 'justice, land and natural resources' (Government of Indonesia and The United Nations Development Programme 2007).

The liberal institutionalist framework that informs such interventions privileges civil society and NGO actors as supporters of a broader 'good- governance' reform agenda. It conceptualises the conflict between citizens or 'claim-holders' and other parties as a failure of proper institutional func- tion, the solution to which is disadvantaged people asking for justice *via institutions* that can act as neutral interventions into conflict. Indeed, the project document explicitly states the assumption that 'governance and democracy are hollow institutional shells unless the populace has the know- ledge of relevant rights and the capacity to realise them' (Government of Indonesia and the United Nations Development Programme 2007, 20). This naively obscures the role of elite powerholders who create hollow institu- tions because it suits their interests.

This ideological understanding and interventions based on it are danger- ous and disempowering for the people identified as intended beneficiar- ies. It assumes that disadvantaged people are to blame for their situation because of their own ignorance, while ignoring the exploitation of corpora- tions. A second dangerous assumption is that existing legal institutions are neutral arbiters that will provide a fair hearing to poor people once they become aware of their formal rights. Just as institutionalist theory dismisses conflicts outside formal institutions, institutionalist interventions delegiti- mise it. Through the system of grants to NGOs, the UNDP-LEAD program provided incentives to NGOs – and the communities that they support – to engage in legalistic approaches to justice instead of more confrontational methods.

To illustrate my critique, we can consider the example of WALHI. After 2007, UNDP-LEAD became the sole funder of WALHI North Maluku, which was then the leading NGO working on issues surrounding Gosowong. D'Hondt et al. (2010, 28–29) argue that UNDP-LEAD was central in convincing WALHI to change tactics from holding demonstrations and blocking and occupying mine sites to seeking legal redress through formal and informal legal avenues. A local activist confirmed this: '[WALHI and AMAN] changed their strategy, working with the legal system, Komnas HAM, go to Jakarta, not direct action.'[38]

WALHI activists were not blind to the risks of depoliticisation and they did not accept the ideological foundation of the LEAD program. We must remember that WALHI and the community surrounding the mine were, by 2007, demoralised by the loss of the Constitutional Court challenge to mining in protected forests and the killing of one protester. One activist told me some NGOs participated in the UNDP-LEAD program because they thought it could be an opportunity to uncover new information (such as water quality and effects of pollution) and to help their grievances reach an international audience. However, instead of being a vehicle for activists to jump scales, like CAA (Community Aid Abroad, now Oxfam Australia) was in the Kelian case, conduct research, or otherwise empower people affected by mining, the UNDP helped undermine resistance to mining through individualised participation in grievance processes.[39]

Cross-class alliances and *adat*

North Halmahera became a new regency (*kabupaten*) in May 2003. Still recovering from the destructive conflict of a few years earlier, the regency held its first elections in 2006. Ir. Hein Namotemo[40] was elected *bupati* (regent) of North Halmahera on a platform including a more significant role for *adat* and Indigenous-friendly development. One of his promises was to open negotiations with NHM about their contribution to regional development.

Part of the problem was the way provincial government elites took advantage of power over newly established and then barely functional *kabupaten* governments to appropriate their resources. Law No. 33/2004 on Revenue Sharing from Natural Resources provides for a complicated distribution of land rent and royalties between national, provincial and regency governments.[41] However, Smith's (2009, 174) research shows that, despite such a precise proscription, from its establishment in 2004 until at least 2008, there were intergovernmental conflicts over transparency and distribution of the monies:

The new North Halmahera district government (where the mine was located) regularly issued complaints to the NHM mining company over the reduced revenue share they actually received when compared with what they were promised in the legislation – it was routinely cut by the provincial government. The district government demanded the goldmine send their revenue share directly, but the company was unable to do this as it contravened legal agreements with the central government.

Namotemo and his administration further argued that NHM, as a hugely profitable foreign-owned gold miner, should make additional contributions to regional development. After one term as *bupati*, little progress had been made; Namotemo had not managed to convince NHM to make additional payments to the North Halmahera government.

The recognition of Indigenous peoples and protections for *adat* in Indonesian law is ambiguous, fragmented and fraught by overlapping conflicts and interests (Li 2014; Wardana 2018; van der Muur et al. 2019). It is beyond the scope of this book to offer a full discussion of these issues. For now, it is enough to say that instead of appealing to national or international legal protections, *adat* supporters organised a political campaign.

This then became an election issue and the *bupati*'s team began recruiting more of the people living around the mine to their campaign. Simultaneous to his term as *bupati*, Namotemo was the chairperson of AMAN's national representative body, and in 2009 facilitated ten communities to form an AMAN branch in North Maluku.[42] Six years after first becoming *bupati* – supported by local groups motivated by interest and identity as Indigenous people, provincial-level politicians, and national allies through AMAN – he managed to secure 1.5% of operating profit for the regency government and 1.1% for the provincial government. This became a new contribution to regional development used by these two levels of government to supplement their development budgets.

Securing this funding was a tremendous success for the *bupati*'s campaigning in North Halmahera based on broad cross-class support for *adat* and development. However, after securing this funding, although continuing to promote the role of *adat* as a unifying ideology in North Halmahera, regency-level support for the more specific concerns of people directly affected by the mine about pollution and respect for sacred sites evaporated.

Nanga Wolla and Ibu Afrida

Namotemo's campaign saw a revival of *adat* and indigeneity as an ideology and legitimising force in conflicts over the use of natural resources in North Halmahera. This can be opposed to the common sense acceptance or resignation to village governance as a mode of participation. The next generation has continued this revival, both as a way of surviving modernity and to claim some of the benefits of it. Gosowong was a traditional forest for hunting and gathering forest products such as wild cloves, fragrant woods, and food until 1997. In the 1940s, apparently small amounts of gold were recovered.[43] Since NHM had been operating, there had always been feelings of resentment from some Pagu Isam people that they had not been acknowledged or compensated as the traditional landowners. Even with the expanded CDE program, and development funding, some resented that they were treated the same as all other people across five *kecematan* when it was their traditional forest that was occupied by NHM. Thus, around 2010, a new movement emerged, led by a charismatic activist.

Ibu Afrida is a schoolteacher from Sosol village in Malifut who has become an *adat* activist. Her story is both remarkable and illustrative of several dynamics within *adat* as a political framework. First, she describes the importance of *adat* as a system regulating social relations:

> We have *adat* law [about] marriage, laws about etiquette, character. We must be polite. We have laws about land, property, like that, we have many traditional regulations. How to look after nature, take care of one another. We also have knowledge, inherited knowledge for example about medicine, about this life, many kinds of cases.[44]

As a conception of the world which ' "organize[s]" human masses, and create[s] the terrain on which men [*sic*] move, acquire consciousness of their position, struggle, etc.' (Gramsci 1971, 377; Q7§21), *adat* can be considered an ideology. It also becomes a basis of education and alliance building:

> I had already made education in every place, meeting with whoever, about recognising our identity as Indigenous people. Starting from our mother language, I gave understanding about the land. It isn't sultan land, it isn't state land. Out of the state and us, we were here earlier. They [community members] understand, after they understand we can begin making maps. After I started education we started territorial mapping. I asked the elders to tell stories. Then we mapped coordinates using GPS.[45]

This land mapping and documenting of stories helped to establish claims of Pagu people as traditional landowners dispossessed by NHM and other non-Indigenous landowners. Ibu Afrida and her allies could then make a claim on NHM:

> So, after that, we went to NHM. We weren't welcomed there so we blockaded. I brought a mass of people who were aware, and we blockaded for 48 hours at the gate … Seven trucks of people, adults and children. 2012. Then it is also important that there was a network like AMAN, Komnas [HAM], journalists … it was all covered by media. Then I was arrested by police … I was taken to

Polres ... It was only one day in Polres because the *bupati* is an *adat* person and the head of AMAN's national board.[46]

Ibu Afrida's ideology, organising, networking and confrontational activism combined to convince NHM that they needed to negotiate. When a manager of community relations came to meet them after her release from the police station, Ibu Frida said:

> 'I want to ask you: This land we call Toguraci and Gosowong. I want to ask you, the names "Toguraci" and "Gosowong", did you bring [them] from Australia or from Jakarta? I think [they were] named by our ... ancestors. So, it means this [is] our land.' If [he] were to say, that there is no acknowledgement by the state [about Indigenous land rights], then don't use this name because that means it is owned by us. And here is the map of our traditional area. Indeed, this map is not yet recognised by the government in Jakarta. But all these sites, sites that are being explored, they are using our names. I asked them not to ... He couldn't answer, he replied 'What do you want?' ... I said 'I want to reconstruct our original culture, I want to document all of it. So that when I am gone, let's say one hundred years from now, I don't remember anymore, it isn't in my brain, but it is written.' Then [the manager] said 'Good idea.'[47]

With the help of a linguist from LIPI (*Lembaga Ilmu Pengetahuan Indonesia*; the Indonesian Institute of Sciences) in Jakarta, Ibu Afrida negotiated with NHM to design a cultural documentation program. They signed a memorandum of understanding to provide Rp2 billion (AU$194,700) in funding from 2013 to 2018 to support the construction, provisioning and activities of a Pagu documentation centre called '*Nanga Wolla*' (our house) in Sosol village, Malifut. Ibu Afrida made her claim, based in a shared ideology (*adat*) and organised through national networks and local demonstrations. Through this struggle, she has been recognised as the first female leader among Pagu people.

The resources that she negotiated with NHM became a source of conflict with some other *adat* figures who are not happy about her growing influence and power and attempted to negotiate alternative agreements with NHM. The Pagu Indigenous group are historically patriarchal, patrilineal and ruled (or guided) by a hereditary aristocracy. Ibu Afrida comes from one of these aristocratic families, but through her grandmother. She is both aware of the tensions and proud of transcending them:

> I have been leading for seven years. It should not be me because women are not allowed. Patrilineal, patriarchal. However, it is me who has never stopped struggling for the existence of Pagu people, for human rights, for Indigenous rights. I don't stop. So, I also struggle for the reconstruction of culture, like with the documentation centre. Because of that the old people respect me. Although until now it is a dynastic system.[48]

So even while claiming to represent an authentic tradition passed down from generation to generation, aspects of this tradition can be challenged and change. The role of AMAN in this is quite significant, as they advocate explicitly for the role of women within *adat* communities across Indonesia. *Adat* is clearly a powerful ideology which can mobilise people through appeals to tradition yet is not as static as most of the literature assumes (for example, Kristiansen and Sulistiawati 2016).

What is most important for the questions posed in this book is that a relatively small group of people, led by a charismatic woman, was able to force a multinational mining company to negotiate. The success of this campaign contains the same elements of other successful campaigns considered in this book: a legitimising ideology, local activism supported by national alliances, legitimising claims to landowning and confrontational tactics which pose a threat to the profitability of mining. And like all other cases, it is also a precarious situation; their power, alliances and networks must be maintained if they are to avoid being forgotten or replaced by another group.

Jalan tikus

AMAN activists did not focus on *adat* to the exclusion of other issues. Indeed, in some ways, they intensified activism around environmental pollution. Ibu Joyce was a member of the North Halmahera parliament at the same time her husband, Hein Namotemo, was *bupati*. She was also the women's organisational coordinator for AMAN North Maluku. In 2011, a group of activists, including Ibu Joyce, followed a winding back road (*jalan tikus*) into NHM's grounds in an attempt to find a rumoured leaking waste pipe. They sneaked in at night, collected evidence but were arrested. They suspected and confirmed that NHM was dishonest about pollution. She said they knew about pollution because of dead banana and coconut trees in the area and they wanted to know what levels of contamination existed, even though NHM said there was no contamination at all. NHM did not provide further information or negotiate about pollution levels.[49] Motivated by these stories, along with consistent complaints by fisherfolk about the disappearance of anchovies from rivers, and complaints of locals falling sick with lumps and itches, AMAN organised some demonstrations in Ternate and received media coverage in 2013 and 2014 (Karim 2013; AMAN 2014). Yet, there was never any significant reaction from NHM.

Juxtaposing AMAN's struggle based in *adat* and advocacy about pollution demonstrates how NHM can control the agenda by permitting some issues to be subject to negotiation – *adat* – while keeping others off the table – pollution. The existence of the mine, its operating area, systems of production and waste disposal are non-negotiable. How NHM contributes to local development is negotiable, but only once the threat of disrupting activities through demonstrations and blockades has been proven. This had the effect of breaking apart the previous coalition that existed around environmental issues, *adat*, lack of development, and small-scale mining, as leaders have incentives to change their demands towards those with more chance of success and generating material benefit.

Participatory environmental monitoring

Before concluding, I want to consider a participatory mechanism that NHM has *not* implemented. Throughout this chapter, I have highlighted how NHM's participatory mechanisms have shaped the agenda of permissible grievances. Grievances about pollution and effects on fisheries close to the mine area have persisted since 1999.

There are only a few publicly available studies on the environmental impacts of NHM's mining activities, and grievance holders do not have the resources to conduct their own research.[50] A study led by Bogor Agricultural University in 2010 found dangerous levels of cyanide and mercury[51] in fish caught in Kao Bay, where any pollution from the Gosowong mine enters the sea (Simbolon et al. 2010).

Newcrest is a signatory to the International Cyanide Management Code for the Manufacture, Transport, and Use of Cyanide in the Production of Gold (the code),[52] a voluntary set of standards against which signatories are audited. Compliance involves self-monitoring and auditing by independent consultants. From 2011 to 2015, monitoring results from the Kobok River, where NHM discharges its wastewater, found cyanide levels

> consistently recorded as being <0.05 mg/L which is greater than the compliance level of <0.022 mg/L ... any releases of solution resulting in a free cyanide concentration of more than 0.022mg/L measured below the mixing zone will be regarded as an environmental emergency event that requires NHM to follow a set process, including raising the alarm, notifying the ERT captain, taking samples and mitigating the release event. ... NHM could not produce evidence that it complied with these requirements, including incident investigation and reporting for each event. As the operation could not show that free cyanide levels at S12KR [the testing site] are less than the compliance level of <0.022mg/L, NHM is now considered to be Non-compliant with this standard of practice.
>
> (Golder Associates 2015, 17)

These levels could be enough to harm and kill fish in the river:

> Concentrations of free cyanide in the aquatic environment ranging from 5.0[53] to 7.2 micrograms per litre reduce swimming performance and inhibit reproduction in many species of fish. ... Concentrations of 20 to 76 micrograms per litre free cyanide cause the death of many species, and concentrations in excess of 200 micrograms per litre are rapidly toxic to most species of fish.
>
> (International Cyanide Management Institute n.d.)

NHM disputes that they have polluted the river, despite these findings, and refuses to release more detailed information. NHM's position is that they release monitoring results to the government and it is the government which chooses not to publicise the reports.[54] Meanwhile the regency government is under-resourced and under-prepared to independently investigate and act upon the data they are presented.

Although there has been periodic agitation by people affected by pollution, WALHI and AMAN, there has not (yet) been enough pressure or publicity about pollution to force NHM to negotiate, investigate, consult or implement a participatory monitoring program. Key allies who agitated for and now receive CDE funding do not have the same interest in confronting accusations of pollution. Because both Indonesian legislation and international standards that apply to NHM are either voluntary, not public, or unenforceable, NHM can choose what issues they engage stakeholders about. Yet this choice is not just a moral or commercial judgement about public good or ethical responsibility. This choice becomes more about how they can best respond to different interests affected by the impacts of mining and the political, social and economic conditions they face. They have effectively shut down debate through avoidance.

Conclusion

The Gosowong gold mine presents an exemplary case of contemporary trends in multinational mining corporations enacting participatory mechanisms. Newcrest's experience – being mired in violent conflict, experimenting with repression, and eventually turning towards participatory CSR guided by international agreements – mirrors the experience of the extractive sector globally. Newcrest and NHM have employed tactics to control conflict, from hiring paramilitary police as security, to attempting sustainable economic development initiatives, and to increasing contributions to regional development. My research shows that NHM is sensitive to demonstrations and is quick to make concessions but very rarely gives in to the specific demands of protesters. Its participatory mechanisms serve two purposes: containing conflict generated by the ongoing disruption rooted in acts of primitive accumulation; and facilitating changes in local relations of production and reproduction more favourable to extractive industries.

Participatory mechanisms implemented by NHM have changed the form of demonstrations from large, confrontational and well-publicised block-ades expressing a collection of grievances to smaller, single-issue, and less widely reported demonstrations. The aims of most demonstrations have also changed – from opposing the expansion or practices of mining to seeking more transparent and efficient forms of participation. Each participatory mechanism implemented by NHM embodied a slightly different consul-tative ideology of representation adapted to local conditions. The village support program fitted with the pre-existing mode of participation – the ideologies of representation and institutionalised patronage networks – embodied in village governance and so was rather successful at redirecting and containing conflict. The sustainable economic development programs, legitimised by sustainability and fitting into regency-level political economic hierarchies, more actively intervened in relations of production, while in the case of Ibu Afrida, it was Newcrest that was receptive to her particularistic ideology rather than the other way around. This diversity of ideologies and institutional structures within this single case underlines that the forms that participation takes is shaped by the receptivity of affected people.

The demoralisation of the failed Constitutional Court case, the kill-ing of a protester, the UNDP-LEAD program, the regional contribution to development, and NHM's sustainable economic development program have all helped to change how particular actors have engaged in conflict. However, it is the village support program that has aligned the interests of village governments with those of NHM and facilitated a depoliticisation of opposition.

In stark contrast to the assumptions of institutionalists, best exempli-fied by the UNDP's LEAD program, people affected by mining, their NGO allies, and politicians representing them have been able to extract many concessions from NHM through direct negotiation and confrontation, espe-cially through organising demonstrations and blockades. Institutional solu-tions and 'good governance' played no role in securing the rights of people affected by mining.

It will be instructive to see if, after its sale from multinational Newcrest to the domestic Indotan Halmahera Bangkit in March 2020 (Brown 2020), NHM maintains similar participatory strategies and alignment with inter-national standards. Any change in strategy as NHM continues to plan for mine closure may provide further evidence of the influence of international self-governance standards and the ideologies embedded within them.

Kulon Progo (Chapter 6) provides an instructive contrast in how and why participatory mechanisms are contested, co-opted, embraced or ignored by people affected by mining. In Kulon Progo most people affected by mining militantly rejected participation, whereas around Gosowong they accepted participation as a way to receive some benefit from the mine. The main reason for this is that the land that NHM is mining was forest, not farmland, and so few people have had their livelihoods directly threatened and they were more receptive to NHM's consultative ideologies. The contestation around Gosowong is not about the existence of the mine but about what is considered a fair contribution to the surrounding communities and who should benefit. Where there was enough ideological common ground between the ideologies of representation adopted by NHM and people affected by mining, on issues such as sustainable community development and support for Indigenous culture, participation produced results for both sides, even as these results represented a process of contestation and compromise. Where there was little ideological receptivity, on environmental pollution, participatory mechanisms were not established, and no compromises were achieved.

In addition to the difference in land conflict, alliances are more vertically organised (cross-class) in Halmahera than in Kulon Progo. This is because of differences in their organisation of agricultural production, histories of organisation and ideologies. It is a product of historically produced social relations of production and reproduction which left people in North Halmahera less experienced in organising autonomously from rulers.

The ideological basis for contestation is similarly different. In Halmahera, indigeneity and *adat* lend themselves to conceptualising struggle as between 'local' people, no matter their class position, and 'outsiders'. The main organisation supporting local people in Halmahera was AMAN, a natural fit as it promotes Indigenous rights across Indonesia. The engagement with AMAN was facilitated by and reinforced *adat* and indigeneity as an identity and ideology, which did not explicitly challenge class relations, whereas in Java, peasant struggles have a much longer history of 'the people' (*rakyat*) struggling against landlords and capital. Together, these comparisons support my argument that the most crucial factors in structuring both opposition to and participation is land, relations of production, histories of organisation and ideology.

Notes

1 Gosowong produced 331,555 ounces of gold in the year to June 2015, from two underground mines, Toguraci and Kencana, established in 2003 and 2006, a processing plant and a rehabilitated open-pit mine (Newcrest 2015).
2 In March 2020, Newcrest announced the sale of its share of NHM to Indotan Halmahera Bangkit (Newcrest 2020). Newcrest stated they sold 100% of their

share rather than divest 51% as required under Indonesian law (Brown 2020). In November 2023, Newcrest was fully acquired by US-based gold and copper miner Newmont Corporation.

3 See Chapter 3 for a detailed discussion on the ICMM Voluntary Principles and Cyanide Management Code.

4 The ethnic classification of people is a fraught endeavour. The Topatimasang (2016) team use the Tobelo language as an ethnic marker that consists of almost all people in North Halmahera excluding Galea and Makian people and extending into East Halmahera and Moroutai. By this classification it includes all people living in the five districts surrounding the Gosowong mine except for transmigrants, who are Makian people living on the coast and Javanese living in interior villages. The Indigenous people living adjacent to the mining area speak a language related to Tobelo and identify as Kao, Pagu or Isam (*adat* leaders, interviews with the author, 7 and 8 September 2017).

5 The sultan's claims to be the patron of Pagu people date back to the sixteenth century (Ibu Afrida, *adat* elder, interview with the author, 7 September 2017).

6 Ibu Afrida, *adat* elder, interview with the author, 7 September 2017.

7 NMH manager of social performance, interview with the author, 24 April 2018; Ibu Afrida, *adat* elder, interview with the author, 12 September 2017.

8 With the potential exception of some forest gardens.

9 The decentralisation and democratisation of the *reformasi* period triggered diverse kinds of conflict across Indonesia. In the words of Vedi Hadiz, 'The new rent-seeking opportunities provided by decentralisation clearly make up the fuel for the often intense levels of conflict that surround contests for control of key institutions of governance at the local level' (2010, 95–96).

10 Malifut would have a majority of Makian citizens while Kao would remain a Kao majoritarian district.

11 NMH manager of social performance, interview with the author, 24 April 2018.

12 Mercury is used by small-scale miners to extract gold, while NHM's industrial process uses cyanide.

13 AMAN activist, interview with the author, 14 March 2017.

14 NMH manager of social performance, interview with the author, 24 April 2018; Ibu Afrida, *adat* elder, interview with the author, 12 September 2017.

15 *Brimob* (Mobile Brigade) is Indonesia's paramilitary and anti-riot police force.

16 WALHI North Maluku activist, interview with the author, 15 September 2017.

17 There are 81 villages in the five districts with approximately 50,000 residents.

18 NMH manager of social performance, interview with the author, 24 April 2018.

19 *Cemat*, North Halmahera, interview with the author, 9 September 2017; *kepala desa*, Kao Barat, interview with the author, 13 September 2017.

20 The district (*kecematan*) governments were responsible for supporting the village teams and distributing the funding. Until 2015, the five *kecematan* governments received one-sixth of the 1% fund for development and administration; after 2015, all funding was channelled directly to villages. *Kecematan* officials, including the *cemat*, are appointed by the *bupati*.

21 Village head, Kao Barat, interview with the author, 13 September 2017; chair of village government business, Kao Barat, interview with the author, 13 September 2017.

22 *Dana desa* is the main allocation of funding from the national government to village governments. The laws governing villages, funding and village structures have recently been reformed with Law No. 6/2014 (see Antlöv et al. 2016; White 2017).

23 Coconut farmers, Kao Barat, interview with the author, 13 September 2017.

24 *Cemat* (sub-district head), North Halmahera, interview with the author, 12 September 2017; village head, Kao Barat, interview with the author, 13 September 2017.

25 Village head, North Halmahera, interview with the author, 21 March 2017.

26 *Kecematan* official, North Halmahera, interview with the author, 23 March 2017; village head, interview with the author, 21 March 2017.

27 Village head, interview with the author, 21 March 2017.

28 Manager of social performance, NHM, interview with the author, 24 April 2018.

29 North Maluku mining inspector, interview with the author, 14 September 2017.

30 Manager of social performance, NHM, interview with the author, 24 April 2018.

31 Village head, interview with the author, 21 March 2007.

32 The implementation date for Regulation No. 41/2016 was December 2018, by which time NHM had redesigned the sustainability program with local community representatives.

33 Manager of social performance, NHM, interview with the author, 24 April 2018.

34 Manager of social performance, NHM, interview with the author, 24 April 2018.

35 Manager of social performance, NHM, interview with the author, 24 April 2018.

36 Coconut farmers, interview with the author, 13 September 2017.

37 Village official, Kao Barat, interview with the author, 13 September 2017.

38 WALHI North Maluku activist, interview with the author, 15 September 2017.

39 WALHI North Maluku activist, interview with the author, 15 September 2017.

40 Ir. Hein Namotemo was a career bureaucrat and junior politician before the conflict. He has been credited with playing an important role in the post-conflict peace process by reviving the role of *adat* as a way to bridge ethnic and religious divides (Duncan 2013, 114).

41 Twenty per cent of both royalties and land rent should be distributed to the national government and 16% to the province (North Maluku). 64% of land rent and 32% of the royalties go to the producing regency (North Halmahera), and the remaining 32% of royalties are divided evenly between all other regencies in the province (Duncan 2007, 729; Agustina et al. 2012, 19).

42 Hein Namotemo, interview with the author, 11 September 2017.

43 Ibu Afrida, *adat* elder, interview with the author, 12 September 2017.

44 Ibu Afrida, *adat* elder, interview with the author, 7 September 2017.
45 Ibu Afrida, *adat* elder, interview with the author, 7 September 2017.
46 Ibu Afrida, *adat* elder, interview with the author, 7 September 2017.
47 Ibu Afrida, *adat* elder, interview with the author, 7 September 2017.
48 Ibu Afrida, *adat* elder, interview with the author, 7 September 2017.
49 Ibu Joyce, ex-member of regional parliament, interview with the author, 9 September 2017; activist, interview with the author, 15 September 2017.
50 See d'Hondt et al. (2010) for a summary of studies conducted before 2010.
51 Cyanide pollution is a result of NHM's industrial goldmining activities, while mercury is used by small-scale miners.
52 See Chapter 4.
53 5.0mcg = 0.005mg.
54 Manager of social performance, NHM, interview with the author, 24 April 2018.

6

Iron resistance in coastal Kulon Progo

This final case study is an example of an exceedingly rare occurrence: a group of people whose land and livelihoods were threatened by a proposal to establish a mine successfully resisted the attempt. They did not merely extract concessions or greater compensation. My other two case studies have demonstrated that participatory mechanisms are enacted by mining companies for two main purposes: first to contain conflict; second to facilitate changes in the means and relationships of production in the area surrounding the mine. In this case study, the mining company, PT Jogja Magasa Iron (JMI), attempted but failed at both. People affected by the mining project organised militant resistance to the mine and consequently it never developed beyond a pilot stage. This demonstrates the significance of decisions taken by people affected by mining about if and how to engage in participatory mechanisms. More interestingly, this case provides an example of how local people can find sources of power apart from corporate invitations to participate, assistance from NGOs or other institutions. This chapter, then, focuses more on the question of why, how and when people affected by mining decide to reject participation and take other courses of action.

The most significant factors explaining the choices of people to resist, and their capacity to do so, are *control* of land, but not necessarily legal ownership; cooperative, non-hierarchical relationships of production and social reproduction; histories and experiences of organisation; ideologies; and alliance structures.

This chapter proceeds in six parts. The first is a history of the area, the mining proposal and the development of mining, including the partially successful land acquisition. The second is a description of the participatory mechanisms that JMI has implemented – *sosialisasi*,[1] village teams, micro-credit *koporasi* (cooperatives), and negotiations for compensation. In presenting empirical data, it will become clear that the mechanisms were all ineffectively implemented because they relied too heavily on alliances with government and elite actors and failed to include local peasants.[2] In the public relations of JMI, the peasants and conflict are entirely ignored, reflecting arrogant attitudes towards rural people. Local peasants were at first not invited and later refused invitations to attend any company-organised events.

The next section turns to focus on the local activist organisation, the PPLP-KP (*Paguyuban Petani Lahan Pantai Kulon Progo*; the Association of Shoreline Farmers Kulon Progo), who have organised local militant

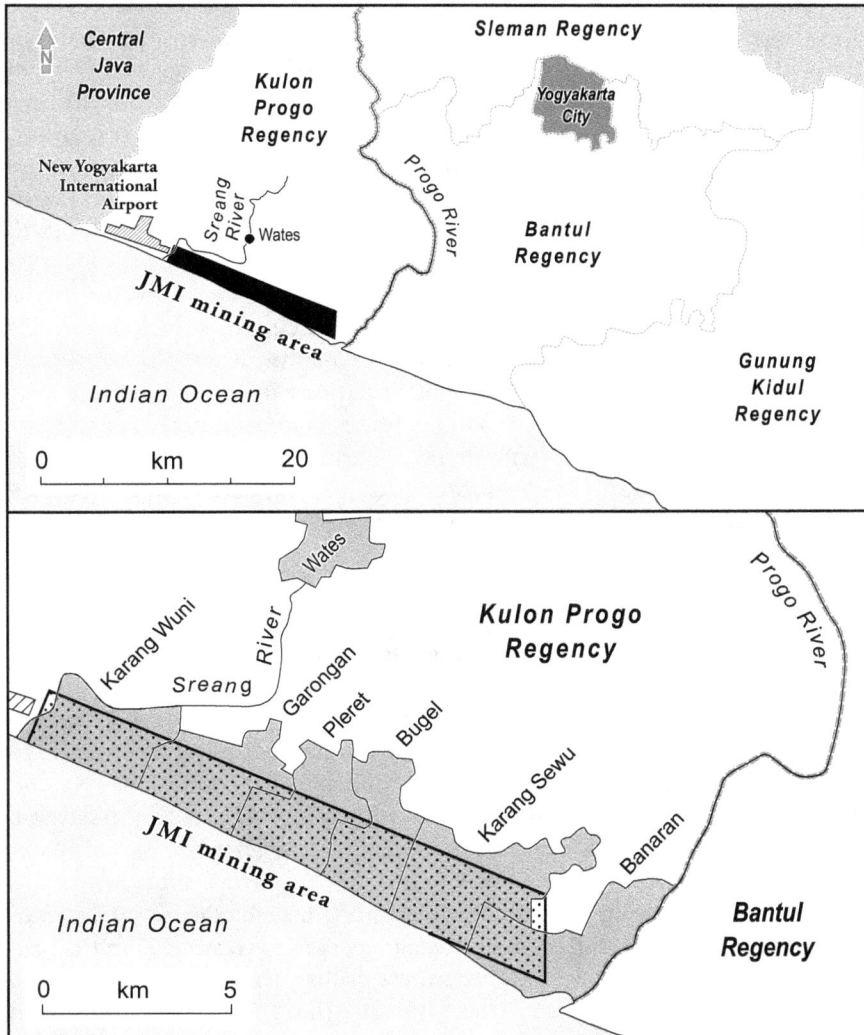

Figure 6.1 Coastal Kulon Progo showing the mining area and affected villages.

resistance and formed alliances with other groups in Indonesia and internationally. Their power results from their independent organisation, militant tactics, and productive management of their land. To explain this, it is necessary to examine the development of their farming methods, organisation and relationships since 1985. This has led to independent organisation of their social relations of production and reproduction and an anarchistic ideology developing among the peasants which translated quickly into a well-organised resistance. The fourth section describes the various alliances the PPLP engaged in and particularly how the most successful alliances were those that fitted best with the peasants' evolving common sense understanding of the world and those that addressed gaps of knowledge and skills in the villages. In the fifth section, an analysis of gender relations and the gendered division of labour lends further weight to the argument that relationships of production and social reproduction help determine the organisation of political groups. Yet this relationship can also be reversed; an analysis of gender roles shows that participation in resistance opened opportunities to create more equitable gendered divisions of labour.

The sixth and final section turns to one of the six villages affected by the mine, Karang Wuni, where the outcome of participatory mechanisms has been the reverse of the other five villages – Banaran, Karang Sewu, Bugel, Pleret and Garongan (Fig. 6.1). Slight variations in land-ownership patterns, ideology and alliances led to first a few, then most peasants participating in negotiations with JMI and finally relinquishing their land. However, the *koporasi* in Karang Wuni is organised democratically and transparently, animated by very similar forms of organisation and ideology as the other villages.

The iron in the sand

Iron was discovered in the dunes on the south coast of Kulon Progo Regency in 1964. Attempts were made to identify exploitable iron sand resources in 1973 and 1975; however, interest evaporated until the mid-2000s (Naidoo et al. 2017, 10). In 2005 PT Jogja Magasa Mining (JMM) began to develop a proposal to exploit the iron in the sand. JMM is described as 'a consortium of individuals, including the Sultan of Yogyakarta' (Indo Mines Ltd 2015, 7). The following year, Indo Mines Limited, a small exploration company listed on the Australian Stock Exchange, made investments in the project, acquiring a 70% stake and began test drilling (Indo Mines Ltd 2006). In 2008, a pilot plant was constructed on site (Indo Mines Ltd 2008), and PT Jogja Magasa Iron (JMI), the operating company jointly owned by Indo Mines and JMM, signed a contract of work (CoW)[3] with the Indonesian government (Indo Mines Ltd 2009, 6). In 2009, Indo Mines secured project finance from the London mining finance company Anglo Pacific plc (Indo Mines Ltd 2016, 39). The mining plan is to extract iron from the 6m-deep coastal sand dunes and produce 2.0Mt/year of pig iron concentrate for 18.5 years from a beneficiation plant, which could then be exported or refined further at a smelter in Indonesia (Naidoo et al. 2017, 27).

Indo Mines' two main partners in this project are the sultan's family, who own 30% of JMI through JMM, and the Pakualaman[4] royal family, who claim ownership of a majority of land in the contract area. Through these initial partners, JMI found allies in the regency and village governments. Between 2012 and 2014, Rajawali Group, a major domestic conglomerate owned by billionaire Peter Sondakh, bought 57.12% of Indo Mines shares (Indo Mines Ltd 2012; 2014). This alliance between international capital, one of the largest domestic corporate conglomerates, provincial royal families, and regency and village governments represents a formidable elite alliance wielding considerable power within Indonesian political and economic structures. This alliance is especially formidable given the extensive patrimonial relationships and deep cultural reverence for the royal families of Yogyakarta (Jati 2013).

The same geological process that made the coastal strip rich in iron also gave it a kind of fertility which local peasants have learnt to harness, growing chillies, vegetables and fruit to provide for their livelihoods. Therefore, the area subject to the proposed mine almost precisely overlaps with farmland supporting a community of approximately 2,000 peasants in 400 families spanning the southern edges of six villages (Widodo 2013, 125). The proposal to mine involved borrowing sections of the land for years at a time, progressively mining the 22km-long, 1.8km-wide contract area (Jati 2013). While each section was being mined the farmers would not have access but would potentially be compensated during that time with other areas of land currently abandoned. However, as detailed below, the actions of peasants prevented further development of the mine from 2008 until Indo Mines' economic position had deteriorated beyond feasibility.

By 2015, the global iron price had fallen,[5] leading Indo Mines to close the pilot plant and focus on 'operating cost optimisation' (Indo Mines Ltd 2015, 7) while still pursuing outstanding approvals. Indo Mines (2015, 11) has stated their intention to make the project compliant with the Equator Principles (Chapter 3). This would entail a higher standard of consultation and participation with mining-affected people while opening up the range of capital investors available to Indo Mines. At the same time, the Indonesian government was overhauling Indonesia's mining laws (see Chapter 3), which changed the CoW system to a licencing system, imposed domestic ownership requirements and restricted the export of unprocessed concentrates.[6] This led one independent expert valuation to discount the value of the project by 80% (Naidoo et al. 2017). By 2017, Indo Mines was facing risks that it might not remain a going concern until Rajawali placed a takeover bid, increasing their ownership to 76.49% and then delisting Indo Mines from the ASX on 21 August 2018 (Chambers 2018). Under the ownership of Rajawali, Indo Mines is still seeking international investors and partners, including potential buyers in China (Jogja Magasa Iron 2020).

Before the fall in global iron prices and reform of mining laws, the most significant obstacles to the mining project were the peasants themselves and complicated land-ownership claims. Despite JMI's powerful political allies, they failed to execute the primitive accumulation (land grab) required to establish the mine. The farmers' struggle is now well over 15 years long and they continue to care for their land (Hernawan et al. 2021).

Land acquisition

Negotiations for land acquisition were complicated by its contested ownership. Within the project area (about 3,000ha), there are three categories of land: certified land owned by individuals or families outright, including homes and some cultivated land; public (state) land including abandonded land; and uncertified cultivated land and heaths (*tegalan*) managed by individuals or families. About 30% of land falls into this third category and is subject to contested claims of ownership (Widodo 2013, 125). On the one hand, the majority of peasants who had been farming there for generations believed themselves to own the land, even though it is not certified, through Indonesia's Basic Agrarian Law of 1960 (BAL/UUPA).[7] On the other hand, the Pakualaman royal family believed themselves to be the rightful landowners through feudal land-ownership traditions reaching back to the Treaty of Giyanti of 1755,[8] and enshrined in the Special Yogyakarta Law of 2012 (UUK).[9]

The BAL is the main legal reference for land title in Indonesia, written as a postcolonial compromise on land reform between the dominant factions in Indonesian politics at the time: the communists, Soekarno's nationalists, and military factions. Land reform provisions include adverse possession of land and redistribution of land owned by absentee landlords, based on the principle that land is a social relation between the people of Indonesia rather than a commodity (Meckelburg 2019, 65). Conflict over land redistribution, including direct action and occupations by peasants, has been a consistent feature of Indonesian politics (Lund and Rachman 2016). The BAL has, however, been interpreted and applied differently by every government since 1960 (Lucas and Warren 2013; McCarthy and Robinson 2016).

On 24 September 1948, Sultan Hamengku Buwono XI, father of the current sultan, declared that the BAL applies in the province of Yogyakarta, implying that peasants working untitled land (*tanah garapan*) are entitled to certification (Aditjondro 2013). However, the Special Yogyakarta Law states that all untitled land in the province of Yogyakarta is owned by the sultanate (Sultan Ground) or the Paku Alam (Paku Alam Ground).[10]

Under the contracts written by JMI and offered to peasants, the land would be formally classified by the BPN (*Badan Pertanahan Nasional*; the national land office) in Kulon Progo. In the areas of contested land ownership, the land would be recognised as being owned by the Paku Alam but with use rights (*hak garap*) belonging to the local peasants. Therefore, for these areas, the peasants needed to sell their use rights to JMI *and* agree that the Paku Alam was the ultimate owner. In return, they would receive land certificates from BPN and compensation (PT Jogja Magasa Iron 2013). JMI's contract of work with the national government entitles them to mine the land for 30 years, during which time rent will be paid to the Paku Alam (Indo Mines Ltd 2015). In areas where land ownership is not contested, peasants have been free to decide whether to sell their land or not. In areas where the peasants are withholding their consent and refusing to certify their land, a stalemate has ensued. JMI is dependent on the Paku Alam and the government enforcing their claims to land ownership. However, at least up to the time of writing, they seem unwilling to move against the organised PPLP. Only in Karang Wuni have negotiations proceeded, events that are discussed in the final section of this chapter.

As it became clear that these peasants would not move aside, JMI attempted to establish participatory mechanisms to control patterns of conflict and to change social relationships within the coastal villages. Yet these failed to effectively engage the peasants whose land was required; indeed they created further divisions and polarisation within and between villages.

Participation failed

Local staff implemented several participatory strategies as part of their community relations efforts. *Sosialisasi* (consultation) meetings were held from 2005, designed to present information about the project, convince the audience of its benefits and identify potential allies. Village teams were established to facilitate activities and give JMI a local presence. *Koporasi*, micro-credit cooperatives, were established in each of the six affected villages. Negotiations for land acquisition were complicated by contested land ownership and resistance.

Sosialisasi

JMI began *sosialisasi* activities in 2005. Peasants whose land would be affected by the mining project were not invited to the initial round of meetings, leaving them to find out about the plan via word of mouth from some who did attend. In contrast, JMI officially invited representatives of village governments, civil servants and local business people who lived and worked outside the contract area.[11] Support from these groups was almost guaranteed, as all would potentially benefit from employment opportunities and community development programs without facing adverse consequences directly.

After it became clear that there was potential for resistance to the mine, JMI made attempts to invite peasants to the meetings. One PPLP member was invited to a *sosialisasi* meeting facilitated by the head of her hamlet and the son of the Paku Alam. When she asked a question about how the mining would affect the height of the dunes and seawater incursions, her question was dismissed, and she was never invited again. She told me: 'Maybe they are afraid my knowledge and questions will provoke other people to think more. They only invite people who agree and nod.'[12] By this stage, PPLP members decided they would not engage with the company. The PPLP protested and blockaded subsequent *sosialisasi* events. On 24 May 2007, the *sosialisasi* team was stuck inside the building which was surrounded by PPLP members until *Brimob*[13] officers cleared the way.

Village teams

JMI established coordinator teams in each affected village. Made up of residents, their role was to consult within the community, convince their neighbours of the mine's benefits, and organise support for JMI. One farmer I interviewed worked his small piece of land before 2006; however, it was not enough to produce an income to support his family. Once he heard rumours about the mining plan in 2005, he attended a *sosialisasi* meeting organised by the Paku Alam:

> There were many questions and many rejections at the start. First, I refused the mine, but then I was unemployed, like lots of other people were unemployed. I asked them what is the benefit, what is the impact on the people here? They told stories. They said that the project would absorb labour.[14]

After six months of consideration, he decided the promise of employment in the mine could be the best way to support his family. He became one of six community coordinators from two villages. Life became hard for him and his family as his village was overwhelmingly anti-mining. He was ostracised from public life and his activities were disrupted, prompting him to move with his family outside the area, until 2015 when the situation was calmer.

PPLP members also talk about 'horizontal conflict' between residents who were pro- and anti-mining. PPLP members refused to attend events organised by anyone they considered pro-mining, ostracised pro-mining neighbours from anti-mining mosques, and stopped their children from playing with their friends if their parents were pro-mining and vice versa.[15] This ostracism was in part a result of a deeply polarising issue dividing a community and in part organised and encouraged by both the PPLP on one side and JMI's community coordinators on the other. In the five villages where there was an overwhelming rejection of mining, this had the effect of completely undermining the work of JMI's community teams. In contrast, in Karang Wuni, the community team fulfilled its functions, ultimately facilitating the acquisition of land by JMI.

Koporasi

In 2011, JMI established *koporasi* in each village. The *koporasi* provide microfinance to members and an official mechanism through which JMI can procure local goods and services (mostly labour or food). Membership is open to all residents of each village, not only those affected by mining. Both functions bring JMI into the field of economic and community development and attempt to create new community interests which are aligned with JMI's.

Each *koporasi* was established with Rp15 million. If they were successfully established after one year, JMI granted another Rp35 million, and if after the end of another year the *koporasi* was still functioning, it was granted a final payment of Rp50 million, bringing the total funding to Rp100 million (total AU$10,164). Eight village *koporasi* received the initial Rp15 million, three received the second grant of Rp35 million and only in Karang Wuni was the final Rp50 million grant made.[16] In all the other villages, it appears that the money was mismanaged or unaccounted for. One village head told me that the initial Rp15 million payment was divided up among friends of the coordinator appointed by JMI.[17] Like with the other participatory mechanisms, PPLP members refused to participate in the *koporasi*. In Karang Wuni, as we will see below, this was not the case. This refusal to participate seems to have both effectively undermined the *koporasi* and left them open to corruption.

Of the participatory mechanisms, the village teams, *sosialisasi*, and support for community events succeeded in finding and securing the support of some allies: village elites, entrepreneurs, some underemployed and some peasants with very small parcels of land. Likewise, the *koporasi* had the potential to align the interests of peasants with JMI's. However, in the areas dominated by the PPLP, all mechanisms were undermined by opposition to mining. Indo Mines misread the situation, believing that the Paku Alam was the unambiguous landowner and that the support of the Paku Alam and sultanate would be enough to secure land for the project. They relied too heavily on an institutional reading of the political situation and the advice of their local partners, who had their own interests and downplayed conflicts with local farmers. Its articulation of consultative problem-solving representation was too narrow to secure legitimacy from affected people.

Unlike in Gosowong, the coastal peasants were not well integrated into existing state or corporate relations of production, reproduction or ideologies. While the participatory strategies of Indo Mines may have fitted well with the ideology and institutions of feudal Yogyakarta, they stood in direct opposition to the peasants' interests and understanding. With the failure of all participatory mechanisms in five out of six villages affected by the mine, the key question becomes why did the coastal peasants from the PPLP choose to militantly reject JMI's participatory mechanisms? Furthermore, what was the base of their power and how were they successful?

Farming is fighting

Peasants living in the area first heard about the project either through rumour or when company people came to collect earth samples. Resistance began almost immediately, when some farmers brought questions to their village governments asking why people were coming to their land without permission or notification.[18] After the debacle of JMI's *sosialisasi* program, several of the hamlet (*pedkuhan*) -based peasants' groups (*kelompok tani*) from six villages met on 1 April 2007 to decide for themselves how to respond to the mining proposal. The inaugural meeting unanimously decided to oppose the development of iron sand mining on their land, to '*bertani atau mati*' (farm or die), and formed the PPLP as the primary organisation of resistance (Widodo 2013, 11). The PPLP adopted a combination of militant confrontation, sabotage, blockades, rejection of mainstream NGOs, and solidarity actions organised through networks of peasants and urban-based activists.

Tactics

Between May 2007 and 2012 the PPLP and their allies engaged in a series of militant direct actions, protests and blockades. During this time, the coastal areas of Kulon Progo became notorious as dangerous places for outsiders to pass through. Roadside posts (*posko*) were constructed all through the

PPLP's area, adorned with anti-mining slogans, from which PPLP members monitored the coming and going of everyone. Parades were organised as both celebrations and demonstrations of support, attracting thousands of farmers who marched, packed into trucks or rode motorbikes without mufflers. Roadblocks were frequently established; anyone suspected of involvement with mining activities was turned away, and *sosialisasi* meetings were blockaded.

On a couple of occasions, at demonstrations at government offices in the regency capital of Wates, ten kilometres to the north, protesters fought with riot police who were attempting to break them up, using improvised weapons like rocks and bamboo against the police batons, tear gas, shields and water cannon. On 23 October 2008, PPLP members protested at the regency parliament Kulon Progo over the issuance of mining licences. They occupied the parliament buildings for three days and three nights. In January 2009, when PPLP organiser Pak Tukijo was on trial,[19] thousands of farmers surrounded the court building, threatening to storm it if he was found guilty. He was found not guilty. The largest demonstration outside Kulon Progo was held at Gadjah Mada University on 21 June 2008, when more than 5,000 people demonstrated about UGM staff providing expert assistance to JMI's environmental assessment and rehabilitation study processes.[20]

Two days after the occupation of the regional parliament, around 300 hired thugs (*preman*) entered the PPLP's area and burnt down several *posko* (road-side resting huts).[21] Fortunately, they left after PPLP members rallied to confront them, and interpersonal violence was avoided.[22] Pak Tukijo was arrested again, following a confrontation between PPLP members in Karang Sewu and JMI employees. This time he was jailed for 28 months from 1 May 2011 (Widodo 2013, 30).

Through these militant tactics, the PPLP managed to hold off development of the mine until the drop in global iron prices forced Indo Mines to suspend operations, Indonesian mining laws changed, and Indo Mines ran out of capital. As activity around the mine site decreased, so too did the frequency of demonstrations. The PPLP still holds parades on their anniversary, attracting thousands of peasants and supporters, as a celebration and as a demonstration that they can still mobilise large crowds.

Even more than these militant actions which stir controversy and made the PPLP infamous, all members interviewed expressed that, for them, their most important and effective strategy is to simply keep farming and managing their land well. One peasant who I interviewed on her land told me:

> Planting and farming are the *most* important, don't let this land be empty. If it is empty, people will think it is not productive, it won't be useful for the people … I think it is more important to manage our land. There are so many discussions, so much theory, the practical is more important.[23]

Likewise, Pak Tukijo, told me:

> Maybe JMI is just waiting for my generation to die – but the younger genera-
> tion will step up as long as the land is productive. If the harvests are good and
> the land is managed well, people will be willing to defend it. ... I'm just scared
> if the harvests fail, then people won't feel so strong and defend their land. That
> is why as long as we keep busy managing the land and don't get distracted, we
> won't be defeated.[24]

Thus the coastal peasants do not allow the attempted land grab or even the
struggle to defeat the mining project distract them from what they are struggling for – their land. Hence the most famous slogan of the PPLP: '*Menanam
adalah melawan!*' (Farming is fighting!). What they are struggling for is the
same as the struggle itself.

Why was the PPLP so successful? Why did they choose militant resistance
to mining? Why did they refuse participation and negotiation with the company and the government? To answer these questions, I turn to explain the
development of the means and relations of production, social reproduction,
ideology and alliances among the peasants.

Sand and chillies

To understand the decisions of people affected by the mining proposal, it is
important to first understand a little about farming systems on the coastal
strip of Kulon Progo.[25] It is the political economy of chilli and vegetable
production along with relationships of production that have given these
communities their staunchly independent and communal character (Jati
2013). Peasants here do not grow rice or sugar cane in irrigated plains like
peasants in most lowland areas of Java, they do not grow tobacco, tea or
coffee like peasants in mountainous areas, and there have never been any
large plantations or forced agriculture on this land. The soil – or rather
sand – on the coastal strip is very different from the soil found on the plains
and mountains of Java and is not suitable to these major agricultural commodities (Kusumaningrum and Mustafa 2015). The farmers grow chillies,
melons, aubergines and other fruit and vegetables. This means that they
are less integrated into the agrarian political economy of Yogyakarta and
are less affected by the government and private conglomerates that control trade in major agricultural products. They are also less integrated into
regency and provincial systems of political patronage.

More significant for our purposes is the history of the development of
farming techniques along the coastal strip, which has occurred since 1985 –
extremely recently compared with other agricultural systems in Yogyakarta
and Java. Before 1985, farming in the '*gersang dan tandus*' (arid and barren)

(Suliadi 2015, 82) coastal strip was extremely marginal. Farming occurred only during the wet season, only very low-value yams, cassavas, peanuts and some corn were cultivated without irrigation, while pandan leaves and bamboo were collected from the wild. In the dry season people searched for work, either as farm labourers in rice fields further north or as migrant labourers in large cities or even abroad. Residents were extremely poor and say they were marginalised from Yogyakarta society as *wong cubung*.[26] This marginalisation is the result of the colonial plantation system, of sugar cane production, and continued feudal systems of land ownership in Yogyakarta, creating landless peasants who moved to the unpopulated southern coastal strip to eke out a living and avoid state control (Yanuardy 2012; Jati 2013).

The story of how current farming practices developed has become something of a local mythology. In 1985, one farmer saw a chilli plant growing in the wild and thought to himself, 'if I nurture this and give it water, it could be very beneficial to the people'.[27] He did nurture the chilli plant; he planted more and found that if you gave them water, they would also grow in the dry season. Once his friends saw his initial success, they joined in the experiment: they dug wells with bamboo, experimented with different crops, talked over coffee after work, formed peasant groups, levelled and cleared the sand dunes and cultivated fields. Slowly, through ongoing cooperation and collective experimentation, they developed new farming techniques. Concrete wells replaced bamboo, plastic pipes and electric pumps replaced watering cans, and the peasants developed a comfortable standard of living.[28] Hard data and statistics on economic development in coastal Kulon Progo are rare and unreliable even in Indonesian and Javanese language sources. The lack of official data from this period confirms the oral histories of older peasants that this was a marginal area, outside the interests of state and corporate actors.

From the early groups that formed to collectively experiment with farming techniques, more formal *kelompok tani* (farming groups) emerged. Organised at hamlet level, each group coordinated planting and harvesting schedules so that labour could be shared across each other's land. They coordinated construction of roads into the farming area to allow better transportation and in the early 2000s they started to introduce more mechanised farming techniques. Some peasants' groups bought tractors and other tools that are collectively shared, while in other places individuals would buy tractors and rent them to their neighbours. Experimentation and land mapping created a 'social collective knowledge' upon which peasants built their success (Yanuardy 2012, 4).

The most significant function of the peasants' groups developed in 2003 when the number of chillies produced grew to be too large to be sold at local markets. *Asosiasi pasar tani* (farmers' market associations) would pool all the chillies harvested at one time and auction them off to the highest bidder

(Rusdiyana and Suminah 2018). This collective auction system meant that chillies could be sold much further afield and that peasants were not competing with one another; instead they increased their bargaining power through collectivised sale and distribution of their produce.[29]

It was this collective process of experimentation, coordination and distribution that the farmers credit with turning wind-swept sand dunes into fertile land and lifting them out of poverty. Whereas older peasants would have been lucky to finish primary education, they now send their children and grandchildren to the city for senior high school and university education, yet their children still aspire to become farmers.[30] It is a remarkable instance of development and poverty eradication over the last 35 years.

Older farmers who led the collective experimentation process starting in 1985 say that the cooperative organisation of farming came about *because* of new methods of cultivation, *during* the process of experimentation.[31] Before 1985, when farming was underdeveloped, there was no coordination, there was no collective organisation or peasants' groups (Kusumaningrum and Mustafa 2015). It was also important that all the shoreline farmers were social outcasts, viewed by inland peasants as isolated and unproductive. While common experiences of being outsiders, working as itinerant and migrant labourers, and living through poverty produced a sense of solidarity, forms of collective organisation only evolved *in response* to the new agricultural practices.

The *kelompok tani* are a central pillar of the coastal communities; they institutionalise the collective, anti-hierarchical spirit of the farming communities. Although decision making in these groups is dominated by men, see below for a description of the gendered division of labour and implications for resistance. Organisers rotate through positions and all profits are distributed back to members. However, what is most remarkable, and perhaps unique in Indonesia, is that since their beginnings in the late 1980s, they have been organised independently of government.[32] Soeharto's government made independent farming organisations illegal; all farming groups had to be organised through village government structures and include representatives from the military. Yet this was never enforced in the coastal area of Kulon Progo. The fact that these independent *kelompok tani* were ignored by the state is further evidence that the coastal area remained outside the interests and political networks of state and capital. It is these groups and the organisational forms that facilitated a rapid formation of the PPLP when the mining company arrived.

This brief historical sketch highlights that the coastal peasants of Kulon Progo have a relatively autonomous history of development, an intense pride in the quality of their crops and land, a system of agriculture that is collectively and independently managed, and peasants' groups that are used to being left alone to determine their own business (Kusumaningrum and Mustafa 2015). That is to say, they have developed collective social relations of production and reproduction independent of state and capital. They also have experiences of working abroad, in cities, as rural day labourers, and more recently as students in the cities. They know what urban and rural poverty is like, understand precarity, and they have witnessed development failures in other areas. Having already succeeded at pulling themselves out of poverty without outside assistance, they were extremely sceptical when a mining company arrived with promises of modernisation.

Ideology

Along with the development of cooperative relations of production and reproduction, the coastal peasants developed ideologically too. Their disposition towards cooperative autonomy and self-development found expression through old and new ideological frames. Mas Widodo, a prominent PPLP organiser, told how one of the first tasks of the PPLP was to refine and increase awareness of '*filosofi tanah*' (philosophy of land):

> We continuously spoke about these things. So that everyone knows that peasants' living space is our land [*ruang hidup petani adalah tanah*] … People must take care of the environment and then the environment will take care of them, protect their life. It is like a mutual connection. So, they understand if somebody wants to take the land or build something or change the function, it will destroy everything.[33]

This philosophy of land developed from experiences with cooperative systems of agricultural production, emphasising custodianship of nature, land and soil as a living resource, anti-hierarchical collective organisation, and self-reliance. It is, of course, also strongly influenced by and integrated back into existing ideological, philosophical and spiritual beliefs. The PPLP became an ideological vehicle in disseminating and sharpening knowledge to help each other understand and react to the mining proposal with coherence.

One peasant interviewed rejected the idea of mining mainly, although not only, because it will destroy traditional sacred places, particular hills and natural springs where people still meditate and conduct rituals specific to those places.[34] A landscape imbued with place-based spiritual practice reinforces and is reinforced by the belief that land is not a commodity to be bought and sold, it serves a higher social function. As one activist put it,

> land is understood not only as the means of production but also as their identity as farmers and living space. If land can be sold, that means it is a commodity. If land is living space [*ruang hidup*], it cannot be sold. Because if you sell your living space, you cannot live.[35]

Land occupies a significant place in the post-colonial left-nationalist imagination of Indonesia (Meckelburg 2019, 67). Land has been forcibly taken by colonialists, multinational corporations and the military, and it has been won back by peasant and union struggle (Lund and Rachman 2016). For peasants with this awareness, land is precious and should not be commodified (see Lucas and Warren 2013, 16–37).

The newest element to be introduced into the ideological mix is anarchism. Although arguably the coastal peasants have long held collective anti-hierarchical tendencies, the word anarchism was brought in when urban activists began supporting the struggle of the PPLP. As a relatively isolated, marginalised, collective and autonomous groups of hamlets, it isn't surprising that the PPLP found friends in anarchists or that anarchists were inspired by the history and philosophy of the PPLP. Anarchism has been significant for lending legitimacy to the PPLP's rejection of both the state and big capital. It has also helped develop their critique of state institutions and NGOs. Anarchists also brought feminist understanding of struggle with them, initiating many conversations about the gendered division of labour in activism and supporting women organisers.[36] Long-term ideological engagement helped to reshape the gendered division of resistance (see below).

None of this is meant to suggest that there is a single grand official ideology of the PPLP. Each individual will adopt a different combination of elements based on their lived experiences. Some are more pious, some more anarchic. To be sure, there are also strongly held beliefs that have hindered the development of an ideology which enables resistance to mining. First among these is the traditional deference usually given to the sultanate and the Paku Alam in Yogyakarta society (Colbron 2016). This belief took a long time to overcome within the PPLP-dominated villages; in Karang Wuni it was one factor in the success of JMI and has been a source of difficulty when searching for allies in Yogyakarta province. Rejection of the sultanate and the Paku Alam has been grounded in the claim that it was the sultan and Paku Alam who first betrayed Javanese tradition to capitalism.

This ideological constellation places peasants as experts at the centre of their own knowledge systems and empowered them to reject the economics and science of the *sosialisasi* meetings, legal systems, academics and even NGOs:

> The peasants of Kulon Progo's coastal beach land are also inventors, developers and protectors of sustainable farming processes. We do not need the babble of whatever professor or engineer with legitimation from the state, school or agency who can only theorise with their theories.
>
> (Widodo 2013, 44)

The ideological constructions of the PPLP are important because they justify and give members confidence to pursue particular tactics and alliances over others. Crucially, this ideological construction is antithetical to the consultative ideologies of representation espoused by JMI and state actors. Peasants rejected ideologies of corporate-led development, they rejected consultative ideologies of representation, and they rejected the feudal ideologies of the Paku Alam. Nevertheless, localised resistance, however well organised and militant, is always vulnerable to investors and their elite allies. The PPLP needed to build alliances of their own.

Alliances

Deep cultural reverence for the royal families in Yogyakarta made it difficult for the PPLP to find sympathy or allies within Yogyakarta (at least initially) and drove them to search for environmentalist, anarchist and international allies (Jati 2013). The PPLP is notoriously sceptical about the involvement of outsiders and NGOs, who they see as bringing their own hidden interests which might not be aligned with the PPLP's. They are critical of NGO attempts to represent them and negotiate or make compromises with corporations. NGOs tend to accept consultative ideologies of representation as an opportunity to have influence, while the PPLP rejected consultation because it precluded their autonomy and democratic rights. PPLP organisers were also reluctant to allow their movement to be used as a vehicle for aspiring politicians or NGO fundraising. The PPLP thus adopted a model for engaging with allies that stipulated allies could act in their respective domains of expertise but could not represent the PPLP outside of strictly agreed guidelines. Alliances formed organically too, based on continuing friendships and long-term connections that were built through mutual struggle. Meanwhile, alliances were forged with other peasants' groups, anarchists, activists and artists across Yogyakarta and Indonesia.

The PPLP was a founding member of the FKMA (*Forum Komunikasi Masyarakat Agraris*; the Agrarian Communities' Communication Forum). They also formed long-term relationships with anarchists, artists and activists in Yogyakarta, Indonesia and globally. JDA (*Jogja Darurat Agraria*; Agrarian Emergency Jogjakarta) was founded by a group of people acting in solidarity with the PPLP. The NGO which has had the biggest impact on the struggle is LBH (*Lembaga Bantuan Hukum*; Legal Aid Indonesia). These allies helped expand the struggle from an isolated land conflict into a challenge to land grabs and the 'exceptional' feudal characteristics of Yogyakarta politics.

Anarchists and solidarity

The PPLP, their militant tactics, opposition to the state and big capital, and autonomous organisation of land became a cause célèbre for anarchists internationally. When I asked about his preference for making alliances with anarchists and other peasants, one PPLP organiser emphasised the friendly informal nature of such connections: 'I am friends with anarchists and peasants, it is nicer, more enjoyable, happier, just like that. Like with other peasants, our minds just meet.'[37]

Anarchist activists worked on the international aspect of the campaign, translating information into English, publishing on blogs and international websites, and through informal international networks. Small demonstrations were organised at Indonesian embassies in London, Athens and Melbourne and at the offices and meetings of Indo Mines in Perth, Australia (Matheos 2011). Declarations of solidarity were sent from France, the Philippines and other places. These international 'solidarity actions' played a limited but important role: once both the Australian and Indonesian companies knew there was international attention, there were no more attacks by *preman* and police violence decreased. PPLP members assume this is because the companies wanted to avoid controversy.

LBH and legal strategy

The most significant NGO ally is LBH (Legal Aid Institute) Yogyakarta, as it plays a specialised role that farmers and other activists cannot easily do for themselves, providing legal education, support and advocacy. With LBH's assistance the PPLP formed a paralegal working group, members of which received basic legal training in 2008. They did this so that the PPLP could build their own understanding of the legal system. These paralegal activists have taken a lead role in educating other PPLP members, as well as in broader public debates to explain that their claims to land rights are based in the Basic Agrarian Law (BAL) and rejecting the Special Yogyakarta Law (UUK).[38]

LBH and PPLP have considered mounting a Constitutional Court challenge to the UUK; however, they view formal legal prospects with pessimism. Neither have they sued the state or company for rights violations. There are several reasons for this. As with LKMTL in Kelian and WALHI in Gosowong, the paralegal team considers the court system in Indonesia to be complicated and corrupt; they do not have confidence in their ability to succeed in court systems when they will surely be outmatched in terms of funding and lawyers by the sultanate.[39] They view courts as enemy terrain. Instead, legal strategies are focused on defending activists and/or farmers who are criminalised because of their campaign work.[40]

In five villages, peasants have not pursued land certification. PPLP members there understand that certifying their land will make it legible, countable and tradeable under the laws of the state, that certification is a step towards enclosure. They also have no faith in any legal institutions to intervene on their behalf in a dispute. They see engagement with the state and corporations as full of risk without corresponding benefits. Instead, they prefer to secure their individual rights through collective action and communal organisation.

Their preferred strategy is to use their legal understanding to strengthen the confidence, legitimacy and assertiveness of the coastal peasants on their home ground. The understanding of BAL and rejection of UUK is integrated into and supports existing ideologies, legitimising the PPLP's ideological position and claims to own the land they are farming (see also Peluso et al. 2008 on the ideological importance of the BAL).

The legal training that the paralegal team received helped the PPLP in other areas. Directly related to the land conflict, the paralegal team helps with legal defences when members are arrested and/or charged by police. This legal support gives members greater confidence to confront police and government. Second, not directly related to the struggle, the paralegal team has also assisted and advocated for members on issues ranging from domestic violence to obtaining driving licences. This helps strengthen the role of the PPLP in the community, especially during periods of relative quiet.

From FKMA to an exceptional Yogyakarta

The PPLP, together with two other location-based groups, formed the FKMA in 2010. One year later there were 15 member groups across Java, Sumatra and Sulawesi. Each of the member groups benefited from the swelling of numbers at their events (Widodo 2013, 77). However, FKMA had its own problems, as farmers from different groups felt different pressures, produced and traded within different political economic conditions and favoured different strategies. This led them to search for other allies who were more directly involved in the struggle against feudal land systems in Yogyakarta.

The sand iron project was the first time that the land ownership provisions contained in the UUK were used as the legal basis of land grabbing in Yogyakarta. Since then it has also been used in Parangkusomo, Watukodok Beach and Temon. While the PPLP was initially isolated as the only group to attack the legitimacy of Sultan Ground and Paku Alam Ground, other allies emerged as they faced their own land conflicts. The multiplication of land conflict in Yogyakarta led to activists, artists and academics in Yogyakarta city becoming more vocal about the sultan and the Paku Alam's abuses of privilege (Colbron 2016). PPLP organisers are now frequent guests at public events, discussions and seminars in Yogyakarta that seek to create a broader resistance to feudal land ownership in Yogyakarta.[41]

Gendered division of labour and activism

The gendered division of labour in farm and domestic work is reflected in community and activist organising.[42] On the farm, women are responsible for planting and harvesting most crops, while men are responsible for the 'heavier' work of preparing the land, construction and applying pesticides.[43] In the household, women are responsible for most, if not all domestic labour, especially preparing food and looking after children. Likewise, at large organised demonstrations women most often play support roles, such as organising food and looking after children. The gendered division of labour and privileging of masculinity also means that men have a more flexible schedule and more available free time, and thus can participate more easily in activist groups and events. The lack of free time and flexibility available to women is a direct barrier to women's participation in decision making and strategy formation.[44] This is mitigated somewhat by the ideology of the PPLP, which respects the spontaneity of each member and each hamlet subgroup. There are important exceptions to this, with some women who can overcome barriers to participation. One PPLP organiser told me her participation is made possible through cooperative arrangements with her neighbours; they will look after her land or children while she is busy with PPLP activities and she does the same for them.

As mentioned above, anarchist allies brought feminist approaches to their organising. One anarcho-feminist activist remarked:

> Even though we have seen a lot of women in the villages that are so brave and smart and have all these great ideas and everything, but they have never been given more spaces to be, to have important roles in the movement ... we haven't found out what is the best way how to break this, you know, traditional views and values about gender in this movement without being offensive.[45]

Solidarity activists did not attempt to impose their feminist values on the PPLP, but consistently held respectful conversations about the gendered division of resistance, while identifying and supporting women organisers.

The struggle itself has had some impact on gender relations among the peasants. Almost every interviewee said that at demonstrations, especially local spontaneous ones, women are often at the front and more militant than men. Demonstrations gave women a chance to prove their strength and bravery. In 2013, in the village of Bugel, one PPLP organiser and several other women formed the first women's farming group (*kelompok tani wan-ita*) in coastal Kulon Progo. Their hope is this group will build the capac-ity of women and facilitate information sharing, to increase their ability to act independently, and work land independently or more equally with their husbands.[46]

Ideological engagements with anarchists, together with the demon-strations of bravery, helped reshape gendered divisions of labour. This is further evidence of the dialectical relationship between social relations of production and activist organisational structure, tactics, ideology and alli-ances. Just as control of land, organisational history, alliances and ideology shape the capacity and desire to resist, so too does resistance reshape those four factors.

Karang Wuni

The exception to the failure of participatory mechanisms to take hold is the village of Karang Wuni, one of the six villages within the mining area. In this village both negotiations to acquire land and *koporasi* were suc-cessful for JMI. There are several factors that explain this: the PPLP was always weaker there; the 'betrayal' of a PPLP organiser; the involvement of NGOs that facilitated participation in corporate processes; the success of the village team; and a reduced ability to withstand intimidation. Initial successes in negotiations for land acquisition and with the *koporasi* sup-ported each other. I will discuss these in sequence below. It is also interest-ing to note that in this village the same collective spirit that led the PPLP to reject mining with such militancy has led to a democratically structured and transparent *koporasi*.

The PPLP and land acquisition in Karang Wuni

JMI conducted negotiations with peasants to acquire land between 2012 and 2013 and signed contracts with all but four families. The PPLP and oppos-ition to the mine was weaker in Karang Wuni from the beginning. PPLP leaders told me that their biggest oversight was not building the organisation there to the level of the other villages. Only a few people from Karang Wuni would attend PPLP events and demonstrations, while local branch meetings suffered from low attendance. On the other hand, a couple of NGOs gained influence and 'deradicalised' or 'tamed' some of the peasants.[47]

There were a couple of key figures who played leadership roles in the Karang Wuni village branch of the PPLP who, at some point, 'changed sides'. These leaders engaged with JMI in negotiations and were involved with NGOs, which encouraged both negotiation with the mining company and land certification to secure farmer's land rights within the complex national and provincial legal systems. Without as strong an organisational base, other PPLP members were less coordinated and militant in their rejection of mining and participation in corporate initiatives. The distinct perspective on NGOs, militancy and negotiation created a split between PPLP organisers in Karang Wuni with those in other villages. According to PPLP organisers, because the organisation was not as strong, people were more easily intimidated or tricked into relinquishing their land.[48]

News of the (former) PPLP organiser selling his use rights to JMI shocked PPLP organisers in the other villages. Described as an influential figure, he became a middleman or broker, encouraging others to relinquish their land too. Before a response could be organised by the PPLP, other peasants followed suit. Among the first was one peasant who owned a larger plot of land and a store. Through quirks of inheritance, he came to own about three times as much land as the average peasant on the coastal strip.[49] His relationship to production and with other peasants changed accordingly as he rented out some land and employed people to work his land.[50] He had more to gain financially from selling land, certification and negotiation with the corporation. After the first wave to accept in early 2013, other peasants followed suit while others tried to hold out. In Karang Wuni, peasants who held out against the mining plans were marginalised within village life. Suliadi (2015, 88–89) quotes one resident stating that 'those who don't agree [with mining] are ostracised. I am not strong enough to face these social sanctions.' Those reluctant to agree felt like they had no other option.

I interviewed one couple who said they were reluctant to relinquish their land even though they could not access it because the surrounding land and access roads were already controlled by JMI. They felt intimidated as excavators would cross into their land and lived in fear of being charged with trespass for walking to their own land. Eventually, they agreed to attend negotiations to see what the offer from JMI would be. They claim they were tricked into signing the agreement to relinquish their land-use rights. They received a one-off payment of Rp75,000 per square metre for 904 square metres of land[51] as well as the loan of an alternative allocation to farm until their original land is returned to them. JMI also has undertaken to return the land to them once mining activities are complete; however, no maximum time is stipulated. At the time of writing, the mine is not operating, yet they are not allowed to use their old land, so it just lies abandoned.[52] Today there are only four families that have not consented to relinquish their land; however, they remain in a stalemate: they cannot access their land because it is surrounded by land controlled by JMI yet have not received compensation either.

Because the contracts with JMI were for the use rights (*hak garap*) (see above) and contained the admission that the Pakualaman royal family is the landowner (*hak milik*), the peasants who did sign contracts are left more vulnerable to further land grabbing. In the village immediately to the west of Karang Wuni, the New Yogyakarta International Airport is currently under construction. Karang Wuni residents worry that their land could be taken again by the Paku Alam for use as hotels, malls and other airport-related infrastructure.[53] Thus the sand iron mining project has triggered land conflicts that have the potential to escalate further beyond the current scope.

The Karang Wuni *koporasi*

The Karang Wuni *koporasi*, formed in 2011, has around 300 members and is further divided into branches, one for each hamlet. Loans, repayments and fees are paid *only* at monthly meetings, which have representation from each of the hamlets (*pedkuhan*). The *koporasi* management board is directly elected by members once a year at their annual general meeting. New members pay a Rp100,000 (AU$9.89) joining fee and each member contributes Rp5,000 (AU$0.49) per month. Members in good standing can borrow up to Rp1 million (AU$98.88),[54] to be paid back over ten months with 1% interest per annum. The maximum limit of the loan can be increased for members who have a good credit rating.[55]

These conditions, especially the requirement that money is only exchanged at monthly meetings, is remarkable. It ensures that this *koporasi* functions transparently to all members. The two members I interviewed were both immensely proud that they had established a transparent and democratic microfinance institution and were continually searching for ways to continue to ensure their *koporasi* operates free of corruption. This, combined with the requirement to pay fees, ensures the active participation of members. These unique processes were designed by members themselves; JMI did not provide strict guidelines about how the *koporasi* should operate.[56]

Inevitably, from 2011, economic interests of Karang Wuni residents began to align with JMI's, smoothing the way for land acquisition negotiations, which started in late 2012. The lack of organised rejection of participation in corporate processes means that there were more people willing to engage in both the *koporasi* and negotiations for land acquisition. The reverse is also true; having relinquished land, peasants needed to access capital to cultivate new land or fund alternative livelihoods, and the *koporasi* provided this opportunity. That is, it helped to smooth the changes in relations of production by funding the creation of alternative avenues for production and reproduction of livelihoods. These practices help make citizens less interested in militantly opposing mining and more likely to demand a

fairer process. They institutionalise alternative means to demand accountability and secure resources while constraining the issues that are available
for discussion.

Peasants in Karang Wuni had established the same patterns of relations
of production and reproduction as those in other villages. However, through
some idiosyncratic circumstances, they were left more receptive to corporate
consultative ideologies of representation. This difference can be explained
further if we return to the theoretical understanding of common sense as

> an amalgam of historically effective ideologies, scientific doctrines and social
> mythologies ... a syncretic historical residue, fragmentary, and contradictory,
> open to multiple interpretations and potentially supportive of very different
> kinds of social visions and political projects.
>
> (Rupert 2006, 93–94)

In all six villages, common sense understandings were based in histories
of Javanese culture; left-nationalist understandings of land; and cooperative and autonomous management of land, production and reproduction.
However, in Karang Wuni, the feudal elements of Javanese culture that
stress deference to elders, upper classes and, above all, the sultan, became
dominant, under the influence of a few landowners who stood to benefit
from the mine's development. This fitted well with modern, individualistic
and corporate ideologies of development and modernity. However, in the
other five villages, deference to the sultan was rejected in favour of traditional Javanese values of land and place and left-nationalist belief in the
right of the people (*rakyat*) to self-determination. These elements were given
additional legitimacy and material support by anarchist allies who helped
expand the struggle to provincial and international scales. In the first village,
peasants lost their land to the mining company, with little compensation,
while in the other five, peasants maintain control and continue to cultivate
their land.

Conclusion

Resistance in coastal Kulon Progo shows how participatory mechanisms
can fail to contain conflict resulting from primitive accumulation – despite
a powerful elite alliance in support of mining. The mode of participation in
this case also significantly differs from those in the other two cases. This is
because of the mining company's close relations with the Sultanate and the
Paku Alam. While still influenced by international governance standards,
ideologies of representation here were more influenced by local feudalism.
This feudalism treated peasants with arrogance, denying them rights to

participate in decisions about mining. Once the mining company realised the mistake of this strategy after peasants began mobilising autonomously from the state and corporation, it was too late and the peasants too powerful.

The basis of the PPLP's power is their organisational capacity directly resulting from the social relationships of production and reproduction developed through collective agricultural experimentation. The capacity and desire of peasants to resist mining are directly related to their control of land, histories of organisation, ideological development and alliances. The independent organisation of the PPLP is rooted in histories of farmers' organisation of finance, production and distribution. This has a strong ideological dimension which has legitimated militant tactics and unconventional alliances with little receptivity to corporate, feudal or consultative ideologies of representation. The PPLP had both the organisational capacity and the belief that they could and should reject any participation in corporate processes. They had the power and alliances to successfully undermine participatory mechanisms and hold off the attempted land grab until the project was suspended.

Even though the mining company's land grab was unsuccessful, it has still disrupted local and even provincial social, economic and political relations. The proposal to mine has triggered latent conflicts over land ownership that until then had no visible expression. With the defeat of the proposal to mine, the main conflict is now about the legitimacy of Sultan Ground/Paku Alam Ground versus peasant rights and the Basic Agrarian Law of 1960. This case also then has implications for literatures on land grabbing and agrarian change in Indonesia and Southeast Asia. However, this is beyond the scope of this book and will be explored elsewhere.

This case demands an emphasis on the importance of the social relations of production and reproduction as factors that create possibilities for action. Rather than a simple source of resources, the relationships that people engage in to make their land productive deeply affect the organisational form of resistance, their ideological development and alliance preferences. Yet the analysis of resistance has also eschewed any deterministic relationship between historical social relations and resistance. Indeed, the examples of LBH's legal training leading to social empowerment and women's participation in resistance leading to changes in gendered divisions of labour show that resistance work also influences the continued evolution of social relations of production and reproduction.

The case of Karang Wuni shows how syncretic common sense understandings of the world can be developed in very different ideological directions. Minor changes in the distribution of land, of leadership quality and ideology can reverse outcomes. In Karang Wuni, corporate participatory mechanisms – the *koporasi* and the village team – have been able to shape how conflict is expressed. Interests between the farmers and the mining company are brought closer together through the loans and work contracts from the *koporasi*. However, it was through negotiations for land acquisition that the company representatives were able to separate out the interests of a couple of influential figures from those who opposed the mine. While this leads some participants to conclude that the conflict has been overcome, it remains latent; the bitterness of the dispossessed may find a new expression in the future. Nevertheless, through participation, the company has negated the risk that conflict poses to its operations in one out of six affected villages. It is also significant that even in the location where resistance is weakest, peasants still have a strong collective, horizontal and independent *koporasi* which they have been able to recreate within corporate participatory mechanisms to smooth disruptions to their social, economic and political conditions. Their independence and organisational experience are manifested within, rather than in opposition to, corporate participatory mechanisms.

Notes

1 *Sosialisasi* could be translated as socialisation or consultation. I use the Indonesian word because 'consultation' connotes a two-way dialog whereas *sosialisasi* is more of an attempt to convince the audience without necessarily asking for their feedback.
2 Throughout this chapter I translate the Indonesian word *petani* as peasant and refer to the small-scale farmers who work their own land and/or land supposedly owned by the Pakualaman royal family as peasants. For further discussion on the politics of peasants and farmers in feudal and capitalist societies, see Wood (1998) and specifically on the Indonesian context, Lucas and Warren (2013).
3 For 3,000ha for 25 years (Yanuardy 2012, 11). The initial CoW spanned eight villages along the south coast of Kulon Progo Regency in the Special Province of Yogyakarta. The two westernmost villages were later excluded because of plans for a state-built airport in that area. Therefore, I only consider events in the six villages that lie west of the Progo River and East of the Bogowonto/ Serang River.
4 Yogyakarta has been ruled by the heads of two royal families, the Sultan and Paku Alam. Since Indonesian independence, Yogyakarta has maintained a special (*istemiwa*) status. It is the only province in Indonesia where the governorship is hereditary, the sultan is the governor and the Paku Alam the vice-governor (Aditjondro 2013; Brown 2003, 63).
5 From December 2014 to October 2015 the price of pig iron in China fell by 30%.
6 See Chapter 4 for detail about changes in Indonesian mining regulations.

7 *Undang-Undang Republik Indonesia No. 5 Tahun 1960 tentang Peraturan Dasar Pokok-Pokok Agraria.*

8 The Treaty of Giyanti ended the sovereignty of Javanese kingdoms and established the Yogyakarta sultanate as subordinate to the Dutch East India Company. Pakualaman was established as a duchy directly responsible to the colonial government in 1813 and given control over territory to the west of the Progo River (Carey 2007, 394; de Jong and Twikromo 2017, 76). This consolidated the pattern of the royal families facilitating land grabs by foreign investors (Brown 2003, 63, 76–77; Meckelburg 2019, 54).

9 *Undang-Undang Republik Indonesia No. 13 Tahun 2012 tentang Keistimewaan Daerah Istimewa Yogyakarta.*

10 Dutch colonial laws Rijksblad Kasultanan No. 16/1918 and Rijksblad Kasultanan No. 18/1918 contained similar provisions and facilitated land grabbing for European-owned factories and plantations before Indonesian independence (Aditjondro 2013, 91).

11 Village head, Kulon Progo, interview with the author, 24 February 2017.

12 PPLP organiser, interview with the author, 27 September 2016.

13 *Brimob* (Mobile Brigade) is Indonesia's paramilitary and riot police force.

14 Shoreline resident, Kulon Progo, interview with the author, 3 March 2017.

15 University student and resident of coastal Kulon Progo, interview with the author, 27 September 2016.

16 Member of Karang Wuni *koporasi*, interview with the author, 3 March 2017.

17 Village head, Kulon Progo, interview with the author, 25 February 2017.

18 PPLP organiser, interview with the author, 21 November 2017.

19 Charged with '*pencemaran nama baik*' (slander or defamation).

20 Solidarity activist, interview with the author, 8 September 2016; see also Aditjondro (2013, 93).

21 Exactly who the attackers were or were hired by is disputed; hamlet head, interview with the author, 3 March 2017.

22 Solidarity activist, interview with the author, 20 September 2016; PPLP organiser, interview with the author, 21 September 2016.

23 PPLP member, interview with the author, 27 September 2016.

24 PPLP organiser, interview with the author, 21 November 2017.

25 These practices are not entirely confined to the regency of Kulon Progo but extend westward along the coast into central and even west Java – the borders are determined by natural geography and history rather than state lines.

26 Javanese word for deprived, sick, uneducated, impoverished people, social outcasts (Widodo 2013).

27 PPLP member, interview with the author, 23 April 2017.

28 PPLP member, interview with the author, 23 April 2017.

29 PPLP member, interview with the author, 23 April 2017.

30 Youth group, interview with the author, 23 April 2017.

31 PPLP member, interview with the author, 23 April 2017.

32 PPLP member, interview with the author, 5 May 2018.

33 Interview with the author, 21 September 2016.

34 Peasant and resident, Kulon Progo, interview with the author, 3 March 2017.
35 Solidarity activist, Yogyakarta, interview with the author, 15 July 2017.
36 Solidarity activist, Yogyakarta, interview with the author, 20 September 2016.
37 Mas Widodo, interview with the author, 21 September 2016.
38 Interviews with three members of PPLP's legal working group, 11 April 2017; LBH Yogyakarta advocate, interview with the author, 13 July 2017.
39 For a detailed discussion of the 'complex, inconsistent, fragmented, unfair and out of touch' system of land law in Indonesia, see Bedner (2016, 64).
40 Interviews with three members of PPLP's legal working group, 11 April 2017; LBH Yogyakarta advocate, interview with the author, 13 July 2017.
41 Solidarity activist, interview with the author, 15 July 2017.
42 Talking about gender and the role of women specifically was the topic of interviews that generated the most divergent responses from participants, therefore these comments are generalisations.
43 Farm labourer, interview with the author, 15 April 2017.
44 PPLP organiser, interview with the author, 12 May 2018.
45 Solidarity activist, Yogyakarta, interview with the author, 8 September 2016.
46 PPLP organiser, interview with the author, 12 May 2018.
47 PPLP member, interview with the author, 24 September 2016.
48 PPLP organiser, interview with the author, 19 April 2017; PPLP organiser, interview with the author, 5 May 2018.
49 The average land holding in Karang Wuni is approximately 0.18ha, with most peasant families owning between 0.08 and 0.26ha.
50 PPLP organiser, interview with the author, 19 April 2017.
51 The total of Rp67.8 million or approximately AU$6,738.
52 Karang Wuni residents, interview with the author, 25 April 2017.
53 PPLP organiser, Karang Wuni, interview with the author, 8 May 2018; peasant and resident, Karang Wuni, interview with the author, 12 May 2018.
54 At average 2013 exchange rates.
55 *Koporasi* member, interview with the author, 9 March 2017; Karang Wuni *koporasi* member, interview with the author, 11 April 2017.
56 *Koporasi* member, interview with the author, 9 March 2017; Karang Wuni *koporasi* member, interview with the author, 11 April 2017.

Conclusion

Extractive accumulation is the collection of processes, from local participatory mechanisms to extractivist strategies and global governance, that
secure the legitimacy and social-governance arrangements ensuring multinational mining corporations' profitability. The theoretical approach in this
book, based in social conflict theory, social reproduction theory, modes of
participation, and the Gramscian concept of common sense, explains the
complexity and diversity in conflict and participation over the social dimensions of mining.

This book has advanced two related arguments:

1. *Multinational mining corporations develop global governance and local
   participatory mechanisms to secure their legitimacy and undermine
   opposition by people affected by mining and non-governmental organisations (NGOs).*

The strategies of mining corporations *and* people affected by mining are
structured by acts of disruption to local economic, social and political relations following acts of primitive accumulation. The evolution of governance
regimes is driven by crises of legitimacy and ongoing cycles of multiscalar
contestation. This directly implicates both corporations and communities in
resistance as governance actors within extractive accumulation.

So, to rephrase the first argument, participatory mechanisms are neither ethical progress nor mere greenwashing. They are a technique used by
multinational mining companies to undermine resistance and create social
relations amenable to extractive accumulation.

2. *People affected by mining will secure more benefit from participation or
   resistance through their control of land, histories of organisation, alliance structures and ideological conceptions of the world.*

Control of land, histories of organisation, alliance structures and ideology
are all internally related through social relations of production and reproduction. Ongoing contestation and participation over land, livelihoods,

ideology and profitability *do not remain confined to local scales but have continuing influence on the evolution of extractivist developmental strategies and global governance networks.* A major implication is that the resistance of people affected by mining, far from being passively determined, is central to the formation of new governance arrangements and the constitution of extractive accumulation.

This Conclusion compares and reviews the theoretical implications of the empirical data of Chapters 2–6. Following this, I expand on implications of this book's findings for social movements and contentious politics, corporate power and global governance, and political participation. I finish by offering reflection on the two most significant issues that any future studies of extractive accumulation would be foolish to ignore: the continued rise of Chinese state-owned corporations and the new boom in critical minerals for green technology.

Primitive accumulation, conflict and scale

The application of the modes of participation framework to the study of multinational mining corporations yields an analysis of their scalar strategies. First is the institutionalisation of modes of participation through standards and mechanisms of corporate self-governance at the global scale (Chapter 2). Second are the specific participatory mechanisms that are implemented at local scales. These are based in globalised modes of participation, influenced by national regulatory regimes and ideologies, but designed in response to local manifestation of conflicts (Chapters 4, 5 and 6). Modes of participation are an attempt to restore or maintain the legitimacy of large-scale corporate mining, contain risky manifestations of conflict, and facilitate changes to political, economic and social relations supportive of extractive capitalism. Participatory mechanisms attempt to change local power relations within affected communities, but they also create new subjectivities, new ideologies and forms of knowledge.

In this book, conflict is understood to originate in acts of primitive accumulation or land grabbing. Yet acts of primitive accumulation have different effects depending on the previous land use of a mining area, the forms of organisation of people affected by mining, and how they relate to pre-existing or latent conflicts (Chapter 1). The establishment of the Kelian mine (Chapter 4) is the most straightforward example of a land grab by a multinational miner entirely disrupting the land and productive, reproductive and subsistence activities of a community. The violent displacement of 4,000 small-scale miners from their land led to them adopting entirely new means of production, reproduction and subsistence, including by making demands of Rio Tinto. The confrontation found multiple expressions as political circumstances, alliances and corporate ideologies shifted.

In Kulon Progo (Chapter 6), the act of primitive accumulation also directly pitted the corporation against peasants within the proposed mining area, and yet was not successful in five out of six affected villages. While peasants militantly rejected the attempted land grab, the proposal triggered latent land conflict between the royal families of Yogyakarta and peasants that then expanded across the province. In Gosowong (Chapter 5), the mining area was forest and there was not a substantial direct threat to the residences or livelihoods of local people. Therefore, the ensuing conflict was concerned with environmental pollution, respect for traditional cultures, and appropriate benefit sharing, and there was less disruption to political, social and economic relations. In each, the original act of primitive accumulation structured the contours of conflict.

In all cases, conflict did not remain confined to local scales, but through alliances with other actors jumped to provincial, national or international scales. In Gosowong (Chapter 5), people affected by mining made a series of shifting alliances with regency politicians and the national NGOs, WALHI and AMAN, in order to extract more benefits from the mine. In Kulon Progo, provincial, national and international alliances played a defensive role by making it harder for the corporation and state actors to use excessive violence during confrontations. However, it is in Kelian (Chapter 4) where the politics of scale are most significant. Alliances were instrumental in bringing the issue to international audiences and forcing KEM to negotiate with people affected by mining. Temporary alliances combined with concurrent challenges from other organisations to Rio Tinto's legitimacy as a responsible corporation and helped prompt the development of a global response to crises. This case was instrumental in the internationalisation of mining activism which drove the reactionary, consultative, participatory agenda of Rio Tinto and coalitions of multinational miners (Chapter 2).

The corporate social responsibility (CSR) techniques developed by Rio Tinto at Kelian with the assistance of the World Bank have since been adopted as global standards, which in turn inform how other mining corporations engage with people in other locations, legitimised through consultative ideologies of representation. Although the primary driver of Newcrest's community development and empowerment program at Gosowong was conflict with local communities, the design of the program was informed by company policy and global standards. The collectively established mode of participation at the global scale thus provides a blueprint for how mining corporations can reconstitute their power in relation to local communities and domestic states. However, rather than being elevated above 'politics', the Gosowong case demonstrates how CSR programs remain susceptible and evolve in reaction to ongoing and new patterns of conflict.

Corporate strategies to undermine resistance

The key strategy of each corporation in response to threatening multiscalar conflicts was to implement participatory mechanisms. Of course, each case also featured violent repression of opposition, yet even in the case of Kelian, where violence was the most severe, participation proved to be a more effective response. A variety of different participatory mechanisms were used: consultation, negotiations for compensation, local employment and procurement agreements, support for *adat*, and education. Conspicuous by its absence from these three cases is any kind of participatory environmental monitoring. Significantly, each corporation implemented participatory community development programs: JMI with microfinance, NHM with its 1% village fund, and KEM with village grants. Although each was structured differently, they all had the effect of generating support and legitimacy for the corporation. They were most effective in gaining legitimacy from people affected by mining where people were already sympathetic or less directly affected – in 27 villages around the Kelian mine, five subdistricts around Gosowong, and Karung Wuni, Kulon Progo – yet had little effect where opposition to the mine was already consolidated.

The common feature of these participatory mechanisms is their base in global governance standards that provide the institutional guidelines and ideological legitimacy for consultative, non-democratic forms of participation at localised corporate sites of participation. Consultative ideologies of representation, and particularistic ideologies where *adat* is concerned, seek the advice of participants or representatives about how to best manage the impacts and opportunities of mining. Corporate consultative ideologies of representation were most successful where they fitted with pre-existing participatory institutions – such as village governance in North Halmahera (Chapter 5). Of course, consultative representation is preferred by mining corporations over democratic representation because they can exclude questions that threaten the continued operation of mining. They operate to smooth conflict and limit what issues are open for discussion and who can discuss them.

Yet, as emphasised in Chapter 2, corporate-sponsored sites of participation are constructed in the shadow of existing and emerging state and autonomous sites of participation. People affected by mining and NGOs strategically choose to either participate in corporate, state or autonomous sites of participation depending on calculated benefits and their capacity.

This shifting between corporate negotiations and legal remedies is a feature of the Kelian and Gosowong cases, while in Kulon Progo peasants opted for purely autonomous participation. Therefore, corporate participatory mechanisms should be designed to offer more benefits or be easier to access than available alternatives.

Land, organisation, alliances and ideology

Participatory mechanisms found varying levels of success in managing conflicts. Here, the reactions of people affected by mining to attempts to elicit their participation are critical. Although there is growing literature detailing what the responses of people affected by mining are to participatory mechanisms, the question of why, how and when groups decide to participate or not, and on what terms, is under-examined (Conde and Le Billon 2017). This section expands on the four factors that I found determine the capacity and desire of people affected by mining to participate or not in corporate processes – all structured by social relations of production. Table 7.1 summarises these findings.

Control of land is the most critical factor in determining the capacity of people affected by mining to resist. Control of land is practical and can be divided into physical control or the ability of groups to exclude other actors; claims which may be based in agrarian law or tradition (*adat*); and legal title or certification. In Kelian, where people affected by mining stood no chance of resisting violent eviction by a combination of military, police and corporate security, it took decades for groups to find alternative sources of power to challenge KEM and demand compensation. In Kulon Progo, peasants' control of their land was not legally recognised – they held no land certificates – however, the density of farming plots together with their physical presence on the land provided them with the capacity to resist not only participation but also the mine's development. In Gosowong, where the mine site was excised from protected forest, people affected by land had neither formal title nor physical control yet were able to establish claims based on traditional ownership as a basis for negotiating compensation.

Following control of land, forms and histories of organisation are the next most crucial factor in the ability of groups of people affected by mining to participate or resist. In Kulon Progo and Kelian, people affected by mining had strong histories of cooperative production, solidarity in social reproduction, and distribution of produce. Their social relations of production, reproduction and subsistence operated independently of state institutions and large capital. These more communal and independent organisational forms transitioned well into organisations of resistance. In the case of Kulon

Table 7.1 Comparison of four factors

Case	Control of land	Histories and forms of organisation	Alliances	Dominant ideologies	Outcome
Kulon Progo 5/6 villages	Yes, legal but uncertified	Cooperative, autonomous from state and corporate capital.	Anarchist networks Legal NGOs Other peasants and groups resisting Sultan Ground	Left-nationalism Javanese 'filosofi tanah' Anarchism	Participation rejected and mining successfully resisted.
Kulon Progo, Karang Wuni	Yes, legal but uncertified	Cooperative, autonomous from state and corporate capital.	Legal and environmental NGOs	Javanese feudalism Developmentalist	Participation not resisted and successful land grab.
Kelian	Yes, informal Evicted by 1992	Cooperative, autonomous from state and corporate capital.	Provincial and national environmental NGOs International NGOs	Left-nationalism Human rights	Eventually successful in negotiating compensation.
Gosowong	No, protected forest	Hierarchical production with state and corporate capital. Cooperative reproduction.	Indigenous peoples' alliance WALHI UNDP Regional politicians	Indigenous rights adat Environmentalism	Secured development goods, but environmental impacts not addressed.

Progo (Chapter 6), peasant groups (*kelompok tani*) which organise production at village and hamlet levels quickly morphed into an effective resistance organisation. In Gosowong, where histories of production and reproduction are bound up in hierarchical forms of rule and appropriation by state actors and capital, organisations were slower to develop and their ability to organise outside corporate and state influence or supervision was curtailed.

Alliances are a further factor in how effectively people affected by mining can campaign if they decide to reject participation – or how much knowledge and support they receive to participate. As mentioned above, national and international allies help conflicts to 'jump scales', where more resources and a wider audience is available. This is especially critical where the opportunities and local sources of power are limited. This is most clear in the Kelian case, because people affected by mining lost their land and livelihoods, and because KEM ensured the support of other villages in West Kutai through community development programs, LKMTL did not have access to resources except the support given by national and international NGOs. The national WALHI alliance including Gosowong, by linking together groups in 13 locations, made it possible to mount a constitutional court challenge to mining in protected forests. Aside from jumping scales, allies also provide material support and knowledge to improve the power of groups within or in opposition to participation. A final important role of alliances is in ideological development. This is most evident in Gosowong, where alliances with both regency politicians and AMAN were based in ideas of defending and promoting *adat* as Indigenous rights. Yet as these alliances proved effective, it also both strengthened *adat* as an organising ideology and facilitated changes in how gender is organised within Pagu culture.

Ideology is the most difficult of the four factors to assess. The ideologies of people affected by mining are both influenced by and influence the three other factors. It is through ideologies, or common sense understandings of the world, that people affected by mining understand their tactics and agency, relationships to land and how they construct organisations and select allies. In Kelian, local organisers looked to redress past grievances and demanded compensation from Rio Tinto. The left-nationalist and even socialist beliefs of LKMTL leadership fitted well with the liberal human rights approach of national and international NGOs, providing common ground to publicise tragedy and claim compensation. Ideologically, both LKMTL and their allies would have preferred a process of justice and accountability; however, the negotiated compensation package was a compromise they had to accept.

Of course, how compatible the common sense understandings of people affected by mining are with consultative ideologies of representation – their ideological receptivity – determines the desire of people affected by mining to participate in corporate processes. In five villages of the Kulon Progo case, the concept of land as a social relation was so central to their understanding of the world (and their livelihoods) that any compromise on this was impossible and they therefore rejected participation.

Ideologies of development, supported by different alliances, stand out as the key factor separating the outcomes in the first five villages from Karang Wuni. In Chapter 6, I explained how common sense understandings of the world are not deterministic but can develop in quite different directions despite similar starting conditions. This depended on how experiences, leadership and outside groups influenced their ideological development, leading one village to accept feudal elements of Javanese culture that stressed deference to the sultan, which fitted well with corporate ideologies of development and modernity, while in the other five villages deference to the sultan was rejected in favour of the PPLP's Javanese '*filosofi tanah*' (philosophy of land) and left-nationalist beliefs in self-determination. In the first village, peasants lost their land to the mining company, with little compensation, while in the other five, peasants maintain control and continue to cultivate their land. Ideological contestation in the field of common sense is tangled with material interests, influencing but not determining decisions and practices of people affected by mining.

The diversity of outcomes

Although the cases examined in this book have many similarities, each produced wildly divergent outcomes. These are explained by the way that acts of primitive accumulation are refracted through evolving contestations over relations of production and social reproduction that spill across multiple political scales. Hence, in coastal Kulon Progo conflict occurred over competing purposes of productive land: it could either be farmed or mined. Peasants believed they were fighting for their lives, hence their slogan '*bertani atau mati!*' (farm or die!). Their capacity and desire based in the four factors discussed above were sufficient to block the mine's development. In Gosowong, conflict and participation are over the distribution of revenues from mining; the land occupied by Newcrest is forest land and the impacts on farming and other productive activities have been either insignificant or indirect. In both Kulon Progo and North Halmahera, the people affected by mining still have access to their land and have adopted more autonomous and representative strategies, respectively. In North Halmahera, this led to obtaining a greater share of benefits of mining.

In Kelian, the small-scale miners and Dayak people were dispossessed of their resources under the New Order dictatorship and they had no power to oppose the military and police violence used to secure the area for Rio Tinto. After *reformasi*, conflict took the form of a campaign to redress previous human rights violations, which entailed participation and mediation. It was the coincidence of international pressure, local mobilisations, the independent investigation and a change in the national regime that opened the political space for LKMTL to act and forced KEM to negotiate compensation. This shows the importance of political context. Under the New Order regime, Rio Tinto could more easily get away with eschewing participation; however, with the emergence of new state-sponsored sites of participation, KEM opened negotiations to avoid the risk of legal action, including potential criminal action against individual managers. For LKMTL and allies, participatory mechanisms were a practical compromise. The justice that they sought was not realistically available. Therefore, when their campaigning led to the offer to participate in negotiations with KEM, they took this opportunity to secure what they could.

The ability of people affected by mining to extract benefits from participation or resistance was the outcome of their ability to exercise power based in their relations of production and social reproduction and how this was amplified or supplemented by alliances. Ideology is the linchpin here, as it determines the receptivity of groups to participatory mechanisms, their desire to participate, resist, or not. But receptivity and desire require the capacity to act, found very practically in control of land and the ability to organise autonomously from state and capital. Alliance then plays the special role of boosting the capacity for action beyond the local scale – a decisive element in resisting or securing more benefits from a mining corporation.

Gendered impacts of mining, participation and resistance

The impacts of conflict, participation and resistance on gendered relations within each affected group was the most varied and unpredictable outcome across the three cases. In Kelian, despite previously enjoying relative equality with male small-scale miners, women were subjected to additional forms of violence and discrimination both during evictions and the mine's operation. Shifts away from communal relations of production, subsistence and reproduction towards corporate and state-mediated development disproportionately disadvantaged women. Unlike in the other two cases, these patterns of disadvantage were not overcome through resistance or participation as there was no social basis for equality.

In Gosowong, NHM's 1% fund reinforced existing social hierarchies, including the dominance of men in village politics. However, the remarkable story of Ibu Afrida shows how the opportunity to participate in the benefits of mining, despite the negative impacts on traditional culture, can produce lasting changes in gendered social and political relations. This also demonstrates how *adat* is not a static traditional construction but may change towards increasing equality, especially when supported by allies. In Kulon Progo, because of the historical gendered division of labour, women were the ones tending the fields and formed the front lines of defence against incursions by the mining corporation. This, combined with long-term engagement with anarcho-feminist allies, led to humble but lasting changes in the gendered division of labour and social reproduction along the five coastal villages. Despite ongoing inequalities, women have now established *kelompok tani wanita* (women's farming groups) and enjoy higher social status compared to before the resistance movement.

While there is much particularity and variance between and among these cases, a closer analysis of gendered impacts of mining, participation and resistance has strengthened and contributed to the theoretical explanation developed in this book. The differentiated power of women and men to participate or resist mining is found in the gendered social relations of production and how these are disrupted by primitive accumulation. However, the gendered division of participation and resistance can also produce changes in social, political and economic relations. Similar conclusions might be drawn about other social divisions, such as age, ethnicity, religion and sexuality and the intersections of these.

For the literature on gendered impacts of mining (Jenkins 2014), these implications follow the call to move past the view of 'women as victims' (Lahiri-Dutt 2011). To move 'beyond victimisation', analysis of gendered legacies of mining must include the effects of participation and resistance that may provide sources of agency (Sinclair 2021). The implication for organisations, regulators and corporations is that gender equality requires deeper changes in economic, political and social structures than compensating for the immediate unequal impacts of mining. Any interventions must be based in awareness of evolving productive and reproductive social relations.

Agency and resistance

The theoretical explanation and empirical data in this book have immediate implications for the study of community–company mining conflicts, but also for the study of corporate power, global governance and political participation more broadly. The most obvious implication for the study of company–community mining conflicts is that understanding the ways that governance standards, corporate policy innovations and participatory mechanisms play out requires actor-oriented methodologies. Institutional interventions, including reform of corporate practices, do not always operate as intended. Participatory mechanisms, including community development programs, are shaped not only by corporate, economic or institutional forces, but the power, decisions and strategies of people affected by mining.

An objective of this research was to move past describing the various reactions and strategies that groups of people affected by mining adopt towards participation to *explain* why, how and when they have the capacity and desire to participate or not. Understanding the diverse outcomes of participation requires an appreciation that the capacity, desires and strategies of people affected by mining matter. This demands an analytical refocusing onto fundamental power asymmetries between actors. The capacity and desire of people affected by mining to participate or not depends on their historically produced social relations of production and reproduction. Empirically, in this study this translated to control of land, forms of organisation, alliance structures and ideological development.

The major implication of this is that the actions and resistance of people affected by mining, far from being passively determined, are central to the formation of new governance arrangements and the constitution of extractive accumulation.

Mining-affected communities can expect better outcomes when they build independent power, either instead of or simultaneous to participating in corporate-controlled mechanisms. There are copious examples of people affected by mining building independent power through grassroots organisations, protest and direct action, alliance building and political campaigning. Maintaining sources of power that are not sanctioned by the state or corporate actors gives mining-affected communities more power to challenge the terms of participation or to demand participation on issues otherwise deemed out of bounds. This is not to suggest that institutional and corporate reform do not matter. Rather, the implication is that improvements in regulation, legislation or corporate policy must be matched by supporting and broadening the base of power of people affected by mining.

To demonstrate these implications, consider free prior informed consent (FPIC) – the most prominent aspirational reform that environmental groups and Indigenous rights campaigners advocate for. FPIC would guarantee people affected by mining the right to consent or reject natural resource projects on their land. If implemented in good faith, FPIC has the potential to upset the dynamics between affected communities and multinational corporations by granting de facto veto rights to communities. This is why the World Bank and multinational mining corporations have deceptively endorsed the right to free prior informed *consultation* (Flemmer and Schilling-Vacaflor 2016).

Prima facie, FPIC might appear to balance corporate power, state sovereignty, and community rights. Aside from documented difficulties with implementation (MacKay 2004; Phillips 2012), we should not expect even radical reforms to transcend the power relations already embedded within contestations over the social dimensions of mining. Where FPIC is granted by a state or international organisation, it is an assertion of power by that institution, ostensibly made in the name of and legitimated by human rights discourse. On the other hand, if communities affected by mining projects mobilise, obtain and assert the power to ensure their consent is respected, they can do this regardless of any institutionalised right to FPIC.

Understanding institutions as the outcome of dynamic social conflict, we cannot expect FPIC to be institutionalised *until* there is a shift in the balance of power between affected communities and mining corporations. Increasing risks to extractive developments that violate the consent of affected people, either on a project level or as a generalised crisis of legitimacy, drive further reform. The point is that groups critical of or opposed to extractive industries will do better to build resilience and alliances to increase their power vis-à-vis mining capital regardless of the existing institutional framework.

Social movements and contentious politics

This book shares a focus on the strategies, motivations and capacities of people affected by mining, local organisations and alliances with social movement literature. Social movement theory approaches to extractive conflicts are valuable for placing these within broader cycles of contentious politics – referred to as 'political opportunity structures', 'resource mobilisation theory' and 'message framing' (e.g. Arce 2014, xvi). This includes the ways that social movements create autonomous sites of participation to build legitimacy and contest the impacts of mining (Dietz 2019). Social movements can then elevate grievances to international scales and create institutional change (Özen and Özen 2009; Byambajav 2015).

Despite much to agree on, the implications of this book are that social movement theory suffers from two blind spots. First, that people affected by mining may resist or participate in ways that are not easily recognisable as 'contentious politics', and may be overlooked by those whose study begins from an analysis of protest movements. This aligns with the political economy literature on 'everyday forms of resistance' and 'everyday political economy' (Scott 1985; Nem Singh and Camba 2016). Second, and most important, social movement scholars are rightly concerned with the capacities of movement organisations, leaders, political opportunities and the processes of resistance (Özen and Özen 2011; Deonandan 2015). However, they are often distracted by moral questions of violent vs non-violent strategies (Kröger 2020). This overlooks the roots of the capacity and desires of

people affected by mining in their social relations of production and reproduction, including historically produced ideologies.

Corporate power and global governance

Much literature on the power of multinational corporations in international
political economy and international relations frames corporate power as
either a zero-sum, in the case of hyperglobalists and sceptics, or positive-sum
game, as in state transformationalist approaches.[1] However, the approach
and empirical results here suggest an analysis of corporate power must go
beyond analyses of globalisation and national-scale conflicts between states
and corporations. Like Welker (2014) and Macdonald (2017), this book
emphasises the ways that corporate power is produced through conflicts
with both local and transnational non-state actors. This understanding is
built on the analysis of corporations as political, social and governance
actors with economic interests (Wilks 2013).

The way that corporations manage their relations with people affected by
their operations and their critics, and the way these techniques are enshrined
in global standards, is the outcome of ongoing and historical conflicts which
traverse multiple political scales. As a collective, multinational mining corporations created governance mechanisms that reconstruct the legitimacy
of the industry as a whole, not merely of individual corporations. The collective exercise of corporate power is important to confront threats of more
stringent regulation by state institutions. Yet this is less about the power
of corporations versus the power of states and more about the competing
interests and powers of corporations versus their critics making opposing
demands of state actors. By epistemologically and methodologically centring conflicts between multinational mining corporations, people affected
by mining and transnational NGOs, global governance is understood as
an expansion of corporate power in response to contestation and crises
(Sinclair 2020).

Although profitability is the primary purpose of corporations, and
although controlling the risks of conflict is undeniably important for profit-
ablility, corporate interests and strategies are not entirely reducible to measurable or predictable effects on profitability. As mining corporations take on
more 'responsibility', their interests expand to include community development and environmental management. This affects an exchange of interest
between mining corporations and people affected by mining. As this cycle
continues, multinational corporations are mutually constituted with the
societies they interact with as they are crisscrossed by diverse interests and
demands (Welker 2014). Participatory mechanisms provide corporations

with the opportunity to enlist community representatives in the service of corporate interests. However, they also provide opportunities for those community representatives to pursue their own interests, sometimes with other community groups and sometimes against the interests of others.

Political participation

The results of this book confirm the explanatory power of the modes of participation framework. I have adapted it to the analysis of corporate sites of participation and explained how modes of participation operate across political scales. This demonstrates that there is fertile ground for applying the framework beyond its proven analysis of political participation as an alternative to democracy in Southeast Asia (Jayasuriya and Rodan 2007; Nguyen 2014; Bal 2015; Rodan 2018).

   Yet, this study also continues to problematise sharp distinctions between 'the state', 'society' and 'corporations'. This emphasises the analytical power of Jessop's (2007, 123) state theory where states are a 'strategic field formed through intersecting power networks'. Indeed, such intersecting power networks also constitute social relations and corporations. For example, in Kulon Progo, the sultan, also the governor of Yogyakarta, owned a significant amount of stock in JMI. In all three cases, boundaries between the state and mining corporations blurred when police and military were paid by the corporations for security services. Even when murders and wrongful arrests, for example, have been proven to have occurred, responsibility is deflected from one party to the other. Therefore, even while demonstrating the utility of corporate sites of participation as an analytical category within the modes of participation framework, these should not be understood as wholly constituted and separate sites. Corporate sites of participation blur into state-sponsored sites and autonomous sites and are constituted in relation to the political opportunities available through alternative sites and modes of participation.

Empirical limitations

The participatory mechanisms, modes of participation and conflicts analysed in this book are immediately relevant to the governance and management of the social dimensions of mining. While multinational corporations in any industry can and do create similar modes of participation, the precise form these take will depend on the historical development and political conflicts surrounding each industry. The degree of success will depend on the dynamic multiscalar contestations surrounding specific issues or industries.

The historic development of global governance in response to crises (described in Chapter 2) that led to the institutionalisation of modes of participation is particular to a subset of powerful multinational corporations. These are the members of the ICMM and signatories to other major international standards and are headquartered in North America, South America, Europe, South Africa, Australia and Japan. Smaller and domestically owned corporations are still influenced by the same global modes of participation, yet they are also more embedded within national and provincial ideologies of representation – as was the case in Kulon Progo. Most importantly, it is yet to be seen how multinational corporations from China, India and Russia will implement CSR in their overseas operations, if they will join existing international associations or if they will create rival standards for participation. The continued growth and influence of China may also 'disturb the international and domestic power relations' (Hatcher 2020, 334) that constitute governance regimes in the extractive industries.[2]

All three cases considered in this book are in Indonesia. I have argued that national legislation and regulation in Indonesia has had little impact on the outcomes of conflict and participation. That is, except in the case of Kelian, where *reformasi* and democratisation were key events in opening opportunities for resistance. This geographic limitation is mitigated by selecting cases from across Indonesia – one in Kalimantan, one in Java and one in Maluku. Each area has very different cultures and economic and political histories, which control for bias. For example, if all had been in Java, it would be almost impossible to separate the effects of corporate participatory mechanisms from the politics of Javanese peasant movements. Yet, while I have argued that we could expect to find similar patterns of conflict in many other countries, the ways that global and regional patterns manifest in different domestic and local contexts remain a matter for empirical investigation.

The point to make about the empirical limitations of this study is that the specific patterns of conflict and participation identified between multinational corporations and people affected by mining in Indonesia should not be extrapolated beyond their limits. However, the framework developed here can continue to be tested and potentially refined to provide insightful explanations for conflict and participation elsewhere and their relationship to dynamic capitalist development.

Future directions

Given the implications and limitations outlined above, there are several directions where future research would prove fruitful. The most immediately obvious avenue is to apply this framework to Chinese-owned multinational mining corporations. As Chinese capital is rapidly expanding internationally, it is critical to understand how different their drivers and mechanisms of participation will be. Especially for state-owned Chinese corporations, will they face a similar crisis of legitimacy to established multinational corporations, or will they produce alternative and competing global standards to manage the environmental and social dimensions of mining?

Especially where Chinese corporations are state owned, what forces will drive integration into or the creation of rival modes of participation at global scales? Early evidence shows that while Chinese mining corporations are not joining international associations or signing up to standards, they are largely conforming to market and social norms of host countries (Gonzalez-Vicente 2012; Carmody 2017). However, if local participatory mechanisms are based in modes of participation institutionalised at the global level, the long-term effects of Chinese refusal to engage global governance associations remains to be seen.

Writing in 2023, a new global boom in exploration and extraction of so-called 'critical minerals' is also underway (Liu et al. 2022; Church and Crawford 2018). This new boom is driven by the urgent need to develop 'green-technologies' like electric vehicles in response to looming climate disaster, but also the powerful forces pushing extractive accumulation within global capitalist systems (Kramarz et al. 2021). What is new and different about 'critical minerals' is their role in new global production networks (GPN) of lithium batteries, electric vehicles and other 'green' technologies (Bridge and Faigen 2022; Bos and Forget 2021). Therefore, future work on extractive accumulation will need a serious engagement with GPNs to understand how the processes of participation, social reproduction and governance in extraction articulate with the energy and auto manufacturing industries.

In conclusion, the overarching, multiscalar political economy analysis of extractive accumulation offers explanations of why new corporate modes of participation emerge and why affected communities decide to participate or resist. The book's findings emphasise the importance of resistance, which is central to the formation of new governance arrangements and the constitution of extractive accumulation. This is an important reminder for scholars, policymakers and activists seeking to address the social and environmental impacts of mining. Increasing the power, agency and organisational capacity of communities affected by mining will be crucial to avoid accelerating land grabbing, pollution, violence and human rights abuse. The new boom in critical minerals and rise of Chinese-based multinational corporations holds great hope of technological and social development away from fossil fuels and climate disaster, but only if communities and activists can organise, resist and create alternative forms of democratic participation in decision-making processes.

Notes

1 See Mikler (2018, 28–33) for a detailed summary of these debates.
2 See Dougherty (2016) on increasing Chinese investment in Latin American extractives.

Glossary

permen	*Peraturan Menteri* – Ministerial regulation.
adat	Traditional or Indigenous systems of law, culture, norms and institutions.
Bertani atau mati!	Farm or die! (PPLP slogan).
Brimob	Mobile Brigade, paramilitary and anti-riot police.
bupati	Regent. The head of a *kabupaten*, elected by citizens.
dana desa	Village fund – dedicated funding paid directly from the national government to village governments for development.
desa	Village, more specifically a defined administrative rural area with an elected head of government, called *kapala desa*. *Desa* are made up of *pedkuhan* (hamlets) and a number of *desa* make up *kecematan* or districts.
kabupaten	Regency. Rural administrative area below province, above district and equivalent to a city.
kecematan	District. Administrative area below province, above village. Sometimes also referred to as a subdistrict.
kelompok tani	Farming group – to coordinate farming activities across a hamlet or village.
kepala desa	Village head. Elected by residents for six-year terms.
koporasi	Cooperative.
Komnas HAM	National Commission for Human Rights.
Menanam adalah melawan!	Farming is fighting! (PPLP slogan).
musyawarah desa	Village consultative assembly. Usually held once a year for village officials to consult residents on development priorities.

Paku Alam	Prince and vice-governor of Yogyakarta, traditional ruler of Pakualaman principality.
penambang rakyat	People's miners. Artisanal and small-scale miners.
petani	Peasant/farmer/agrarian smallholder.
sosialisasi	Socialisation. Unlike in English, *sosialisasi* has more of an intentional connotation, and could include consultation.
preman	Gangsters. Often hired by politicians and corporations to perform dirty work.

References

Abercrombie, Nicholas, Stephen Hill and Bryan S. Turner. 1994. *The Penguin Dictionary of Sociology*. London: Penguin.

ACFOA. 1995. 'Trouble at Freeport: Eyewitness Accounts of West Papuan Resistance to the Freeport-McMoRan Mine in Irian Jaya, Indonesia and Indonesian Military Repression: June 1994 – February 1995'. Canberra: Australian Council for Overseas Aid (ACFOA) [Human Rights Office].

Aditjondro, George Junus. 2013. 'Epilog: SG dan PAG, Penumpang Gelap RUUK Yogyakarta'. In *Menanam Adalah Melawan!*, by Widodo, 91–94. Yogyakarta, Indonesia: Paguyuban Petani Lahan Pesisir Kulon Progo and Tanah Air Beta.

Agustina, Cut Dian, Ehtisham Ahmad, Dhanie Nugroho and Herbert Siagian. 2012. *Political Economy of Natural Resource Revenue Sharing in Indonesia*. Asia Research Centre Working Paper 55. London: London School of Economics & Political Science.

Ali, Saleem H., Damien Giurco, Nicholas Arndt, Edmund Nickless, Graham Brown, Alecos Demetriades, Ray Durrheim et al. 2017. 'Mineral Supply for Sustainable Development Requires Resource Governance'. *Nature* 543 (7645).

Allen, Matthew G. 2018. *Resource Extraction and Contentious States: Mining and the Politics of Scale in the Pacific Islands*. Singapore: Palgrave Macmillan.

AMAN. 2014. 'Cemari Lingkungan, Pemerintah Didesak Putus Kontrak Karya PT NHM'. *AMAN Maluku Utara* (blog). 11 February 2014. http://amanmalut.blogs pot.com.au/2014/02/cemari-lingkungan-pemerintah-didesak_11.html. Accessed 2 April 2024.

Anas, Titik, Hal Hill, Dionisius Narjoko and Chandra Tri Putra. 2022. 'The Indonesian Economy in Turbulent Times'. *Bulletin of Indonesian Economic Studies* 58 (3): 241–71. https://doi.org/10.1080/00074918.2022.2133344.

Angelbeck, Bill. 2008. 'Archaeological Heritage and Traditional Forests within the Logging Economy of British Columbia'. In *Earth Matters: Indigenous Peoples, the Extractive Industries and Corporate Social Responsibility*, edited by Ciaran O'Faircheallaigh and Saleem Ali, 123–41. Sheffield: Greenleaf.

Antlöv, Hans, Anna Wetterberg and Leni Dharmawan. 2016. 'Village Governance, Community Life, and the 2014 Village Law in Indonesia'. *Bulletin of Indonesian Economic Studies* 52 (2): 161–83. https://doi.org/10.1080/00074 918.2015.1129047.

Anugrah, Iqra. 2019. 'Standing for Parliament, and against Mining in Kalimantan'. *New Mandala* (blog). 16 April. www.newmandala.org/standing-for-parliament-and-against-mining-in-kalimantan/. Accessed 19 March 2024.

Arce, Moisés. 2014. *Resource Extraction and Protest in Peru*. Pittsburgh, PA: University of Pittsburgh Press.

Arellano-Yanguas, Javier. 2011. 'Mining and Conflict in Peru; Sowing the Minerals, Reaping a Hail of Stones'. In *Social Conflict, Economic Development and the Extractive Industry: Evidence from South America*, edited by Anthony Bebbington, 89–111. New York: Routledge.

Aspinall, Edward. 2007. 'The Construction of Grievance: Natural Resources and Identity in a Separatist Conflict'. *Journal of Conflict Resolution* 51 (6): 950–72.

———. 2013. 'The Triumph of Capital? Class Politics and Indonesian Democratisation'. *Journal of Contemporary Asia* 43 (2): 226–42. https://doi.org/10.1080/00472336.2012.757432.

———. 2015. 'Inequality and Democracy in Indonesia'. *Kyoto Review of Southeast Asia* 17. http://kyotoreview.org/issue-17/inequality-and-democracy-in-indonesia/. Accessed 19 March 2024.

Aspinall, Edward, and Noor Rohman. 2017. 'Village Head Elections in Java: Money Politics and Brokerage in the Remaking of Indonesia's Rural Elite'. *Journal of Southeast Asian Studies* 48 (1): 31–52. https://doi.org/10.1017/S002246341 6000461.

Atkinson, Jeffrey. 1998. *Undermined: The Impact of Australian Mining Companies in Developing Countries*. Melbourne: Community Aid Abroad.

Atkinson, Jeffrey, Annabel Brown and James Ensor. 2001. *Mining Ombudsman Annual Report 2000–2001*. Melbourne: Oxfam Community Aid Abroad Australia.

Auty, Richard M. 1993. *Sustaining Development in Mineral Economies: The Resource Curse Thesis*. New York: Routledge.

Ayelazuno, Jasper Abembia. 2014. 'The "New Extractivism" in Ghana: A Critical Review of Its Development Prospects'. *Extractive Industries and Society* 1 (2): 292–302. https://doi.org/10.1016/j.exis.2014.04.008.

Bachriadi, Dianto. 1998. *Merana Di Tengah Kelimpahan, Pelanggaran-pelanggaran HAM Pada Industri Pertambangan di Indonesia [Languishing Amongst Abundance, Human Rights Violations in the Indonesian Mining Industry]*. Jakarta: ELSAM.

———, ed. 2012. *Dari Lokal Ke Nasional Kembali, Kembali Ke Lokal: Perjuangan hak atas tanah di Indonesia*. Bandung: ARC.

Bachriadi, Dianto, and Erwin Suryana. 2016. 'Land Grabbing and Speculation for Energy Business: A Case Study of ExxonMobil in East Java, Indonesia'. *Canadian Journal of Development Studies/Revue canadienne d'études du développement* 37 (4): 578–94. https://doi.org/10.1080/02255189.2016.1197825.

Baker, Jacqui. 2013. 'The Parman Economy: Post-Authoritarian Shifts in the Off-Budget Economy of Indonesia's Security Institutions'. *Indonesia* 96 (Special Issue: Wealth, Power, and Contemporary Indonesian Politics): 123–50.

Baker, Janelle Marie, and Clinton N. Westman. 2018. 'Extracting Knowledge: Social Science, Environmental Impact Assessment, and Indigenous Consultation in the Oil Sands of Alberta, Canada'. *Extractive Industries and Society* 5 (1): 144–53. https://doi.org/10.1016/j.exis.2017.12.008.

Bal, Charanpal S. 2015. 'Production Politics and Migrant Labour Advocacy in Singapore'. *Journal of Contemporary Asia* 45 (2): 219–42. https://doi.org/10.1080/00472336.2014.960880.

Ballard, Chris, and Glenn Banks. 2003. 'Resource Wars: The Anthropology of Mining'. *Annual Review of Anthropology* 32 (January): 287–313.

Bank Indonesia. 2023a. 'Nilai ekspor menurut komoditas [Value of export by commodity]'. In *Statistik Ekonomi dan Keuangan Indonesia [Indonesian Economic and Financial Statistics]*. Jakarta: Bank Indonesia. www.bi.go.id/seki/tabel/TABEL5_10.pdf.

———. 2023b. 'Produk Domestik Bruto Menurut Lapangan Atas Dasar Harga Berlaku [Gross Domestic Product by Industrial Origin at Current Prices]'. In *Statistik Ekonomi Dan Keuangan Indonesia [Indonesian Economic and Financial Statistics]*. Jakarta: Bank Indonesia. www.bi.go.id/seki/tabel/TABEL7_1.pdf.

Barron, Patrick, Muhammad Najib Azca and Tri Susdinarjanti. 2012. *After the Communal War: Understanding and Addressing Post-Conflict Violence in Eastern Indonesia*. Yogyakarta, Indonesia: CSPS.

Barrow, C. J. 2010. 'How Is Environmental Conflict Addressed by SIA?' *Environmental Impact Assessment Review* 30 (5): 293–301. https://doi.org/10.1016/j.eiar.2010.04.001.

Batha, Emma. 2000. 'Death of a River'. *BBC*, 15 February, online edition. http://news.bbc.co.uk/2/hi/europe/642880.stm. Accessed 19 March 2024.

Bebbington, Anthony, ed. 2011. *Social Conflict, Economic Development and the Extractive Industry: Evidence from South America*. New York: Routledge.

Bebbington, Denise Humphreys. 2011. 'State-Indigenous Tensions over Hydrocarbon Development in the Bolivian Chaco'. In *Social Conflict, Economic Development and the Extractive Industry: Evidence from South America*, edited by Anthony Bebbington, 134–52. New York: Routledge.

Bedner, Adrian. 2016. 'Indonesian Land Law: Integration at Last? And for Whom?' In *Land and Development in Indonesia: Searching for the People's Sovereignty*, edited by John F. McCarthy and Kathryn Robinson, 63–88. Singapore: ISEAS-Yusof Ishak Institute.

Bezanson, Kate, and Meg Luxton. 2006. *Social Reproduction: Feminist Political Economy Challenges Neo-Liberalism*. Montreal: McGill-Queen's University Press.

Bhattacharya, Tithi. 2017a. 'Introduction: Mapping Social Reproduction Theory'. In *Social Reproduction Theory: Remapping Class, Recentering Oppression*, edited by Tithi Bhattacharya, 1–20. London: Pluto. https://doi.org/10.2307/j.ctt1vz494j.

———, ed. 2017b. *Social Reproduction Theory: Remapping Class, Recentering Oppression*. London: Pluto. https://doi.org/10.2307/j.ctt1vz494j.

Bice, Sara. 2016. *Responsible Mining: Key Principles for Industry Integrity*. New York: Routledge.

Bieler, Andreas, and Adam David Morton. 2018. *Global Capitalism, Global War, Global Crisis*. Cambridge: Cambridge University Press.

Birks, Melanie. 2014. 'Practical Philosophy'. In *Qualitative Methodology: A Practical Guide*, edited by Jane Mills and Melanie Birks, 17–29. London: SAGE.

Bond, Carol, and Lisa Kelly. 2021. 'Returning Land to Country: Indigenous Engagement in Mined Land Closure and Rehabilitation'. *Australian Journal of Management* 46 (1): 174–92. https://doi.org/10.1177/0312896220919136.

Borras, Saturnino M., and Jennifer C. Franco. 2013. 'Global Land Grabbing and Political Reactions "From Below"'. *Third World Quarterly* 34 (9): 1723–47. https://doi.org/10.1080/01436597.2013.843845.

Bos, Vincent, and Marie Forget. 2021. 'Global Production Networks and the Lithium Industry: A Bolivian Perspective'. *Geoforum* 125 (October): 168–80. https://doi.org/10.1016/j.geoforum.2021.06.001.

Breslin, Shaun, and Helen E. S. Nesadurai. 2018. 'Who Governs and How? Non-State Actors and Transnational Governance in Southeast Asia'. *Journal of Contemporary Asia* 48 (2): 187–203. https://doi.org/10.1080/00472 336.2017.1416423.

Bridge, Gavin, and Erika Faigen. 2022. 'Towards the Lithium-Ion Battery Production Network: Thinking beyond Mineral Supply Chains'. *Energy Research & Social Science* 89 (July): 102659. https://doi.org/10.1016/j.erss.2022.102659.

Brown, Colin. 2003. *A Short History of Indonesia: The Unlikely Nation?* Crows Nest, NSW: Allen & Unwin.

Brown, Tamara. 2020. 'Finalisation of Gosowong Sale'. Market Release. Melbourne: Newcrest Mining.

Brueckner, Martin, and Marian Eabrasu. 2018. 'Pinning down the Social License to Operate (SLO): The Problem of Normative Complexity'. *Resources Policy* 59: 217–26. https://doi.org/10.1016/j.resourpol.2018.07.004.

Brueckner, Martin, and Lian Sinclair. 2019. 'International Experiences with Social Licence Contestations'. In *Eco-activism and Social Work: New Directions in Leadership and Group Work*, edited by Dyann Ross, Martin Brueckner, Marilyn Palmer and Wallea Eaglehawk, 111–22. London: Routledge.

Bua, Yuliana Datu. 2004. 'With KEM and the Rio Tinto Foundation'. In *The KEM Experience*, edited by Terry Holland, 126–27. Tasmania: Forty South.

Bünte, Marco. 2018. 'Building Governance from Scratch: Myanmar and the Extractive Industry Transparency Initiative'. *Journal of Contemporary Asia* 48 (2): 230–51. https://doi.org/10.1080/00472336.2017.1416153.

Burton, Bob. 2001. 'When Corporations Want to Cuddle'. In *Moving Mountains: Communities Confront Mining and Globalization*, edited by Geoff Evans, James Goodman and Nina Lansbury, 109–24. Otford, NSW: Mineral Policy Institute and Otford Press.

Byambajav, Dalaibuyan. 2015. 'The River Movements' Struggle in Mongolia'. *Social Movement Studies* 14 (1): 92–97. https://doi.org/10.1080/14742 837.2013.877387.

Čakardić, Ankica. 2017. 'From Theory of Accumulation to Social-Reproduction Theory: A Case for Luxemburgian Feminism'. *Historical Materialism* 25 (4): 37–64. https://doi.org/10.1163/1569206X-12341542.

Campbell, Bonnie, and Pascale Hatcher. 2019. 'Neoliberal Reform, Contestation and Relations of Power in Mining: Observations from Guinea and Mongolia'. *Extractive Industries and Society* 6 (3): 642–53. https://doi.org/10.1016/j.exis.2019.06.010.

Carey, P. B. R. 2007. *The Power of Prophecy: Prince Dipanagara and the End of an Old Order in Java, 1785–1855*, 2nd ed. Leiden, Netherlands: KITLV.

Carmody, Pádraig. 2017. 'The Geopolitics and Economics of BRICS' Resource and Market Access in Southern Africa: Aiding Development or Creating Dependency?' *Journal of Southern African Studies* 43 (5): 863–77. https://doi.org/10.1080/03057070.2017.1337359.

Carroll, Toby, and Darryl S. L. Jarvis. 2015. 'The New Politics of Development: Citizens, Civil Society, and the Evolution of Neoliberal Development Policy'. *Globalizations* 12 (3): 281–304. https://doi.org/10.1080/14747731.2015.1016301.

Casson, Anne. 2001. *Decentralisation of Policies Affecting Forests and Estate Crops in Kutai Barat District, East Kalimantan*. Jakarta: Center for International Forestry Research (CIFOR). https://doi.org/10.17528/cifor/001056.

CFMEU Mining and Energy Division, dir. 1998. *Naked into the Jungle: A Documentary Film on Rio Tinto, Workers and Communities*. Sydney: Summerhill Films.

Chamas, Zena, Farid Ibrahim and Toby Mann. 2022. 'Indonesia Has Passed Laws Banning Sex Outside Marriage. Here's a Breakdown of the New Laws and What Effect They May Have'. *ABC News*, 6 December. www.abc.net.au/news/2022-12-07/indonesia-bans-sex-outside-marriage-explained-criminal-code/101738 418. Accessed 19 March 2024.

Chambers, Peter. 2018. 'Removal of Indo Mines from ASX'. Announcement to shareholders. Sydney: Indo Mines.

Church, Clare, and Alec Crawford. 2018. *Green Conflict Minerals: The Fuels of Conflict in the Transition to a Low-Carbon Economy*. International Institute for Sustainable Development. IISD.org. Accessed 19 March 2024.

Cochrane, Glynn. 2017. *Anthropology in the Mining Industry: Community Relations after Bougainville's Civil War*. Cham, Switzerland: Palgrave Macmillan.

Colbron, Cally. 2016. 'The Sultan of Development?' *Inside Indonesia* (blog). 8 February. www.insideindonesia.org/the-sultan-of-development. Accessed 19 March 2024.

Colley, Peter. 2001. 'Political Economy of Mining'. In *Moving Mountains: Communities Confront Mining and Globalization*, edited by Geoff Evans, James Goodman and Nina Lansbury, 19–36. Otford, NSW: Mineral Policy Institute and Otford Press.

Conde, Marta, and Philippe Le Billon. 2017. 'Why Do Some Communities Resist Mining Projects While Others Do Not?' *Extractive Industries and Society* 4 (2017): 681–97.

Cooke, Bill, and Uma Kothari. 2001. *Participation: The New Tyranny?* London: Zed.

Coumans, Catherine. 2008. 'Realising Solidarity: Indigenous Peoples and NGOs in the Contested Terrains of Mining and Corporate Accountability'. In *Earth Matters: Indigenous Peoples, the Extractive Industries and Corporate Social Responsibility*, edited by Ciaran O'Faircheallaigh and Saleem Ali, 42–66. Sheffield: Greenleaf.

Danielson, Luke. 2002. *Breaking New Ground: Mining, Minerals, and Sustainable Development: The Report of the MMSD Project*. London: Earthscan. http://pubs.iied.org/9084IIED. Accessed 19 March 2024.

Darling, Peter. 1995. 'Kelian – Indonesia's Largest Gold Operation'. *Engineering & Mining Journal* 196 (10): 28–30.

Dashwood, Heather S. 2013. 'Global Private Governance: Explaining Initiatives in the Global Mining Sector'. In *The Handbook of Global Companies*, edited by John Mikler, 456–72. Chichester: John Wiley & Sons.

Davis, Bill W. J. N. 2004. 'KEM's First Leader'. In *The KEM Experience*, edited by Terry Holland, 39. Tasmania: Forty South.

de Jong, Edwin, and Argo Twikromo. 2017. 'Friction within Harmony: Everyday Dynamics and the Negotiation of Diversity in Yogyakarta, Indonesia'. *Journal of Southeast Asian Studies; Singapore* 48 (1): 71–90. http://dx.doi.org.libproxy.murdoch.edu.au/10.1017/S0022463416000485.

d'Hondt, Laure Y. 2010. 'Seeking Environmental Justice in North Maluku: How Transformed Injustices and Big Interests Get in the Way'. *Law, Social Justice and Global Development Journal* 15 (2010): 1–19.

d'Hondt, Laure Y., Sangaji M. Syahril and others. 2010. 'Environmental Justice in Halmahera Utara: Lost in Poverty, Interests and Identity'. https://openaccess.leidenuniv.nl/handle/1887/18052. Accessed 19 March 2024.

Deonandan, Kalowatie. 2015. 'Evaluating the Effectiveness of the Anti-Mining Movement in Guatemala: The Role of Political Opportunities and Message Framing'. *Canadian Journal of Latin American and Caribbean Studies/Revue canadienne des études latino-américaines et caraïbes* 40 (1): 27–47. https://doi.org/10.1080/08263663.2015.1031472.

Devi, Bernadetta, and Dody Prayogo. 2013. 'Mining and Development in Indonesia: An Overview of the Regulatory Framework and Policies'. International Mining for Development Centre. http://im4dc.org/wp-content/uploads/2013/09/Mining-and-Development-in-Indonesia.pdf. Accessed 19 March 2024.

Dietz, Kristina. 2019. 'Direct Democracy in Mining Conflicts in Latin America: Mobilising against the La Colosa Project in Colombia'. *Canadian Journal of Development Studies/Revue canadienne d'études du développement* 40 (2): 145–62. https://doi.org/10.1080/02255189.2018.1467830.

Digges, Andrew, and Steven Brown. 2021. 'Managing the EV Nickel Pickle'. *Transition Economist*, 15 December. https://pemedianetwork.com/hydrogen-economist/articles/sponsored-content/2021/managing-the-ev-nickel-pickle/. Accessed 19 March 2024.

DISR. 2023. 'Critical Minerals Strategy 2023–2030'. Australian Government Department of Industry, Science and Resources. www.industry.gov.au/sites/default/files/2023-06/critical-minerals-strategy-2023-2030.pdf. Accessed 19 March 2024.

Doornbos, Martin. 2001. '"Good Governance": The Rise and Decline of a Policy Metaphor?' *Journal of Development Studies* 37 (6): 93–108.

Dougherty, Michael L. 2016. 'From Global Peripheries to the Earth's Core: The New Extraction in Latin America'. In *Mining in Latin America: Critical Approaches to the New Extraction*, edited by Kalowatie Deonandan and Michael L. Dougherty, 3–24. London: Routledge.

Down to Earth. 2004. 'Mining in Protected Forests – Government Gives Way to Mining Industry Pressure'. *Down to Earth* (blog). May. www.downtoearth-indonesia.org/story/mining-protected-forests-government-gives-way-mining-industry-pressure. Accessed 19 March 2024.

———. 2005. 'Legal Challenge to Mining in Protected Forests'. *Down to Earth* (blog). May. www.downtoearth-indonesia.org/story/legal-challenge-mining-protected-forests. Accessed 19 March 2024.

Drake, Phillip. 2012. *Composing Disaster/Disastrous Compositions: Nature, Politics and Indonesia's Mud Volcano.* Ph.D. thesis, University of Hawai'i.

———. 2016. *Indonesia and the Politics of Disaster: Power and Representation in Indonesia's Mud Volcano.* London: Routledge. https://doi.org/10.4324/978131 5525136.

Duncan, Christopher R. 2003. 'Untangling Conversion: Religious Change and Identity among the Forest Tobelo of Indonesia'. *Ethnology* 42 (4): 307. https://doi.org/10.2307/3773831.

———. 2007. 'Mixed Outcomes: The Impact of Regional Autonomy and Decentralization on Indigenous Ethnic Minorities in Indonesia'. *Development and Change* 38 (4): 711–33.

———. 2013. *Violence and Vengeance: Religious Conflict and Its Aftermath in Eastern Indonesia.* Ithaca, NY: Cornell University Press.

Eames, Mike. 2017. 'Newcrest Joins ICMM as Its 25th Company Member'. International Council on Mining and Metals, 1 November 2017, Media Release edition. www.icmm.com/en-gb/news/2017/newcrest-joins-icmm. Accessed 25 March 2018.

EITI Indonesia. 2022. *Report of EITI Indonesia 2019–2020.* Jakarta: Extractive Industries Transparency Initiative Indonesia. https://eiti.org/documents/indonesia-2019-2020-eiti-report. Accessed 19 March 2024.

Elbra, Ainsley. 2014. 'Interests Need Not Be Pursued If They Can Be Created: Private Governance in African Gold Mining'. *Business and Politics* 16 (2): 247–66. https://doi.org/10.1515/bap-2013-0021.

———. 2017. *Governing African Gold Mining: Private Governance and the Resource Curse.* London: Springer.

Elias, Juanita, John M. Hobson, Lena Rethel and Leonard Seabrooke. 2016. 'Conclusion'. In *The Everyday Political Economy of Southeast Asia*, edited by Juanita Elias and Lena Rethel, 239–60. Cambridge: Cambridge University Press.

Elias, Juanita, and Lena Rethel. 2016. *The Everyday Political Economy of Southeast Asia.* Cambridge: Cambridge University Press.

Engels, Friedrich. 1986. *The Origin of the Family, Private Property and the State.* London: Penguin.

Engineering & Mining Journal. 2014. 'Weighing the Costs of Indonesia's Export Ban'. *Engineering & Mining Journal* 215 (9): 103–7.

Erb, Maribeth. 2016. 'Mining and the Conflict over Values in Nusa Tenggara Timur Province, Eastern Indonesia'. *Extractive Industries and Society* 3 (2): 370–82. https://doi.org/10.1016/j.exis.2016.03.003.

Escobar, Arturo. 2001. 'Culture Sits in Places: Reflections on Globalism and Subaltern Strategies of Localization'. *Political Geography* 20 (2): 139–74. https://doi.org/10.1016/S0962-6298(00)00064-0.

Evans, Geoff, James Goodman and Nina Lansbury. 2001. 'Introduction'. In *Moving Mountains: Communities Confront Mining and Globalization*, edited by Geoff Evans, James Goodman and Nina Lansbury. Otford, NSW: Mineral Policy Institute and Otford Press.

Everingham, Jo-Anne, Deanna Kemp, Saleem Ali, Gillian Cornish, Marcia Langton and Bruce Harvey. 2016. *Why Agreements Matter: A Resource Guide for Integrating Agreements into Communities and Social Performance Work at Rio Tinto.* Melbourne: Rio Tinto in partnership with the Centre for Social Responsibility in Mining, University of Queensland. https://cdn-rio.dataweavers.io/-/media/content/documents/sustainability/corporate-policies/rt-why-agreements-matter.pdf?rev=005e2e8256c948c49e454dfea246b3cd. Accessed 3 April 2024.

Fanthorpe, Richard, and Christopher Gabelle. 2013. *Political Economy of Extractives Governance in Sierra Leone.* World Bank. https://openknowledge.worldbank.org/handle/10986/16726. Accessed 19 March 2024.

Federici, Silvia Beatriz. 2004. *Caliban and the Witch.* New York: Autonomedia.

Ferguson, Sarah, dir. 2016. 'Catastrophic Failure'. *Four Corners.* Sydney: ABC Television. www.abc.net.au/news/2016-03-01/catastrophic-failure/7199824. Accessed 19 March 2024.

Fife, Wayne. 2005. *Doing Fieldwork: Ethnographic Methods for Research in Developing Countries and Beyond.* Basingstoke: Palgrave Macmillan.

Filer, Colin, John Burton and Glenn Banks. 2008. 'The Fragmentation of Responsibilities in the Melanesian Mining Sector'. In *Earth Matters: Indigenous Peoples, the Extractive Industries and Corporate Social Responsibility*, edited by Ciaran O'Faircheallaigh and Saleem Ali, 163–79. Sheffield: Greenleaf.

Filer, Colin, and Pierre-Yves Le Meur, eds. 2017. *Large-Scale Mines and Local-Level Politics: Between New Caledonia and Papua New Guinea.* Canberra: ANU Press.

Filer, Colin, and Martha Macintyre. 2006. 'Grass Roots and Deep Holes: Community Responses to Mining in Melanesia'. *Contemporary Pacific* 18 (2): 215–32.

Filippini, Michele. 2017. *Using Gramsci: A New Approach.* Translated by Patrick J. Barr. London: Pluto.

Fjellborg, Daniel, Karin Beland Lindahl and Anna Zachrisson. 2022. 'What to Do When the Mining Company Comes to Town? Mapping Actions of Anti-Extraction Movements in Sweden, 2009–2019'. *Resources Policy* 75 (March): 102514. https://doi.org/10.1016/j.resourpol.2021.102514.

Flemmer, Riccarda, and Almut Schilling-Vacaflor. 2016. 'Unfulfilled Promises of the Consultation Approach: The Limits to Effective Indigenous Participation in Bolivia's and Peru's Extractive Industries'. *Third World Quarterly* 37 (1): 172–88. https://doi.org/10.1080/01436597.2015.1092867.

Fletcher, Brett. 2012. 'Welcome to Gosowong Gold Mine'. Presented at the OZMINE 2012 Sustainable and Responsible Mining: ASEAN and Australia in Synergy, Jakarta, 17 April. https://web.archive.org/web/20140225064838/https://www.austrade.gov.au/ArticleDocuments/1418/ozmine2012-Terry-Pilch-Presentation.pdf.aspx. Accessed 3 April 2024.

Fox, Jonathan A., and L. Dave Brown. 2000. *The Struggle for Accountability: The World Bank, NGOs, and Grassroots Movements*, 2nd ed. Cambridge, MA: MIT Press.

Franks, Daniel M., Rachel Davis, Anthony J. Bebbington, Saleem H. Ali, Deanna Kemp and Martin Scurrah. 2014. 'Conflict Translates Environmental and Social Risk into Business Costs'. *Proceedings of the National Academy of Sciences of the United States of America* 111 (21): 7576–81.

Frederiksen, Tomas, and Matthew Himley. 2020. 'Tactics of Dispossession: Access, Power, and Subjectivity at the Extractive Frontier'. *Transactions of the Institute of British Geographers* 45 (1): 50–64. https://doi.org/10.1111/tran.12329.

Freischlad, Nadine. 2022. 'Mud to Musk: Bakrie & Brothers Plans Comeback with EV Play'. *The Ken Southeast Asia*, 26 July. https://the-ken.com/sea/story/mud-to-musk-bakrie-brothers-plans-comeback-with-ev-play/. Accessed 19 March 2024.

GBA. 2022. 'GBA Battery Passport: The Human Rights Index'. Version 1.0. Global Battery Alliance. www.globalbattery.org/media/publications/gba-humanrightsindex-v1rev1.pdf. Accessed 19 March 2024.

Gellert, Paul K. 2019. 'Neoliberalism and Altered State Developmentalism in the Twenty-First Century Extractive Regime of Indonesia'. *Globalizations* 16 (6): 894–918. https://doi.org/10.1080/14747731.2018.1560189.

Ghifari, Deni. 2023. 'Indonesia Braces for Possible WTO Case over Bauxite Export Ban'. *Jakarta Post*, 19 June, online edition. www.thejakartapost.com/business/2023/06/19/indonesia-braces-for-possible-wto-case-from-china-over-bauxite-export-ban.html. Accessed 19 March 2024.

Gobby, Jen, Leah Temper, Matthew Burke and Nicolas von Ellenrieder. 2022. 'Resistance as Governance: Transformative Strategies Forged on the Frontlines of Extractivism in Canada'. *Extractive Industries and Society* 9 (March): 100919. https://doi.org/10.1016/j.exis.2021.100919.

Golder Associates. 2015. *Gosowong Gold Mine Rectification Audit Summary Audit Report.* https://web.archive.org/web/20201029102734/https://www.cyanidecode.org/sites/default/files/pdf/NewcrestGosowongSAR2015.pdf. Accessed 3 April 2024.

Gonzalez-Vicente, Ruben. 2012. 'Mapping Chinese Mining Investment in Latin America: Politics or Market?' *China Quarterly* 209 (March): 35–58. https://doi.org/10.1017/S0305741011001470.

Government of Indonesia and The United Nations Development Programme. 2007. *Legal Empowerment and Assistance for the Disadvantaged (LEAD) Project Document.* Jakarta. https://web.archive.org/web/20220714050649/https://info.undp.org/docs/pdc/Documents/IDN/00043641_LEAD.pdf. Accessed 3 April 2024.

Gramsci, Antonio. 1971. *Selections from the Prison Notebooks.* Edited and translated by Hoare Quentin and Geoffery Nowell-Smith. New York: International Publishers.

———. 1996. *Prison Notebooks.* Edited and translated by Joseph A. Buttigieg. Vol. 2. 3 vols. New York: Columbia University Press.

Green, Marshall. 1965. 'Telegram 1290 from American Embassy Jakarta'. Jakarta: American Embassy. https://nsarchive.gwu.edu/document/15705-document-9-telegram-1290-american-embassy. Accessed 3 April 2024.

Grzybowski, Alex. 2012. *Extractive Industries and Conflict: Toolkit and Guidance for Preventing and Managing Land and Natural Resource Conflict.* The United Nations Interagency Team for Preventative Action. www.un.org/en/land-natural-resources-conflict/pdfs/GN_Extractive.pdf. Accessed 19 March 2024.

Guáqueta, Alexandra. 2013. 'Harnessing Corporations: Lessons from the Voluntary Principles on Security and Human Rights in Colombia and Indonesia'. *Journal of Asian Public Policy* 6 (2): 129–46. https://doi.org/10.1080/17516234.2013.814306.

Guarneros-Meza, Valeria. 2022. 'Governance, Participation, and Hegemony: Governing Cananea and the Sonora River Region'. *Latin American Perspectives*, June, 0094582X221106146. https://doi.org/10.1177/0094582X221106146.

Guggenheim, Scott. 2006. 'Crises and Contradictions: Understanding the Origins of a Community Development Project in Indonesia'. In *The Search for Empowerment: Social Capital as Idea and Practice at the World Bank*, edited by Anthony Bebbington, Michael Woolcock and Scott Guggenheim, 111–44. Bloomfield, CT: Stylus.

Guichaoua, Yvan. 2012. 'Elites' Survival and Natural Resource Exploitation in Nigeria and Niger'. In *The Developmental Challenges of Mining and Oil: Lessons from Africa and Latin America*, edited by Rosemary Thorp, Stefania Battistelli, Yvan Guichaoua, Jose Carlos Orihuela and Martiza Pardes, 131–67. New York: Palgrave Macmillan.

Hadiz, Vedi R. 2010. *Localising Power in Post-Authoritarian Indonesia: A Southeast Asia Perspective.* Stanford, CA: Stanford University Press.

Hadiz, Vedi R., and Richard Robison. 2013. 'The Political Economy of Oligarchy and the Reorganization of Power in Indonesia'. *Indonesia* 96 (1): 35–57. https://doi.org/10.5728/indonesia.96.0033.

Hall, Derek. 2013. 'Primitive Accumulation, Accumulation by Dispossession and the Global Land Grab'. *Third World Quarterly* 34 (9): 1582–1604. https://doi.org/10.1080/01436597.2013.843854.

Hall, Rebecca Jane. 2016. 'Reproduction and Resistance: An Anti-Colonial Contribution to Social-Reproduction Feminism'. *Historical Materialism* 24 (2): 87–110. https://doi.org/10.1163/1569206X-12341473.

Hall, Ruth, Marc Edelman, Saturnino M. Borras, Ian Scoones, Ben White and Wendy Wolford. 2015. 'Resistance, Acquiescence or Incorporation? An Introduction to Land Grabbing and Political Reactions "from Below"'. *Journal of Peasant Studies* 42 (3–4): 467–88. https://doi.org/10.1080/03066 150.2015.1036746.

Hamby, Chris. 2016. 'The Billion-Dollar Ultimatum. 2. Secrets of a Global Super Court'. *BuzzFeed News*. Online. www.buzzfeed.com/chrishamby/the-billion-dol lar-ultimatum. Accessed 19 March 2024.

Hameiri, Shahar. 2019. 'Institutionalism beyond Methodological Nationalism? The New Interdependence Approach and the Limits of Historical Institutionalism'. *Review of International Political Economy*. https://doi.org/10.1080/09692 290.2019.1675742.

Hameiri, Shahar, and Lee Jones. 2015. *Governing Borderless Threats: Non-Traditional Security and the Politics of State Transformation*. Cambridge: Cambridge University Press.

———. 2020. 'Theorising Political Economy in Southeast Asia'. In *The Political Economy of Southeast Asia: Politics and Uneven Development under Hyperglobalisation*, edited by Toby Carroll, Shahar Hameiri and Lee Jones, 4th ed. Cham, Switzerland: Palgrave Macmillan. https://doi.org/10.1007/ 978-3-030-28255-4.

Hameiri, Shahar, Caroline Hughes and Fabio Scarpello. 2017. *International Intervention and Local Politics: Fragmented States and the Politics of Scale*. Cambridge: Cambridge University Press.

Hanlon, Gerard. 2008. 'Rethinking Corporate Social Responsibility and the Role of the Firm – On the Denial of Politics'. In *The Oxford Handbook of Corporate Social Responsibility*, edited by Andrew Crane, Abagail McWilliams, Dirk Matten, Jeremy Moon and Donald S. Siegel, 156–72. Oxford: Oxford University Press.

Harker, John. 2003. 'Intervention is Served: The US Federal Alien Torts Claims Act and the Irony of Ironies'. *Cambridge Review of International Affairs* 16 (1): 155–64. https://doi.org/10.1080/0955757032000075762.

Harsono, Norman. 2020. 'Explainer: New Rules in Revised Mining Law'. *Jakarta Post*, 14 May, online edition. www.thejakartapost.com/news/2020/05/14/explainer-new-rules-in-revised-mining-law.html. Accessed 19 March 2024.

Harvey, David. 2003. *New Imperialism*. London: Oxford University Press.

Hatcher, Pascale. 2012. 'Taming Risks in Asia: The World Bank Group and New Mining Regimes'. *Journal of Contemporary Asia* 42 (3): 427–46. https://doi.org/ 10.1080/00472336.2012.687630.

———. 2014. *Regimes of Risk: The World Bank and the Transformation of Mining in Asia*. New York: Palgrave Macmillan.

———. 2015. 'Neoliberal Modes of Participation in Frontier Settings: Mining, Multilateral Meddling, and Politics in Laos'. *Globalizations* 12 (3): 322–46. https://doi.org/10.1080/14747731.2015.1016305.

———. 2020. 'The Political Economy of Southeast Asia's Extractive Industries: Governance, Power Struggles and Development Outcomes'. In *The Political Economy of Southeast Asia: Politics and Uneven Development under Hyperglobalisation*, edited by Toby Carroll, Shahar Hameiri and Lee Jones, 4th ed. Cham, Switzerland: Palgrave Macmillan. https://doi.org/10.1007/ 978-3-030-28255-4.

Hatcher, Pascale, and Etienne Roy Grégoire. 2022. 'Governance of Extractive Industries'. In *Handbook on Governance and Development*, edited by Wil Hout and Jane Hutchinson. Cheltenham: Edward Elgar. https://doi.org/10.4337/9781789908756.00029.

Haufler, Virginia. 2017. 'Governing Conflict through Transnational Corporations: The Case of Conflict Minerals'. In *Transnational Actors in War and Peace: Militants, Activists, and Corporations in World Politics*, edited by David Malet and Miriam J. Anderson, 61–83. Washington, DC: Georgetown University Press.

Heiner, Michael, David Hinchley, James Fitzsimons, Frank Weisenberger, Wayne Bergmann, Tina McMahon, Joseph Milgin et al. 2019. 'Moving from Reactive to Proactive Development Planning to Conserve Indigenous Community and Biodiversity Values'. *Environmental Impact Assessment Review* 74 (January): 1–13. https://doi.org/10.1016/j.eiar.2018.09.002.

Hernawan, rf Koes, Cahyo Purnomo Edi, Lusia Arumingtyas, Mariyana Ricky and Soetana Monang Hasibuan. 2021. 'Indonesian Farmers Resisting an Iron Mine Run up against a Sultan'. *Mongabay Environmental News*, 28 October. https://news.mongabay.com/2021/10/indonesian-farmers-resisting-an-iron-mine-run-up-against-a-sultan/. Accessed 19 March 2024.

Hickey, Samuel, and Giles Mohan. 2005. 'Relocating Participation within a Radical Politics of Development'. *Development and Change* 36 (2): 237–62.

Hobson, John M., and Leonard Seabrooke. 2001. 'Everyday IPE: Revealing Everyday Forms of Change in the World Economy'. In *Everyday Politics of the World Economy*, edited by John M. Hobson and Leonard Seabrooke, 1–24. Cambridge: Cambridge University Press. https://doi.org/10.1017/CBO9780511491375.001.

Hopes, Michael. 2004a. 'KEM's Pioneer Women'. In *The KEM Experience*, edited by Terry Holland, 48. Tasmania: Forty South.

———. 2004b. 'Pius, the Man'. In *The KEM Experience*, edited by Terry Holland, 178–79. Tasmania: Forty South.

———. 2004c. 'The Early Days from the 1940s to the Mid-1980s'. In *The KEM Experience*, edited by Terry Holland, 23–24. Tasmania: Forty South.

Horowitz, Leah S. 2008. '"It's up to the Clan to Protect": Cultural Heritage and the Micropolitical Ecology of Conservation in New Caledonia'. *Social Science Journal* 45 (2): 258–78. https://doi.org/10.1016/j.soscij.2008.03.005.

———. 2011. 'Interpreting Industry's Impacts: Micropolitical Ecologies of Divergent Community Responses'. *Development and Change* 42 (6): 1379–91. https://doi.org/10.1111/j.1467-7660.2011.01740.x.

———. 2015. 'Culturally Articulated Neoliberalisation: Corporate Social Responsibility and the Capture of Indigenous Legitimacy in New Caledonia'. *Transactions of the Institute of British Geographers* 40 (1): 88–101. https://doi.org/10.1111/tran.12057.

Huber, Isabelle. 2022. 'Indonesia's Battery Industrial Strategy'. *Centre for Strategic and International Studies*, 4 February. www.csis.org/analysis/indonesias-battery-industrial-strategy. Accessed 19 March 2024.

Hutchison, Jane, and Ian Wilson. 2020. 'Poor People's Politics in Urban Southeast Asia'. In *The Political Economy of Southeast Asia: Politics and Uneven Development under Hyperglobalisation*, edited by Toby Carroll, Shahar Hameiri and Lee Jones, 4th ed. Cham, Switzerland: Palgrave Macmillan. https://doi.org/10.1007/978-3-030-28255-4.

Hutchison, Jane, Wil Hout, Caroline Hughes and Richard Robison. 2014. *Political Economy and the Aid Industry in Asia*. Basingstoke: Palgrave Macmillan.

ICEM. 1997. *Rio Tinto Tainted Titan: The Stakeholders' Report*. Brussels: International Federation of Chemical, Energy, Mine and General Workers' Unions.

ICMM. 2015. 'Sustainable Development Framework: ICMM Principles', revised ed. London: International Council on Mining and Metals. https://web.archive.org/web/20200226000737/https://www.icmm.com/website/publications/pdfs/comm itments/revised-2015_icmm-principles.pdf. Accessed 3 April 2024.

———. 2022. *Mining Contribution Index* (MCI), 6th ed. London: International Council on Mining and Metals. www.icmm.com/website/publications/pdfs/social-performance/2022/research_mci-6-ed.pdf?cb=16134. Accessed 19 March 2024.

———. 2023. *Mining Principles Performance Expectations*. London: International Council on Mining and Metals. www.icmm.com/website/publications/pdfs/min ing-principles/mining-principles.pdf?cb=59962. Accessed 19 March 2024.

———. n.d. 'Our History'. *International Council on Metals and Mining* (blog). https://web.archive.org/web/20200527151740/https://www.icmm.com/en-gb/about-us/our-organisation/annual-reviews/our-history. Accessed 3 April 2024.

———. n.d. 'Our Members'. International Council on Mining and Metals. www.icmm.com/en-gb/our-story/our-members. Accessed 16 October 2023.

IEA. 2022. *The Role of Critical Minerals in Clean Energy Transitions*. Revised version. The International Energy Agency. www.iea.org/data-and-statistics/data-product/the-role-of-critical-minerals-in-clean-energy-transitions-2. Accessed 19 March 2024.

Indo Mines Ltd. 2006. *Annual Report*. https://web.archive.org/web/20230303114 306/www.indomines.com.au/assets/Uploads/Annual-Report-2006.pdf. Accessed 3 April 2024.

———. 2008. *Annual Report*. https://web.archive.org/web/20231028064628/http://www.indomines.com.au/assets/Uploads/2008-Annual-Report.pdf. Accessed 3 April 2024.

———. 2009. *Annual Report*. https://web.archive.org/web/20231028064810/http://www.indomines.com.au/assets/Uploads/091030-Annual-Report.pdf. Accessed 3 April 2024.

———. 2012. *Annual Report*. https://web.archive.org/web/20180320092031/http://www.indomines.com.au/assets/release/2012/2012-Annual-Report2.pdf. Accessed 3 April 2024.

———. 2014. *Annual Report*. https://web.archive.org/web/20180320092021/http://www.indomines.com.au/investor-relations/annual-reports/period/2014. Accessed 3 April 2024.

———. 2015. *Annual Report*. https://web.archive.org/web/20180320092016/http://www.indomines.com.au/investor-relations/annual-reports/period/2015. Accessed 3 April 2024.

———. 2016. *Annual Report*. https://web.archive.org/web/20180320092011/http://www.indomines.com.au/investor-relations/annual-reports/period/2016. Accessed 3 April 2024.

International Cyanide Management Institute. n.d. 'Environmental & Health Effects'. In *Cyanide Facts*. International Cyanide Management Institute. https://cyanidec ode.org/cyanide-facts. Accessed 27 February 2018.

International Longshore and Warehouse Union. 2010. 'Rio Tinto: A Shameful History of Human and Labour Rights Abuses and Environmental Degradation

Around the Globe'. *London Mining Network* (blog). 20 April. http://londonmi ningnetwork.org/2010/04/rio-tinto-a-shameful-history-of-human-and-labour-rights-abuses-and-environmental-degradation-around-the-globe/. Accessed 19 March 2024.

IRMA. 2018. 'IRMA Standard for Responsible Mining'. Initiative for Responsible Mining Assurance. https://responsiblemining.net/wp-content/uploads/2018/07/IRMA_STANDARD_v.1.0_FINAL_2018-1.pdf. Accessed 19 March 2024.

Jaskoski, Maiah. 2020. 'Participatory Institutions as a Focal Point for Mobilizing: Prior Consultation and Indigenous Conflict in Colombia's Extractive Industries'. *Comparative Politics* 52 (4): 537–56.

———. 2022. *The Politics of Extraction: Territorial Rights, Participatory Institutions, and Conflict in Latin America*. Oxford: Oxford University Press.

JATAM. 2009. 'JATAM Condemns the Violence at a Proposed Australian-Owned Iron Mine'. Translation: www.minesandcommunities.org/article.php?a=9631. Accessed 19 March 2024.

———. 2020. 'Omnibus Law: Oligarch's Legal Holy Book * JATAM'. *JATAM* (blog). 17 October. www.jatam.org/en/omnibus-law-oligarchs-legal-holy-book/. Accessed 19 March 2024.

———. 2022. 'Sufferings of Residents and Environment behind the Business Transactions of Tesla and Chinese Companies in Indonesia * JATAM'. *JATAM* (blog). 10 August. www.jatam.org/en/sufferings-of-residents-and-environment-behind-the-business-transactions-of-tesla-and-chinese-companies-in-indonesia/. Accessed 19 March 2024.

Jati, Wasisto Raharjo. 2013. 'Predatory Regime Dalam Ranah Lokal: Konflik Pasir Besi Di Kabupaten Kulon Progo'. *Jurnal Demokrasi Dan HAM* 10 (1): 85–111.

Jayasuriya, Kanishka, and Garry Rodan. 2007. 'Beyond Hybrid Regimes: More Participation, Less Contestation in Southeast Asia'. *Democratization* 14 (5): 773–94. https://doi.org/10.1080/13510340701635647.

Jenkins, Katy. 2014. 'Women, Mining and Development: An Emerging Research Agenda'. *Extractive Industries and Society* 1 (2): 329–39. https://doi.org/10.1016/j.exis.2014.08.004.

Jessop, Bob. 2006a. 'Gramsci as a Spatial Theorist'. In *Images of Gramsci: Connections and Contentions in Political Theory and International Relations*, edited by Andreas Bieler and Adam David Morton, 27–43. New York: Routledge.

———. 2006b. *The Strategic-Relational Approach: An Interview with Bob Jessop Interview by Joo Hyoung Ji*. http://bobjessop.org/2014/12/02/the-strategic-rel ational-approach-an-interview-with-bob-jessop/. Accessed 19 March 2024.

———. 2007. *State Power*. Cambridge: Polity.

Jogja Magasa Iron. 2020. 'Paparan Perkembangan Proyek Pengolahan Dan Pemurnian Pasir Besi Kulonprogo [Presentation of the Development of the Kulonprogo Iron Sand Processing and Refining Project]'. Presented at the Rapat Pertemuan dengan Bupati Kulonprogo, Kulon Progo, Yogyakarta, 20 July.

Karim, Anton Abdul. 2013. 'Tercemar Limbah, Warga Menderita Benjol-benjol'. KOMPAS.com, 11 December, online edition. https://regional.kompas.com/read/2013/12/11/0718408/Tercemar.Limbah.Warga.Menderita.Benjol-benjol. Accessed 2 April 2024.

Kellow, Aynsley. 2007. 'Privilege and Underprivilege: Counterveiling Groups, Policy and Mining Industry at the Global Level'. In *Global Public Policy: Business and the Countervailing Powers of Civil Society*, edited by Karsten Ronit, 110–31. Abingdon: Routledge.

KEM. 2007. *Pembayaran Ganti Rugi PT KEM Kepada Masyarakat Kelian Sejak Tahun 1986 Sampai 1998 [PT KEM Compensation Payments to the Kelian Community since 1986 until 1998]*. Compensation Report. Proses Penyelesaian Tuntutan Ganti Rugi Masyarakat. Samarinda, Indonesia: PT Kelian Equatorial Mining.

Kemp, Deanna, Jane Gronow, Vanessa Zimmerman, Julie Kim, Allan Lerberg Jørgensen and Nora Götzmann. 2013. *Why Human Rights Matter*. London: Rio Tinto. https://cdn-rio.dataweavers.io/-/media/content/documents/sustainability/corporate-policies/rt-why-human-rights-matter-en.pdf?rev=fe3c3dc45efa4e2c9 09b6f325b660537. Accessed 3 April 2024.

Kennedy, Danny. 2001. 'Rio Tinto: Global Compact Violator'. *CorpWatch* (blog). 13 July. https://web.archive.org/web/20060210191115/http://corpwatch.org/arti cle.php?id=622. Accessed 2 April 2024.

Kerkvliet, Benedict J. Tria. 1990. *Everyday Politics in the Philippines: Class and Status Relations in a Central Luzon Village*. Berkeley: University of California Press.

Kirsch, Stuart. 2014. *Mining Capitalism: The Relationship between Corporations and their Critics*. Oakland: University of California Press.

Koch, Natalie, and Tom Perreault. 2019. 'Resource Nationalism'. *Progress in Human Geography* 43 (4): 611–31. https://doi.org/10.1177/0309132518781497.

Koman, Veronica. 2020. *The 2019 West Papua Uprising: Protests against Racism and for Self-Determination*. London: TAPOL. www.tapol.org/sites/default/files/The%202019%20West%20Papua%20Uprising.pdf. Accessed 19 March 2024.

KPA. 2019. *Masa Depan Reforma Agraria Melampaui Tahun Politik: Catatan Akhir Tahun 2018 [The Future of Agrarian Reform Beyond the Year in Politics: 2018 Annual Report]*. Jakarta: Konsortium Pembaruan Agraria.

———. 2022. *Catatan Akhir Tahun 2021: Penggusuran Skala Nasional (PSN) [2021 Annual Report: National Scale Evictions]*. Jakarta: Konsortium Pembaruan Agraria.

Kramarz, Teresa, Susan Park and Craig Johnson. 2021. 'Governing the Dark Side of Renewable Energy: A Typology of Global Displacements'. *Energy Research & Social Science* 74 (April): 101902. https://doi.org/10.1016/j.erss.2020.101902.

Kristiansen, Stein, and Linda Sulistiawati. 2016. 'Traditions, Land Rights, and Local Welfare Creation: Studies from Eastern Indonesia'. *Bulletin of Indonesian Economic Studies* 52 (2): 209–27. https://doi.org/10.1080/00074 918.2015.1129049.

Kröger, Markus. 2020. *Iron Will: Global Extractivism and Mining Resistance in Brazil and India*. Ann Arbor: University of Michigan Press. https://doi.org/10.3998/mpub.11533186.

Kurniawan, Nanang Indra, Päivi Lujala, Ståle Angen Rye and Diana Vela-Almeida. 2022. 'The Role of Local Participation in the Governance of Natural Resource Extraction'. *Extractive Industries and Society* 9 (March): 101029. https://doi.org/10.1016/j.exis.2021.101029.

Kusumaningrum, Juliman Foor Z., and Dalvi Mustafa. 2015. 'Social Quality Masyarakat Lahan Pasir Pantai Pada Aspek Social Empowerment Di Kecamatan Panjatan Kabupaten Kulonprogo [Social Quality of Sand Land Community on Social Aspect of Empowerment in Panjatan Sub-District, Kulonprogo Regency]'. *Agriekonomika* 4 (1): 1–9. https://doi.org/10.21107/agriekonomika.v4i1.669.

Lahiri-Dutt, Kuntala, ed. 2011. *Gendering the Field: Towards Sustainable Livelihoods for Mining Communities*. Vol. 6. Canberra: ANU Press. www.jstor.org/stable/j.ctt24h9g4.

———. 2012. 'Digging Women: Towards a New Agenda for Feminist Critiques of Mining'. *Gender, Place & Culture* 19 (2): 193–212. https://doi.org/10.1080/0966369X.2011.572433.

———. 2018. 'Extractive Peasants: Reframing Informal Artisanal and Small-Scale Mining Debates'. *Third World Quarterly* 39 (8): 1561–82. https://doi.org/10.1080/01436597.2018.1458300.

Langlois, Anthony J. 2022. *Sexuality and Gender Diversity Rights in Southeast Asia*. Cambridge: Cambridge University Press. https://doi.org/10.1017/9781108933216.

Leal, Pablo Alejandro. 2007. 'Participation: The Ascendancy of a Buzzword in the Neo-Liberal Era'. *Development in Practice* 17 (4–5): 539–48. https://doi.org/10.1080/09614520701469518.

Leifsen, Esben, Maria-Therese Gustafsson, Maria A. Guzmán-Gallegos and Almut Schilling-Vacaflor. 2017. 'New Mechanisms of Participation in Extractive Governance: Between Technologies of Governance and Resistance Work'. *Third World Quarterly* 38 (5): 1043–57. https://doi.org/10.1080/01436597.2017.1302329.

Leith, Denise. 2003. *The Politics of Power: Freeport in Suharto's Indonesia*. Honolulu: University of Hawai'i Press.

Leiva, Fernando. 2019. 'Economic Elites and New Strategies for Extractivism in Chile'. *European Review of Latin American and Caribbean Studies* 108 (December): 131–52. https://doi.org/10.32992/erlacs.10511.

Li, Fabiana. 2015. *Unearthing Conflict: Corporate Mining, Activism, and Expertise in Peru*. Durham, NC: Duke University Press.

Li, Tania. 2014. *Land's End: Capitalist Relations on an Indigenous Frontier*. Durham, NC: Duke University Press.

Li, Tania M. 1996. 'Images of Community: Discourse and Strategy in Property Relations'. *Development and Change* 27 (3): 501–27. https://doi.org/10.1111/j.1467-7660.1996.tb00601.x.

Li, Tania Murray. 2011. 'Centering Labor in the Land Grab Debate'. *Journal of Peasant Studies* 38 (2): 281–98. https://doi.org/10.1080/03066150.2011.559009.

Liu, Wenjuan, Datu B. Agusdinata, Hallie Eakin and Hugo Romero. 2022. 'Sustainable Minerals Extraction for Electric Vehicles: A Pilot Study of Consumers' Perceptions of Impacts'. *Resources Policy* 75 (March): 102523. https://doi.org/10.1016/j.resourpol.2021.102523.

Lucas, Anton, and Carol Warren. 2013. *Land for the People: The State and Agrarian Conflict in Indonesia*. Athens: Ohio University Press.

Lund, Christian, and Noer Fauzi Rachman. 2016. 'Occupied! Property, Citizenship and Peasant Movements in Rural Java'. *Development and Change* 47 (6): 1316–37. https://doi.org/10.1111/dech.12263.

Luxembourg, Rosa. 1951. *The Accumulation of Capital*. Translated by Agnes Schwarzschild. London: Routledge and Keegan Paul.

Lynch, Owen James, and Emily Harwell. 2002. *Whose Resources? Whose Common Good?: Towards a New Paradigm of Environmental Justice and the National Interest in Indonesia*. Washington, DC: Center for International Environment Law (CIEL) in collaboration with Association for Community and Ecologically-Based Law Reform.

Macdonald, Ingrid, and Brendan Ross. 2002. *Mining Ombudsman Annual Report 2001–2002*. Melbourne: Oxfam Community Aid Abroad Australia.

———. 2003. *Mining Ombudsman Annual Report 2003*. Melbourne: Oxfam Community Aid Abroad Australia.

MacDonald, Kate. 2017. 'Containing Conflict: Authoritative Transnational Actors and the Management of Company-Community Conflict'. In *Transnational Actors in War and Peace: Militants, Activists, and Corporations in World Politics*, edited by David Malet and Miriam J. Anderson, 197–214. Washington, DC: Georgetown University Press.

MacKay, Fergus. 2004. 'Indigenous Peoples' Right to Free, Prior and Informed Consent and The World Bank's Extractive Industries Review'. *Sustainable Development Law and Policy* 4 (2): 43–65.

Magenda, Burhan. 1991. *East Kalimantan: The Decline of a Commercial Aristocracy*. Ithaca, NY: Cornell Modern Indonesia Project.

Mahy, Petra. 2011a. *Gender Equality and Corporate Social Responsibility in Mining: An Investigation of the Potential for Change at Kaltim Prima Coal, Indonesia*. Ph.D. thesis, Australian National University.

———. 2011b. 'Sex Work and Livelihoods: Beyond the "Negative Impacts on Women" in Indonesian Mining'. In *Gendering the Field: Towards Sustainable Livelihoods for Mining Communities*, edited by Kuntala Lahiri-Dutt, 6: 49–66. Canberra: ANU Press.

Maimunah, Siti, and Sarah Agustiorini. 2020. 'From the Commons to Extractivism and Back: The Story of Mahakam River in Indonesia – Undisciplined Environments'. 15 October. https://undisciplinedenvironments.org/2020/10/15/from-the-commons-to-extractivism-and-back-the-story-of-mahakam-river-in-indonesia/. Accessed 19 March 2024.

Mangkoedilaga, Benjamin, Muridan S. Widjojo and Azas T. Nainggolan. 2000. *Laporan Hasil Investigasi Masalah Hak Asasi Manusia di Sekitar Wilayah Pertambangan PT Kelian Equatorial Mining, Kabupaten Kutai Barat, Kalimantan Timur, Indonesia [Report of Results from the Investigation into Problems with Fundamental Human Rights in the Mining Area of PT Kelian Equatorial Mining, West Kutai Regency, East Kalimantan, Indonesia]*. Jakarta: Komnas HAM.

Manheim, Jarol B. 2001. *The Death of a Thousand Cuts: Corporate Campaigns and the Attack on the Corporation*. Mahwah, NJ: Lawrence Erlbaum.

Marx, Karl. 1990. *Capital: A Critique of Political Economy, Volume 1*. Translated by Ben Fowkes. London: Penguin Books in association with New Left Review.

Matheos, Reyhard. 2011. 'A Tale of Sand: A Hidden Ecological Struggle in Yogyakarta'. *Latitudes* (blog). 15 June. https://web.archive.org/web/20111106132538/https://latitudes.nu/a-tale-of-sand-a-hidden-story-of-ecological-struggle-in-yogyakarta/. Accessed 3 April 2024.

May, Christopher. 2020. *A Research Agenda for Corporations*. Cheltenham: Edward Elgar. www.elgaronline.com/monobook/9781788977524.00005.xml. Accessed 3 April 2024.

McCarthy, John F., and Kathryn Robinson. 2016. *Land and Development in Indonesia: Searching for the People's Sovereignty*. Singapore: ISEAS-Yusof Ishak Institute.

McKenna, Kylie. 2015. *Corporate Social Responsibility and Natural Resource Conflict*. London: Taylor and Francis.

McSorley, Jean, and Rick Fowler. 2001. 'Mineworkers on the Offensive'. In *Moving Mountains: Communities Confront Mining and Globalization*, edited by Geoff Evans, James Goodman and Nina Lansbury, 165–80. Otford, NSW: Mineral Policy Institute and Otford Press.

Meckelburg, Rebecca. 2019. *Subaltern Agency and the Political Economy of Rural Social Change*. Ph.D. thesis, Murdoch University. https://researchrepository.murd och.edu.au/id/eprint/57177/1/Meckelburg2019.pdf. Accessed 19 March 2024.

———. 2021. 'Women at the Frontlines: Women's Unrecognised Leadership Role in Indonesia's COVID-19 Response Policy'. Policy Briefing – SEARBO. Canberra: ANU Coral Bell School.

Mentan, Tatah. 2018. *The Open Veins of Africa: The Dynamics of Extractive Accumulation by Dispossession in 21st Century Africa*. Mankon, Bamenda: Langaa Research & Publishing CIG.

Mikler, John. 2018. *The Political Power of Global Corporations*. Cambridge: Polity.

Mills, Jane. 2014. 'Methodology and Methods'. In *Qualitative Methodology: A Practical Guide*, edited by Melanie Birks and Jane Mills, 31–47. London: SAGE.

Mine Closure Steering Committee. 2002. 'MCSC Communique No. 8'. Kelian Equatorial Mining.

———. 2003. 'Kumpulan Komunike Komite Pengarah Pengakhiran Tambang (KPPT) [Collection of Communiques of the Mine Closure Steering Committee]'. Kelian Equatorial Mining.

Moody, Roger. 1992. *The Gulliver File: Mines, People and Land: A Global Battlefield*. London: International.

———. 2007. *Rocks and Hard Places*. London: Zed.

Moore, Madelaine. 2023a. 'A Time of Reproductive Unrest: The Articulation of Capital Accumulation, Social Reproduction, and the Irish State'. *New Political Economy* 28 (1): 112–25. https://doi.org/10.1080/13563467.2022.2084518.

———. 2023b. *Water Struggles as Resistance to Neoliberal Capitalism: A Time of Reproductive Unrest*. Manchester: Manchester University Press. https://doi.org/ 10.7765/9781526165992.

Morse, Ian. 2021. 'Indonesia Has a Long Way to Go to Produce Nickel Sustainably'. *China Dialogue*, 28 May. https://chinadialogue.net/en/pollution/indonesia-has-a-long-way-to-go-to-produce-nickel-sustainably/. Accessed 19 March 2024.

Muhammad, Chalid, Siti Maimunah, Aminuddin Kirom, Helvi Lystiani, Hasanuddin, Andre S. Wijaya, Tracy Glynn and Endi Biaro Haeruddin. 2005. *Tambang & Kemiskinan: kasus-kasus pertambangan di Indonesia 2001–2003 [Mining and Poverty Mining Cases in Indonesia]*. South Jakarta, Indonesia: Jaringan Advokasi Tambang (JATAM).

Murdoch, Jonathan, and Terry Marsden. 1995. 'The Spatialization of Politics: Local and National Actor-Spaces in Environmental Conflict'. *Transactions of the Institute of British Geographers*, New Series, 20 (3): 368–80. https://doi.org/ 10.2307/622657.

Mzembe, Andrew Ngawenja, and Yvonne Downs. 2014. 'Managerial and Stakeholder Perceptions of an Africa-Based Multinational Mining Company's Corporate Social Responsibility (CSR)'. *Extractive Industries and Society* 1 (2): 225–36. https://doi.org/10.1016/j.exis.2014.06.002.

Nagar, Anirudha. 2021. 'The Juukan Gorge Incident: Key Lessons on Free, Prior and Informed Consent'. *Business and Human Rights Journal* 6 (2): 377–83. https:// doi.org/10.1017/bhj.2021.18.

Naidoo, Trivindren, Dmitry Pertel and Wayne Ghavalas. 2017. *Independent Technical Specialist's Report Valuation of the Jogjakarta Pig Iron Project Held by Indo Mines Limited*. Valuation CSA Global Report no. R430.2017. Perth, Australia: CSA Global.

Nem Singh, Jewellord, and France Bourgouin. 2013. 'Introduction: Resource Governance at a Time of Plenty'. In *Resource Governance and Developmental States in the Global South*, edited by Jewellord Nem Singh and France Bourgouin, 1–18. London: Palgrave Macmillan.

Nem Singh, Jewellord, and Alvin A. Camba. 2016. 'Neoliberalism, Resource Governance and the Everyday Politics of Protests in the Philippines'. In *The Everyday Political Economy of Southeast Asia*, edited by Juanita Elias and Lena Rethel, 49–71. Cambridge: Cambridge University Press. https://doi.org/10.1017/CBO9781316402092.003.

Newcrest. 2010. *Newcrest Sustainability Report 2010*. Melbourne: Newcrest Mining. https://web.archive.org/web/20170228090152/www.newcrest.com.au/media/sustainability_reports/Sustainability_Report_2010.pdf. Accessed 3 April 2024.

———. 2011. *Newcrest Sustainability Report 2011*. Melbourne: Newcrest Mining. https://web.archive.org/web/20170228090132/http://www.newcrest.com.au/media/sustainability_reports/Newcrest-Sustainability-Report-2011.pdf. Accessed 3 April 2024.

———. 2012. *Technical Report on the Gosowong Property in North Maluku Province Indonesia*. Company Announcement, Toronto Stock Exchange. Melbourne: Newcrest Mining. www.asx.com.au/asxpdf/20120302/pdf/424s1t6 jryxg9y.pdf. Accessed 19 March 2024.

———. 2015. *2015 Sustainability Report*. Melbourne: Newcrest Mining. www.newcrest.com/sites/default/files/2019-10/151222_Newcrest%202015%20Sustainability%20Report.pdf. Accessed 19 March 2024.

———. 2016. 'History | Newcrest Mining Limited'. Delivering Our Future. www.newcrest.com.au/about-us/history. Accessed 22 July 2016.

———. 2017. *2017 Newcrest Sustainability Report*. Melbourne: Newcrest Mining. www.newcrest.com/sites/default/files/2019-10/17_Newcrest%20Sustainability%20Report.pdf. Accessed 19 March 2024.

———. 2020. *Quarterly Report for the Three Months Ended 31 March 2020*. Melbourne, Australia: Newcrest Mining. www.newcrest.com/sites/default/files/2020-04/200430_Newcrest%20Mar%2020%20Quarterly%20Report%20-%20Market%20Release%20.pdf. Accessed 19 March 2024.

'Newmont, Indonesia Settle Pollution Lawsuit'. 2006. *Mining Engineering* 58 (3): 16.

Nguyen, Tu Phuong. 2014. 'Business Associations and the Politics of Contained Participation in Vietnam'. *Australian Journal of Political Science* 49 (2): 334–49. https://doi.org/10.1080/10361146.2014.896317.

North, Douglass C. 1990. *Institutions, Institutional Change, and Economic Performance*. Cambridge: Cambridge University Press.

———. 2005. *Understanding the Process of Economic Change*. Princeton, NJ: Princeton University Press.

Nugraha, Indra. 2013. 'Konflik Agraria 2013 Meningkat, 21 Warga Tewas, 30 Tertembak'. *Mongabay*, 22 December, online edition. www.mongabay.co.id/2013/12/22/konflik-agraria-2013-meningkat-21-warga-tewas-30-tertembak/. Accessed 19 March 2024.

Nurcahyana, Yudhi, Pius Erick Nyompe, Valentinus Tingang, Yustinus Dullah, Gabriel Oktavianus, S. SH Rusulan and Sigit Wibobo. 2008. *Status Penyelesaian Tuntutan Ganti Rugi Masyarakat oleh PT KEM, [Status of Demands for*

Compensation of the Community to PT KEM]. Samarinda, Indonesia: PT Kelian Equatorial Mining.

Nursyamsi, Aisyah, Anisa Dewi Anggriani and Yulia Adiningsih, dirs. 2019. *Mosi Tidak Percaya [Motion of No Confidence]*. Part 2. Watchdoc Documentary. www.youtube.com/watch?v=QOHSxgPIqEE. Accessed 19 March 2024.

Nyompe, Pius Erick. 2003. 'The Closure of the Kelian Gold Mine and the Role of the Business Partnership for Development/World Bank'. Presented at the EIR's Eminent Person meeting on Indigenous Peoples, Extractive Industries and the World Bank, Oxford, April 15. www.forestpeoples.org/sites/fpp/files/publication/2010/08/eirinternatwshopindonesiacaseengapr03.pdf. Accessed 19 March 2024.

O'Faircheallaigh, Ciaran. 2008. 'Negotiating Cultural Heritage? Aboriginal – Mining Company Agreements in Australia'. *Development and Change* 39 (1): 25–51. https://doi.org/10.1111/j.1467-7660.2008.00467.x.

———. 2015. *Negotiations in the Indigenous World: Aboriginal Peoples and the Extractive Industry in Australia and Canada*. London: Routledge.

O'Faircheallaigh, Ciaran, and Saleem Ali. 2008. *Earth Matters: Indigenous Peoples, the Extractive Industries and Corporate Social Responsibility*. Sheffield: Greenleaf.

Ong, Thuy. 2016. 'Samarco Disaster: BHP Billiton "Encouraged" by Samarco Dam Remediation but Still Intends to Appeal $8b Civil Claim'. *ABC News*, 14 July. www.abc.net.au/news/2016-07-14/bhp-billiton-encouraged-by-samarco-dam-remediation/7630118. Accessed 19 March 2024.

Osburg, Thomas, and René Schmidpeter. 2013. *Social Innovation : Solutions for a Sustainable Future*. Dordrecht: Springer.

Özen, Hayriye, and Şükrü Özen. 2011. 'Interactions in and between Strategic Action Fields: A Comparative Analysis of Two Environmental Conflicts in Gold-Mining Fields in Turkey'. *Organization & Environment* 24 (4): 343–63. https://doi.org/10.1177/1086026611426343.

Özen, Şükrü, and Hayriye Özen. 2009. 'Peasants Against MNCs and the State: The Role of the Bergama Struggle in the Institutional Construction of the Gold-Mining Field in Turkey'. *Organization* 16 (4): 547–73. https://doi.org/10.1177/1350508409104508.

Park, Susan. 2014. 'Institutional Isomorphism and the Asian Development Bank's Accountability Mechanism: Something Old, Something New; Something Borrowed, Something Blue?' *Pacific Review* 27 (2): 217–39. https://doi.org/10.1080/09512748.2014.882394.

Peluso, Nancy Lee. 1992. 'Structures of Access Control, Repertoires of Resistance'. In *Rich Forests, Poor People: Resource Control and Resistance in Java*. Berkeley: University of California Press.

Peluso, Nancy Lee. 2016. 'The Plantation and the Mine: Agrarian Transformation and the Remaking of Land and Smallholders in Indonesia'. In *Land and Development in Indonesia: Searching for the People's Sovereignty*, edited by John F. McCarthy and Kathryn Robinson, 35–59. Singapore: ISEAS-Yusof Ishak Institute.

Peluso, Nancy Lee, Suraya Afiff and Noer Fauzi Rachman. 2008. 'Claiming the Grounds for Reform: Agrarian and Environmental Movements in Indonesia'. *Journal of Agrarian Change* 8 (2–3): 377–407. https://doi.org/10.1111/j.1471-0366.2008.00174.x.

Perreault, Tom. 2018. 'The Plantation and the Mine: Comment on "After the Land Grab: Infrastructural Violence and the 'Mafia System' in Indonesia's Oil Palm Plantation Zone" by Tania Li'. *Geoforum* 96: 345–47. https://doi.org/10.1016/j.geoforum.2018.02.025.

Phillips, Ruth. 2001. 'Engagement or Confrontation?' In *Moving Mountains: Communities Confront Mining and Globalization*, edited by Geoff Evans, James Goodman and Nina Lansbury, 181–94. Otford, NSW: Mineral Policy Institute and Otford Press.

———. 2012. 'Non-Government Organisations in a Sustainable Relationship for Sustainable Mining? The Australian NGO Perspective on What Happened after the MMSD Initiative'. *Third Sector Review* 18 (1): 171–93.

Power, Thomas. 2020. 'Assailing Accountability: Law Enforcement Politicisation, Partisan Coercion and Executive Aggrandisement under the Jokowi Administration'. In *Democracy in Indonesia: From Stagnation to Regression?*, edited by Eve Warburton and Thomas Power, 277–302. Singapore: ISEAS–Yusof Ishak Institute. www.cambridge.org/core/books/democracy-in-indonesia/assailing-accountability-law-enforcement-politicisation-partisan-coercion-and-executive-aggrandisement-under-the-jokowi-administration/4728FD73C06B2482A1C25D964F101941. Accessed 19 March 2024.

Power, Thomas, and Eve Warburton. 2020. 'The Decline of Indonesian Democracy'. In *Democracy in Indonesia: From Stagnation to Regression?*, edited by Eve Warburton and Thomas Power, 1–20. Singapore: ISEAS–Yusof Ishak Institute. www.cambridge.org/core/books/democracy-in-indonesia/decline-of-indonesian-democracy/0B0ED35DBA70167AD948258981AFAAEF. Accessed 19 March 2024.

Prno, Jason, and Scott D. Slocombe. 2012. 'Exploring the Origins of "Social License to Operate" in the Mining Sector: Perspectives from Governance and Sustainability Theories'. *Resources Policy* 37 (3): 346–57. https://doi.org/10.1016/j.resourpol.2012.04.002.

PT Jogja Magasa Iron. 2013. 'Perjanjian pelepasan, pengalihan, dan penyerahan hak garap, lahan garapan, serta tanaman garapanya di atas tanah Paku Alam Ground ("PAG") di desa Karangwuni, Kecematan Wates, Kabupaten Kulon Progo, Daerah Istimewa Yogyakarta 029/PAG/04/KW/XI/2013/B5'.

PT Nusa Halmahera Minerals. 2015. 'Pelaksanaan Program Pengembangan Masyarakat Dalam Persiapan Penutupan Tambang, PT Nusa Halmahera Minerals (PTNHM)'s Corporate Social Responsibility (CSR) Program'. Presented at the Presentation to ESDM (Ministry of Energy and Natural Resources), ESDM, 12 May.

PwC. 2015. *Mining in Indonesia Investment and Taxation Guide May 2015 – 7th Edition*. Jakarta: PriceWaterhouseCoopers. www.pwc.com/id/en/publications/assets/mining-in-indonesia-2015.pdf. Accessed 19 March 2024.

———. 2018. *Mining in Indonesia: Investment and Taxation Guide May 2018 10th Edition*. Jakarta: PriceWaterhouseCoopers. www.pwc.com/id/en/publications/assets/eumpublications/mining/mining-guide-2018.pdf. Accessed 19 March 2024.

———. 2022. *Mining in Indonesia: Investment and Taxation Guide 2022 12th Edition*. PriceWaterhouseCoopers. www.pwc.com/id/en/energy-utilities-mining/assets/mining/mining-guide-2022.pdf. Accessed 19 March 2024.

———. 2023. *Mine 2023: 20th Edition, the Era of Reinvention*. www.pwc.com.au/industry/mining/global-mine-2023/global-mine-2023-report.pdf. Accessed 19 March 2024.

Rachmayana. 2004. 'Women's Rights and the Mine'. In *The KEM Experience*, edited by Terry Holland, 182–83. Tasmania: Forty South.

Regan, Anthony J. 1998. 'Causes and Course of the Bougainville Conflict'. *Journal of Pacific History* 33 (3): 269–85. https://doi.org/10.1080/00223349808572878.

Rio Tinto. 2015. *Working for Mutual Benefit: Sustainable Development 2015.* London. https://cdn-rio.dataweavers.io/-/media/content/documents/invest/repo rts/sustainable-development-reports/rt-sustainable-development-2015.pdf?rev= 2ca7665e5565408fa7c02f663bbfc2ab. Accessed 3 April 2024.

Rivera Andía, Juan Javier, and Cecilie Vindal Ødegaard. 2019. 'Introduction: Indigenous Peoples, Extractivism, and Turbulences in South America'. In *Indigenous Life Projects and Extractivism: Ethnographies from South America*, edited by Cecilie Vindal Ødegaard and Juan Javier Rivera Andía, 1–50. Cham, Switzerland: Springer. https://doi.org/10.1007/978-3-319-93435-8.

Robinson, Geoffrey. 1998. 'Rawan Is as Rawan Does: The Origins of Disorder in New Order Aceh'. *Indonesia* 66 (October): 127–57. https://doi.org/10.2307/3351450.

Robinson, Kathryn. 2016. 'Mining, Land and Community Rights in Indonesia'. In *Land and Development in Indonesia: Searching for the People's Sovereignty*, edited by John F. McCarthy and Kathryn Robinson, 63–88. Singapore: ISEAS-Yusof Ishak Institute.

Robison, Richard. 2009. *Indonesia: The Rise of Capital.* Jakarta: Equinox.

Robison, Richard, and Vedi R. Hadiz. 2004. *Reorganising Power in Indonesia: The Politics of Oligarchy in an Age of Markets.* London: RoutledgeCurzon.

Roche, Charles, Howard Sindana and Nawasio Walim. 2019. 'Extractive Dispossession: "I Am Not Happy Our Land Will Go, We Will Have No Better Life"'. *Extractive Industries and Society* 6 (3): 977–92.

Rodan, Garry. 2012. 'Competing Ideologies of Political Representation in Southeast Asia'. *Third World Quarterly* 33 (2): 311–32. https://doi.org/10.1080/01436 597.2012.666014.

———. 2018. *Participation Without Democracy: Containing Conflict in Southeast Asia.* Ithaca, NY: Cornell University Press.

Rodan, Garry, Kevin Hewison and Richard Robison. 2006. *The Political Economy of South-East Asia: Markets, Power and Contestation*, 3rd ed. Melbourne: Oxford University Press.

Roseberry, William. 1989. *Anthropologies and Histories: Essays in Culture, History, and Political Economy.* New Brunswick, NJ: Rutgers University Press.

Ross, Michael L. 2018. 'The Politics of the Resource Curse: A Review'. In *The Oxford Handbook of the Politics of Development*, edited by Carol Lancaster and Nicolas van de Walle, 200–23. Oxford: Oxford University Press.

Rosser, Andrew, and Donni Edwin. 2010. 'The Politics of Corporate Social Responsibility in Indonesia'. *Pacific Review* 23 (1): 1–22. https://doi.org/10.1080/09512740903398314.

Rupert, Mark. 2006. 'Reading Gramsci in an Era of Economic Globalising Capitalism'. In *Images of Gramsci: Connections and Contentions in Political Theory and International Relations*, edited by Andreas Bieler and Adam David Morton, 89–103. New York: Routledge.

Rusdiyana, E., and Suminah. 2018. 'An Adaptation Strategy of Sandland Peasants in Yogyakarta toward Climate Change'. *IOP Conference Series: Earth and Environmental Science* 129 (March): 012040. https://doi.org/10.1088/1755-1315/129/1/012040.

Rushdi, Muhammad, Apditya Sutomo, Pius Ginting and Masri Anwar. 2021. *Fast and Furious for Future: The Dark Side of Electric Vehicle Battery Components and their Social and Ecological Impacts in Indonesia.* Rosa Luxembourg Stiftung.

www.rosalux.de/fileadmin/images/publikationen/Studien/Fast_and_Furious_for_Future.pdf. Accessed 19 March 2024.

Sachs, Jeffrey D., and Andrew M. Warner. 1999. 'The Big Push, Natural Resource Booms and Growth'. *Journal of Development Economics* 59 (1): 43–76. https://doi.org/10.1016/S0304-3878(99)00005-X.

Salim, Agus, Wahidah R. Bulan, Bejo Untung, Indro Laksono and Karen Brock. 2017. 'Indonesia's Village Law: Enabler or Constraint for More Accountable Governance?' Making All Voices Count Research Report. Brighton: Institute of Development Studies.

Schonhardt, Sara, and Austen Hufford. 2016. 'Newmont Mining to Sell Indonesian Mine for $1.3 Billion'. *Wall Street Journal*, 30 June. www.wsj.com/articles/newmont-mining-to-sell-indonesian-mine-for-920-million-1467285254. Accessed 19 March 2024.

Scott, James C. 1985. *Weapons of the Weak*. New Haven, CT: Yale University Press.

———. 2012. *Two Cheers for Anarchism: Six Essay Pieces on Autonomy, Dignity, and Meaningful Work and Play*. Princeton, NJ: Princeton University Press.

Sears, Alan. 2016. 'Situating Sexuality in Social Reproduction'. *Historical Materialism* 24 (2), 138–63. https://doi.org/10.1163/1569206X-12341474.

Setiawan, Ken M. P. 2022. 'Vulnerable but Resilient: Indonesia in an Age of Democratic Decline'. *Bulletin of Indonesian Economic Studies* 58 (3): 273–95. https://doi.org/10.1080/00074918.2022.2139168.

Setijadi, Charlotte. 2021. 'The Pandemic as Political Opportunity: Jokowi's Indonesia in the Time of Covid-19'. *Bulletin of Indonesian Economic Studies* 57 (3): 297–320. https://doi.org/10.1080/00074918.2021.2004342.

Shapiro, Tricia. 2010. *Mountain Justice: Homegrown Resistance to Mountaintop Removal, for the Future of Us All*. Chico, CA: AK Press.

Simbolon, Domu, Silvanus Maxwel Simange and Sri Yulina Wulandari. 2010. 'Kandungan Merkuri Dan Sianida Pada Ikan Yang Tertangkap Dari Teluk Kao, Halmahera Utara'. *Ilmu Kelautan: Indonesian Journal of Marine Sciences* 15 (3): 126–34.

Sinclair, L., J. Pope, S. Holcombe, L. Hamblin, D. Pershke, R. J. Standish, M. E. Kragt, F. Haslam McKenzie and R. E. Young. 2022. *Towards a Framework for Regional Cumulative Impact Assessment*. Final Report. Foundational Project 1.1. Perth, Australia: CRC TiME. https://crctime.com.au/macwp/wp-content/uploads/2022/04/Project-1.1_Final-Report_14.04.22_approved.pdf. Accessed 19 March 2024.

Sinclair, Lian. 2020. 'The Power of Multinational Mining Corporations, Global Governance and Social Conflict'. In *MNCs in Global Politics: Pathways of Influence*, edited by John Mikler and Karsten Ronit, 139–58. Cheltenham: Edward Elgar. https://doi.org/10.4337/9781789903232.00015.

———. 2021. 'Beyond Victimisation: Gendered Legacies of Mining, Participation, and Resistance'. *Extractive Industries and Society* 8 (3): S2214790X21000058. https://doi.org/10.1016/j.exis.2021.01.005.

Singh, Kavaljit. 2011. 'Corporate Accountability: Is Self-Regulation the Answer?' In *Relations of Global Power: Neoliberal Order and Disorder*, edited by Gary Teeple and Stephen McBride, 60–72. Toronto: University of Toronto Press.

Slater and Gordon. 2018. 'Ok Tedi – Entering Uncharted Territory'. Blog. 7 August. www.slatergordon.com.au/blog/ok-tedi-entering-uncharted-territory. Accessed 19 March 2024.

Smith, Claire Querida. 2009. *The Contested State and Politics of Elite Continuity in North Maluku, Indonesia (1998–2008)*. Ph.D. thesis, London School of Economics and Political Science.

Smith, Neil. 2003. 'Remaking Scale: Competition and Cooperation in Pre-National and Post-National Europe'. In *State/Space: A Reader*, edited by Neil Brenner, Bob Jessop, Martin Jones and Gordon Macleod, 225–38. Oxford: Blackwell.

———. 2008. *Uneven Development: Nature, Capital, and the Production of Space*, 3rd ed. Athens: University of Georgia Press.

Stiglitz, J. 2003. 'Globalization and the Economic Role of the State in the New Millennium'. *Industrial and Corporate Change* 12 (1): 3–26. https://doi.org/10.1093/icc/12.1.3.

Suliadi. 2015. 'Resistensi petani terhadap pertambangan pasir besi di karangwuni Kulon Progo'. *Sosiologi Reflektif* 9 (2): 79–102.

Swyngedouw, Erik, and Nikolas C. Heynen. 2010. 'Urban Political Ecology, Justice and the Politics of Scale'. *Antipode* 35: 898–918.

Symon, Andrew. 2007. 'Petroleum and Mining in Southeast Asia: Managing the Environmental and Social Impacts'. *Southeast Asian Affairs*, 77–100. www.jstor.org/stable/27913327.

Syukri, Muhammad. 2024. 'Indonesia's New Developmental State: Interrogating Participatory Village Governance'. *Journal of Contemporary Asia* 54 (1): 1–23. https://doi.org/10.1080/00472336.2022.2089904.

Szablowski, David. 2007. *Transnational Law and Local Struggles: Mining, Communities and the World Bank*. Oxford: Hart.

Tapsell, Ross. 2012. 'Old Tricks in a New Era: Self-Censorship in Indonesian Journalism'. *Asian Studies Review* 36 (2): 227–45.

'The Equator Principles III'. 2013. www.equator-principles.com/. Accessed 19 March 2024.

Thompson, E. P. 1978. 'Eighteenth-century English Society: Class Struggle without Class?' *Social History* 3 (2): 133–65. https://doi.org/10.1080/03071027808567424.

Thorp, Rosemary, Stefania Battistelli, Yvan Guichaoua, Jose Carlos Orihuela and Martiza Pardes. 2012. *The Developmental Challenges of Mining and Oil: Lessons from Africa and Latin America*. New York: Palgrave Macmillan.

Tilley, Lisa. 2021. 'Extractive Investibility in Historical Colonial Perspective: The Emerging Market and Its Antecedents in Indonesia'. *Review of International Political Economy* 28 (5): 1099–1118. https://doi.org/10.1080/09692290.2020.1763423.

Tingay, Mark. 2015. 'Initial Pore Pressures under the Lusi Mud Volcano, Indonesia'. *Interpretation* 3 (1): 33–49. https://doi.org/10.1190/INT-2014-0092.1.

Topatimasang, Roem, ed. 2016. *Orang-Orang Kalah: Kisah Penyingkiran Masyarakat Adat Kepulauan Maluku*, revised ed. Yogyakarta, Indonesia: INSISTPress.

Torres-Wong, Marcela, and Adrian Jimenez-Sandoval. 2022. 'Indigenous Resource Governance as an Alternative to Mining: Redefining the Boundaries of Indigenous Participation'. *Extractive Industries and Society* 9 (March): 101001. https://doi.org/10.1016/j.exis.2021.101001.

UNDP. 2008. 'National Strategy on Access to Justice – LEAD Fact Sheet'. UNDP. Jakarta. www.snap-undp.org/lepknowledgebank/Public%20Document%20Library/National%20Strategy%20on%20Access%20to%20Justice%20-%20LEAD%20Fact%20Sheet.pdf. Accessed 19 March 2024.

Usman. 2016. 'The Bloodshed in North Halmahera: Roots, Escalation and Reconciliation'. *Journal of Indonesian Social Sciences and Humanities* 6 (2): 1–11.

van der Muur, Willem, Jacqueline Vel, Micah R. Fisher and Kathryn Robinson. 2019. 'Changing Indigeneity Politics in Indonesia: From Revival to Projects'. *Asia Pacific Journal of Anthropology* 20 (5): 379–96. https://doi.org/10.1080/14442 213.2019.1669520.

Veltmeyer, Henry, and James F. Petras. 2014. *The New Extractivism: A Post-Neoliberal Development Model or Imperialism of the Twenty-First Century?* London: Zed.

Verweijen, Judith, and Alexander Dunlap. 2021. 'The Evolving Techniques of the Social Engineering of Extraction: Introducing Political (Re)Actions "from above" in Large-Scale Mining and Energy Projects'. *Political Geography* 88 (June): 102342. https://doi.org/10.1016/j.polgeo.2021.102342.

Veza, Ibham, Mohd Azman Abas, Djati Wibowo Djamari, Noreffendy Tamaldin, Fitri Endrasari, Bentang Arief Budiman … and Muhammad Aziz. 2022. 'Electric Vehicles in Malaysia and Indonesia: Opportunities and Challenges'. *Energies* 15 (7): 2564. https://doi.org/10.3390/en15072564.

Vogel, David. 2007. *The Market for Virtue: The Potential and Limits of Corporate Social Responsibility*. Washington, DC: Brookings Institution Press.

Voluntary Principles Initiative. 2022. '10 Steps to Maintain Security in Compliance with Human Rights'. Voluntary Principles on Security and Human Rights. www.voluntaryprinciples.org/wp-content/uploads/2022/05/7060_VP_101Guide_P42.pdf. Accessed 19 March 2024.

Waagstein, Patricia Rinwigati. 2011. 'The Mandatory Corporate Social Responsibility in Indonesia: Problems and Implications'. *Journal of Business Ethics* 98 (3): 455–66.

Wanvik, Tarje Iversen. 2014. 'Encountering a Multidimensional Assemblage: The Case of Norwegian Corporate Social Responsibility Activities in Indonesia'. *Norsk Geografisk Tidsskrift – Norwegian Journal of Geography* 68 (5): 282–90. https://doi.org/10.1080/00291951.2014.964761.

Warburton, Eve. 2014. 'In Whose Interest? Debating Resource Nationalism in Indonesia.' *Kyoto Review of Southeast Asia* 15. http://kyotoreview.org/yav/in-whose-interest-debating-resource-nationalism-in-indonesia/. Accessed 19 March 2024.

———. 2016. 'Jokowi and the New Developmentalism'. *Bulletin of Indonesian Economic Studies* 52 (3): 297–320. https://doi.org/10.1080/00074918.2016.1249262.

———. 2019. 'A New Developmentalism in Indonesia?' In *The Indonesian Economy in Transition: Policy Challenges in the Jokowi Era and Beyond*, edited by Hal Hill and Siwage Dharma Negara, 34–56. Singapore: ISEAS–Yusof Ishak Institute. www.cambridge.org/core/books/indonesian-economy-in-transition/new-developmentalism-in-indonesia/BE1ACED8AC34EB3B6864AABA0A2885D4. Accessed 19 March 2024.

Warburton, Eve, and Thomas Power, eds. 2020. *Democracy in Indonesia: From Stagnation to Regression?* Singapore: ISEAS–Yusof Ishak Institute. www.cambridge.org/core/books/democracy-in-indonesia/assailing-accountability-law-enforcement-politicisation-partisan-coercion-and-executive-aggrandisement-under-the-jokowi-administration/4728FD73C06B2482A1C25D964F101941. Accessed 19 March 2024.

Wardana, Agung. 2018. 'Legal Engineering in a Contest over Space in Bali'. *Australian Journal of Asian Law* 19 (1): 1–12.

———. 2021. 'UU Pertambangan Mineral Dan Batubara: Negasi Berlanjut Terhadap Hak Atas Lingkungan Hidup Yang Baik Dan Sehat'. Indonesian Supreme Court Decision No. 37/PUU-XIX/2021.

———. 2022. 'The Indonesian Paradox in the Anthropocene'. *Asia Pacific Journal of Environmental Law* 24 (2): 230–84.

Watchman, Paul Q., Angela Delfino and Juliette Addison. 2007. 'EP 2: The Revised Equator Principles: Why Hard-Nosed Bankers are Embracing Soft Law Principles'. *Law and Financial Markets Review* 1 (2): 85–113.

Welker, Marina. 2009. '"Corporate Security Begins in the Community": Mining, the Corporate Social Responsibility Industry, and Environmental Advocacy in Indonesia'. *Cultural Anthropology* 24 (1): 142–79.

———. 2014. *Enacting the Corporation: An American Mining Firm in Post-Authoritarian Indonesia*. Berkeley: University of California Press.

Wesley, Anthea, and Diana MacCallum. 2014. 'The Political Economy of Corporate Social Responsibility in the Resource Sector in Western Australia. A Case Study of the Proposed James Price Point LNG Precinct'. In *Resource Curse or Cure?*, edited by Martin Brueckner, Angela Durey, Robyn Mayes and Christof Pforr, 59–73. Berlin: Springer.

White, Ben. 2017. 'The Myth of the Harmonious Village'. *Inside Indonesia* 128 (May). www.insideindonesia.org/editions/edition-128-apr-jun-2017/the-myth-of-the-harmonious-village. Accessed 19 March 2024.

White, Sarah C. 1996. 'Depoliticising Development: The Uses and Abuses of Participation'. *Development in Practice* 6 (1): 6–15. https://doi.org/10.1080/0961 452961000157564.

Widodo. 2013. *Menanam Adalah Melawan!* Yogyakarta, Indonesia: Paguyuban Petani Lahan Pesisir Kulon Progo and Tanah Air Beta.

Wijaya, Trissia, and Lian Sinclair. 2024. 'An EV-fix for Indonesia: The green development-resource nationalist nexus'. *Environmental Politics* https://doi.org/10.1080/09644016.2024.2332129.

Wilks, Stephen. 2013. *The Political Power of the Business Corporation*. Cheltenham: Edward Elgar.

Wilson Becerril, Michael. 2021. *Resisting Extractivism: Peruvian Gold, Everyday Violence, and the Politics of Attention*. Nashville, TN: Vanderbilt University Press.

Wilson, Chris. 2008. *Ethno-Religious Violence in Indonesia: From Soil to God*. London: Routledge.

Wilson, Jeffrey D. 2015. 'Understanding Resource Nationalism: Economic Dynamics and Political Institutions'. *Contemporary Politics* 21 (4): 399–416. https://doi.org/10.1080/13569775.2015.1013293.

Winanti, Poppy S., and Rachael Diprose. 2020. 'Reordering the Extractive Political Settlement: Resource Nationalism, Domestic Ownership and Transnational Bargains in Indonesia'. *Extractive Industries and Society* 7 (4): 1534–46. https://doi.org/10.1016/j.exis.2020.08.015.

Wood, Ellen Meiksins. 1998. 'The Agrarian Origins of Capitalism'. *Monthly Review* 50 (3): 14–31.

World Bank. 2003. *Striking a Better Balance: Volume 1. The World Bank Group and Extractive Industries*. Washington, DC: World Bank. https://openknowledge.worldbank.org/handle/10986/17705. Accessed 19 March 2024.

————. 2014. *The World Bank in Extractive Industries: 2013 Annual Review*. Washington, DC: World Bank Group.

World Bank Group. 2004. *Striking a Better Balance – the World Bank Group and Extractive Industries: The Final Report of the Extractive Industries Review – World Bank Group Management Response*. Washington, DC: World Bank Group.

World Bank and International Finance Corporation. 2002. 'It's Not Over When It's Over: Mine Closure around the World'. http://siteresources.worldbank.org/INTOGMC/Resources/notoverwhenover.pdf. Accessed 19 March 2024.

Wright, Christopher. 2012. 'Global Banks, the Environment, and Human Rights: The Impact of the Equator Principles on Lending Policies and Practices'. *Global Environmental Politics* 12 (1): 56–77.

Yanuardy, Dian. 2012. 'Commoning, Dispossession Projects and Resistance: A Land Dispossession Project for Sand Iron Mining in Yogyakarta, Indonesia'. Presented at the International Conference on Global Land Grabbing II, Department of Development Sociology at Cornell University, Ithaca, NY, 17 October.

Yin, Robert K. 2003. *Case Study Research: Design and Methods*, 3rd ed. London: SAGE.

Zanden, Jan Luiten van, and Daan Marks. 2012. *An Economic History of Indonesia: 1800–2010*. London: Routledge. https://doi.org/10.4324/978020 3126196.

Zhou, Qian. 2022. 'Indonesia to Ban Bauxite Exports from June 2023: An Explainer'. *ASEAN Business News*, 28 December. www.aseanbriefing.com/news/indonesia-to-ban-bauxite-export-from-june-2023/. Accessed 19 March 2024.

Index

EU authorised representative for GPSR:
Easy Access System Europe, Mustamäe tee 50,
10621 Tallinn, Estonia
gpsr.requests@easproject.com